China Vision

Praise for China Vision

Daniel Wagner presents a brisk, provocative, and thought-provoking account of China's resurgence, contending that Beijing harbors a zero-sum conception of geopolitics and is moving swiftly and purposefully to achieve global preeminence. He envisions neither the wholesale erosion of the postwar system, nor the total triumph of a Chinese successor, but rather a protracted negotiation between American and Chinese concepts of order. Minimizing the security risks that inhere in any such process will be among this century's foremost strategic imperatives.

- Ali Wyne, policy analyst, RAND Corporation (USA)

Policy makers in Southeast Asia will find *China Vision* a handy guide to help them navigate the complex terrain of dealing with a stubborn mega-power. The Philippines, for one, can learn from the experiences of its neighbors and other countries especially after its overwhelming victory in its maritime dispute against China. Daniel Wagner provides the readers a broad sweep of China's imperious behavior, filled with examples and written in accessible prose, making his case clear: this Asian giant plays by its own rules. He cites pushbacks against China by a few countries and the tough challenges that lay ahead. *China Vision* gives leaders and governments in this region a big nudge to take this global power to account for disregarding international law. It's time to listen to Wagner's voice.

Marites Dañguilan Vitug, author of *Rock Solid: How the Philippines Won its Maritime Case against China* and editor-at-large of Rappler (Philippines)

China Vision is a comprehensive and useful work on the most important political flashpoints in the country today. From core foreign affairs issues such as China's territorial disputes in the South China Sea to its cyber warfare capabilities and its race to achieve AI supremacy, Wagner's book is extensive yet digestible. It is particularly refreshing with its contextualized, realistic evaluation of Beijing's intentions and agenda, allowing us to walk with eyes wide open into the Chinese century.

Cindy Yu, China Specialist, The Spectator (UK)

China Vision is an extremely comprehensive and detailed view of modern China, highlighting the positives and negatives, and I recommend it to anyone looking for some on the ground perspectives from a seasoned professional. As a regular China commentator, it was useful for me to challenge some of my own perspectives on the country. Understanding China is important for all of us. Daniel has covered a lot of ground in this book. I enjoyed reading it.

David Thomas, CEO, Think Global (Australia)

Daniel Wagner has unpacked the various dynamics underpinning China's monumental ascent in a manner simultaneously holistic, of practical relevance, and hugely enjoyable to read. He is among a growing body of nuanced authors and scholars that remain refreshingly wary of the shouting from the rooftops about Chinese state collapse, and from those that envision a classical Sinica on the basis of geopolitical linearity. His take is grounded in many years spent working and living across Asia, and details several critical facets of this transformative phenomenon; from historical and geopolitical analysis to cyber security risks and social and cultural psychology, this book is a must read.

Aditya Ramachandran, analyst, FutureMap (Singapore)

Anyone considering reading a book entitled *China Vision: China's Crusade to Create a World in its Own Image* is probably well aware that the US-China economic relationship, after years of worsening frictions, went off the rails in 2018 when Washington and Beijing exchanged a few rounds of tit-for-tat tariffs that now ensnare $360 billion of two-way trade. Ongoing negotiations to end the trade war notwithstanding, the question of what it will take—indeed, whether it is even possible—to get relations back on track cannot be answered properly without US policymakers and opinion leaders first coming to terms with China's methods, its thinking, and its vision.

Political scientist and longtime China watcher Daniel Wagner has done a masterful job painting a picture of a country that—by cultural inclination and one-party leadership—is forward-looking, determined, and methodical in its inexorable quest to regain the global stature it once held and reshape the world in its image. It is difficult to imagine a US polity that will not react, or overreact, to a rising challenger subverting an order that was instrumental to its own rise, while aiming to reshape the world in its image.

Wagner notes: "China is in a unique position to influence the global economy and the future course of globalization. The question is whether it will do so responsibly, and at what cost for other countries?" The narrative throughout the book implies an answer: China will do whatever it perceives to be in its own interest, which may or may not be simpatico with the interests of others, so it is incumbent upon the US and other countries to wake up, rise to the challenge, and push back against a China that is clever, cunning, and often usurpatory.

With dozens of anecdotes, Wagner describes how China wields its asymmetric power in Africa, Eurasia, and elsewhere without regard to local needs, expectations, or norms. From infrastructure projects related to its Belt and Road initiative to commodity contracts in Africa to promises of financial support in Latin America in exchange for diplomatic recognition, Beijing is weaving a web of relationships that ultimately leave its partner countries financially indebted or otherwise beholden to China.

The book then pivots to China's assertive determination in staking its territorial claims vis-à-vis Japan, India, Vietnam, the Philippines and Malaysia, and notes US deference to China's provocative actions as providing space for more expansive Chinese claims.

The details surrounding Beijing's dogged commitment to obtaining technology by any means and at all costs are well-documented in the book, as is the Chinese government's commitment to cyber malfeasance, cyber espionage, and cyber warfare. Wagner explains how China's recent cybersecurity and national security laws give government officials carte blanche to examine foreign companies' information, communications technology products, and to review source code, all under the guise of ensuring the products are "secure and controllable".

Meanwhile, given what he characterizes as massive disparities in government directed investments in the technologies of the future, Wagner believes the race for supremacy in fields like artificial intelligence and quantum computing will ultimately be lost to China. Given the digital surveillance and military (including the space weapons) applications of these technologies, that is more than mildly disconcerting.

Wagner reminds us that our complacency created this mess: "For decades China has, because of its size and importance, gotten away with things that most nations would never even have attempted. It has been able to do so because, in part, it made itself the world's largest center of manufacturing and its largest importer, implying that no other nation had the cojones to stand up to Beijing, for fear of economic retribution. _The world has itself to blame for giving China that power_."

At least, in the US, there appears to have been an awakening to the fact that China under Xi Jinping is not the same poor country that went desperately searching for reforms in the late 1970s in order to reverse the economic and social catastrophes of the Great Leap Forward and the Cultural Revolution. The argument that market reforms would encourage China to liberalize and be "more like us" no longer carries any weight. China is now a moderately rich country that will soon have the world's largest economy. Its government is headed by a "president for life", who eschews market reforms, promotes state-owned enterprises, surveilles its citizens, exports its surveillance technology to developing country autocracies, runs brutal reeducation camps, and shows no interest—as is thematic in the book—in deviating from China Vision.

However, Wagner ends on a relatively optimistic note:

"What we are witnessing in the slugfest between China and the US is neither the imminent demise of the US-led post-War global order nor swift imposition of a new order based on China's unique view of the world. The post-War order was not created and did not come to define the global legal, regulatory, trade, and investment regime of the past 70 years in one fell swoop. It was the result of decades of carefully crafted multilateral diplomacy that will not simply be unraveled by a single Chinese or American president. If it is truly to be redefined, that, too, will take decades, and implies the ongoing complicity of scores of countries."

This is a very good book. It provides ample details on all of the major issue groups dominating China's relationship with the world: trade, technology, security, and geopolitics. Readers should come away worried, hopeful, and motivated.

- Dan Ikenson, director, the CATO Institute's Stiefel Center for Trade Policy Studies (USA)

China Vision is a good account of the Chinese Communist Party's domestic heavy-handedness and foreign diplomacy-via-blank-check. The two are interconnected, as China's crackdown on internal dissidents informs how it treats foreign countries and human rights activists who dare to oppose it. Through China's Belt and Road Initiative, wherein China loans billions of infrastructure dollars to developing nations, it can control them via a carrot-and-stick approach. China's spy state apparatus is also being used to sabotage foreign humanitarian organizations, religious groups, governments, and companies. The CCP is in the process of exporting its surveillance state blueprint to other interested authoritarian states, setting the stage for a cold war between China and its client dictatorships versus Western democracies. The People's Liberation Army is preparing for this possibility with a huge naval buildup in the contested South China Sea, aided by all of the "civilian" ports that it is building there under the auspices of the BRI. Daniel Wagner's book does a good job of explaining these geopolitical trends in a concise and even-handed way. He explains how colonialism and the Cold War helped to shape China's cynical outlook on the world and does not exaggerate China's capabilities. Anyone in politics, technology, economics, or the NGO sphere will learn a lot from this book.

- Russell Whitehouse, Executive Editor, International Policy Digest (USA)

Also by Daniel Wagner

AI Supremacy

Virtual Terror

Global Risk Agility and Decision-making

Managing Country Risk

Political Risk Insurance Guide

A repository of his published work (including more than 600 articles on current affairs and risk management) may be found at: www.countryrisksolutions.com.

China Vision

China's Crusade to Create
a World in its Own Image

Daniel Wagner

Cover design: Anna Zayco

www.annazayco.com; aniazayco@gmail.com

This book is dedicated to the Chinese people, who deserve to have a government that is not dedicated, first and foremost, to the perpetuation of its own existence at their expense, and that respects and practices widely accepted international norms rather than seeking to create and enforce its own set of rules.

Acknowledgements

I am grateful to Daniel Ikeson of the CATO Institute, Ali Wyne of RAND, Marites Vitug of Rappler, Cindy Yu of The Spectator, Aditya Ramachandran of FutureMap, David Thomas of Think Global, and Russell Whitehouse of the International Policy Digest for taking the time to review this book.

A special thanks to Anna Zayco for her incredible artwork and design of the book cover.

Contents

Abbreviations

1MDB	1 Malaysia Development Berhad
ADB	Asian Development Bank
AI	Artificial Intelligence
AIIB	Asian Infrastructure Investment Bank
ASAT	Anti-satellite
ASEAN	Association of Southeast Asian Nations
BRI	Belt and Road Initiative
BRICS	Brazil, Russia, India, China, and South Africa
CCP	Chinese Communist Party
CCTV	Closed-circuit Television
CFIUS	Committee on Foreign Investment in the United States
CSAC	Cybersecurity Association of China
DAMO	Discovery, Adventure, Momentum, and Outlook
DARPA	United States Defense Advanced Research Projects Agency
DoD	United States Department of Defense

EU	European Union
FDI	Foreign Direct Investment
FIRRMA	Foreign Investment Risk Review Modernization Act
FOCAC	Forum on China-Africa Cooperation
GCC	Gulf Cooperation Council
GDP	Gross Domestic Product
GNI	Gross National Income
GSD	PLA General Staff Department
HIPC	Highly Indebted Poor Countries
HP	Hewlett-Packard
HPM	High-power Microwave
IBM	International Business Machines
ICJ	International Court of Justice
IMF	International Monetary Fund
IP	Intellectual Property
ITU	International Telecommunications Union
KMT	Kuomintang
MDB	Multilateral Development Bank
ML	Machine Learning
MNEs	Multinational Enterprises
MSS	China's Ministry of State Security
MST	China Ministry of Science and Technology
NASA	United States National Aeronautics and Space Administration

NSA	United States National Security Agency
OECD	Organization of Economic Cooperation and Development
OFDI	Outward Foreign Direct Investment
OPM	United States Office of Personnel Management
PLA	People's Liberation Army
PCJ	Permanent Court of Arbitration
R&D	Research and Development
RAT	Remote Access Trojan
SGR	Standard Gauge Railway
SMBs	Small and Medium-Sized Businesses
SOE	State-owned Enterprise
SSF	China's Strategic Support Force
ToS	Terms of Service
UN	United Nations
UNCLOS	United Nations Convention on the Law of the Seas
US	United States
USG	United States Government
UUV	Unmanned Underwater Vehicle
VPN	Virtual Private Network
WTO	World Trade Organization

Prologue

I am a great admirer of the Chinese people, whose willpower, determination, and hard work should be the envy of the world. I have a variety of concerns about how the Chinese government treats its people, but the subject of this book is primarily about how the government acts towards the rest of the world.

My analysis of China in this book is based on having visited the country dozens of times since 1986, being a long-time student of China, and having written scores of articles about it for many years. My examination of how the Chinese government views the world, manipulates the global system for its own benefit, and is in the process of creating a China-centric future is derived from that foundation.

To better understand my frame of reference, consider that, during my time living and working in Asia for most of the first decade of this century, I traveled to China on a routine basis – sometimes monthly – and mostly for business. During that time, I was part of a team of people working to help get a massive hydroelectric project off the ground in Nepal, which was to utilize Chinese financing, engineering, construction, and insurance to build a facility that would deliver power to northern India.

At the time, this was a radical concept. Sino-Indian relations have been at odds for decades and, given their geographical proximity, competitive orientation, and historical conflicts, the notion of collaborating on a development project for the primary benefit of India and Nepal was unheard of. Never before had China, India, and Nepal dared to pursue such an undertaking, and never before had Chinese resources been critical to such a massive project's success in tiny Nepal.

Yet the project was an excellent example of how the Chinese government can be, and often is, forward thinking and ahead of its time. That is part of what gives the Chinese a unique view of and orientation toward the world. That orientation, and China's growing presence and power on the global stage, are the primary reasons why I decided to write this book. China has always fascinated me. I admire the Chinese peoples' prowess, curiosity about the world, and how boldly and brashly they sometimes act.

Few other countries yield as much influence and command such respect. This is, of course, at least in part, due to China's geographical, population, and economic size, but it is about more than that. It is about China's place in history and what the Chinese people no doubt consider to be their own conception of Manifest Destiny; except, in this case, that destiny is about spreading China's influence, governing philosophy, and resources around the world.

Beijing's purpose in doing so appears to be a combination of things. As is the case with many countries, China seeks to secure abundant natural resources to power its fantastic growth. It also pursues preferential trading rights and bilateral relationships with a broad swathe of the world's nations and desires to project its power well beyond its borders. You might be inclined to ask, how is that different from the US, for example? The biggest difference is that China wants the world to play by its own set of rules, which is often in direct contrast to the global norms that have been established – with China's participation, it is worth adding – since the 1940s.

The book is filled with examples that illustrate this point. For now, consider in this context China's self-proclaimed leadership in the ongoing global climate change discussions. As the world's largest polluter and consumer of coal to fuel its power plants, for many years China was a passive participant in these discussions. The US withdrawal from the Paris Agreement on Climate Change provided an opening for Beijing to assume a more robust position in the talks. But it decided to step up to the plate *while it remains the world's biggest carbon emitter and its carbon emission levels continue to rise.*

China wants to become the leading voice for developing countries on the subject of climate change and carbon emissions as its greatest *offender*, promoting the concept of a dual set of standards for developed and developing countries – more stringent for developed countries and less so for developing countries. So, which is China: a developed or a developing country? Depending on the subject, the Chinese government would have the world's nations believe that it is both. Beijing wants to be developing countries' advocate in climate change negotiations as it promotes and invests in coal-fired power plants throughout the developing world – promoting some of the worst forms of carbon emissions in these countries, all of which are *signatories to the Paris Agreement, which calls for a net global reduction by 2050! China's own target for beginning to reduce carbon emissions does not even commence until after 2030, which is incompatible with the Agreement's targets and objectives!*[1]

Some would call this chutzpah. I call it getting away with what you can. The truth is, for decades, because of its size and importance, China has gotten away with things that most nations would never even have attempted. It has been able to do so because, in part, it made itself the world's largest center of manufacturing and its largest importer, implying that no other nation had the cojones to stand up to Beijing, for fear of economic retribution. It is important to point out, however, that <u>the world has itself to blame for giving China that power</u>.

No one forced thousands of global companies to establish production operations in China. Once it became well understood that operating there can be extremely challenging, and that it can be a decade or more before many foreign firms have any real chance of becoming profitable (if at all), in most any other country, these firms could have made the decision to leave. No one forced them to stay there, but they were either greedy, stubborn, or just plain dumb. I have heard many stories of foreign companies that were raked over the coals by dishonest joint venture partners, overly zealous regulators, or the judicial system in China.

A lot of countries also have themselves to blame for allowing things to get so out of hand with China. The US fell into the habit of merely scolding Beijing for its plethora of objectionable behaviors. President Obama scolded Beijing when, in 2015, it was discovered that the Chinese had hacked and stolen the highly sensitive personal information of more than 22 million current and former US government employees and their families from the Office of Personnel Management (OPM). A stronger response was certainly warranted. As is noted in Chapter 6, there have been numerous instances where the US failed to exert a more robust response to China's antics. For that reason, I am pleased to finally see President Trump call China what it is – a thief of intellectual property on an institutionalized state level.

That said, China is, and will remain, a force to be reckoned with. It is important that the world has its eyes wide open about what China is, and is not. It is my hope that readers of this book will carefully consider the case that I am making here for China to be held responsible and taken to task when it recklessly breaches international standards, laws, and norms of behavior. If the world fails to do so, Beijing can only be expected to continue doing the same, while methodically implementing its own set of rules that it expects the world to abide by. Its vision of the world – China Vision – is intended to ensure that, once China becomes the world's largest economy and most important political force, it stays on top. It is incumbent on the rest of the world to ensure that China Vision does not become the de facto standard by which the world order and new normal continues to evolve.

1 China and the World

There is no doubt that this is China's century. Anyone who refuses to believe it is in denial. That may bother some people in the West, such as Americans, who might have a difficult time imagining that their long-held title as the world's largest economy and most powerful nation is about to be supplanted by a communist country that, they perceive, excels in the theft of intellectual property and does not play by the same rules as most of the rest of the world.

However, from the perspective of China's government and many of its people, China's is simply re-assuming the leading role it has had in global trade and investment numerous times throughout its history. For hundreds of years before the US even came into existence, the title of world's largest economy was either held by China or India, which together accounted for as much as 50% of global gross domestic product (GDP). For example, in 1400, it is estimated that China accounted for approximately 30% of the global economy; in 1500, that figure was 25%; in 1700, it was 22%.[1] In 1820, China's economy was 6 times larger than Britain's and almost 20 times the GDP of the US.[2]

This air of inevitability has served to influence how China has approached a range of issues, from adherence to the international rule of law and respect for maritime boundaries to human rights and consideration of the environment. The truth is, China often operates by its own interpretation of the rules that have been nearly universally accepted by the world's nations. It sees nothing wrong with doing so and has become masterful at breaching established norms of international behavior – whether in commerce, diplomacy, or military engagement – to suit its own particular vision of the world: China Vision.

China Vision is an integral part of how China is climbing back on top of the world stage. It is all about seeing the world from China's own lens and wanting to superimpose its unique manner of functioning into its relationship with the rest of the world. China Vision is about more than mere competition on the global stage, however; *it is simultaneously about the evisceration of Western-crafted norms in pursuit of China's long-term objective: to become the world's leading political, economic, military, and technological power by 2050.*

If that sounds like a highly ambitious goal, it is, and yet, China is well on its way to achieving nearly all of it, with the possible exception of outstripping the US and Russia as the world's leading military powers by the middle of this century. The US and Russia are simply too far ahead of China in their own ability to project their power militarily. China does not even yet have a fully functional blue-water navy, although it is in the process of creating one. But that is not stopping China's leaders from having the *ambition* to surpass Moscow and Washington in that regard.

That said, China has presided over nothing short of an economic miracle since 1960, and the Chinese government deserves a lot of credit for it. The Chinese Communist Party (CCP) has lifted the vast majority of its people out of abject poverty and transformed the country from what many considered to be a backwater, largely rural, developing country into an urban, manufacturing global powerhouse. In 1960, China's GDP was approximately $60 billion and its Gross National Income (GNI) per capita was just $70. By 2016, its GDP was in excess of $11 trillion and its GNI per capita was more than $8,200.[3] While one could easily brush this off by saying that, from the 1960 levels, there was only one direction in which its indicators could go (up), especially given the tremendous labor power implied by being the world's most populous country, there is no denying that the Chinese government's transformation of China's economy is nothing short of miraculous.

While China may ultimately fall short of its goal of becoming supreme in all of the previously mentioned areas, it is proceeding apace and has many of its near-and-medium-term goals in its sights. Beijing intends to become a high-income country by 2030. It has its Sustainable Development Goals mapped out for 2030 and, by that time, China intends to

2

become the world's undisputed leader in Artificial Intelligence (AI), which will set the stage for its future economic development.

As we approach the end of this second decade of the 21st century, while many of the world's leading political powers and pundits have been busy opining about when (not if) China will become the world's largest economy (estimated to be by the middle of the next decade), China has been busy becoming the world's leading de facto economic and political power. It has been running circles around the US in places like Africa and the Middle East, quietly establishing strong bilateral relations with the regions' governments, spreading money around, strengthening trading relationships, and cementing long-term contracts to extract and/or obtain a long-term supply of natural resources.

At the same time, it has also been busy in the corridors of the world's multilateral institutions, quietly establishing its prominence and exerting its influence in how development loans are disbursed. Although China held just 4.5% of the World Bank's voting power (compared with 16% by the United States (US))[4] in 2018, and it contributed just 5% toward the United Nation's (UNs) regular budget in 2015 (compared with 22% by the US), Beijing is punching well above its weight in these and other multilateral organizations. Suffice it to say that very little of consequence gets done at the World Bank, the UN, the Asian Development Bank (ADB), or any number of other such organizations without the wink and nod of Beijing.

Apart from having become so influential in these postwar bastions of economic power, Beijing has been instrumental in creating two new development banks – the Asian Infrastructure Investment Bank (AIIB) and the New Development Bank – both of which are based in China and are beginning to wield considerable clout in the global development arena. Both banks are starting to supplant the other multilateral development banks (MDBs) in a meaningful way. Yet, they are doing it with China Vision – sometimes bypassing conventional Western-created financial institutions and implementing a Chinese approach to development lending.

Chinese foreign direct investment (FDI) tends to differ from widely accepted international standards in three primary ways. First, Chinese investment tends to be concentrated in countries with poor governance environments. Second,

Chinese companies do not, in general, subscribe to global standards of environmental and social safeguards. And third, China remains relatively closed to foreign investment in many sectors, in contrast to its partners in both the developed and developing worlds.

The Organization of Economic Cooperation and Development (OECD) calculates an index of FDI restrictiveness for OECD countries and major emerging markets. In 2014, the Index showed that, among the BRICS countries (Brazil, Russia, India, China, and South Africa), for each economy and some of its major industries, China was by far the most closed economy among them.[5] *So, on one hand, it seeks to invest in countries that will swing the doors wide open for Chinese investors, but when it comes to inbound investment, China's doors are among the most tightly closed among developing countries.*

Beijing has also deployed China Vision to redefine what is considered 'normal' in bilateral economic and political relations. The dispensation of foreign aid in the postwar era had been largely defined by the West in terms of an orientation toward democracy and respect for human rights. China has become an increasingly significant foreign aid donor without much consideration for the type of government or whether it is in the habit of abusing its power or people. What matters most to Beijing is whether a given country has whatever China needs and is in a position to deliver it. If a country has both of these things, Chinese money flows.

This has given Beijing a considerable advantage over some of its Western brethren, who have ended up tripping over themselves with what often tends to be a cookie-cutter approach to defining whether a given country passes the smell test in terms of acceptable Western notions of democracy and human rights. *China has expertly identified the flaws and frailties of the Western model of politics and diplomacy to craft its own version, based on its own values, rules, and norms – which generally do not include democracy and human rights.*

One might argue that China is really no different than any other leading nation, in that it determines what matters, what its preferred rules of engagement are, and who it prefers its allies to be. It then sees how far it can go to realize its own ambitions in its own way. China cannot be blamed for doing that. But what makes China Vision different from the vision of any other leading nation is that *Beijing appears to know no boundaries in its quest for economic, political, technological, and military supremacy.* From establishing and maintaining relations with North Korea and Iran to the Democratic Republic of Congo and Venezuela – *Beijing will do whatever it takes to establish a good working relationship to satisfy its needs, irrespective of the type of government, depth of corruption, or nature of the forms of abuse that may proliferate in a given country.*

The Chinese Mindset

The famous American Sinologist Lucian Pye has observed that the Chinese believe that individuals are generally highly partisan, have hidden agendas, and will act in devious ways, consistent with their biases and preferences. Such an orientation can be extended to how the Chinese view the business world and international relations. Consider the Chinese mindset vis-à-vis business. Chinese businesses operate with the understanding that their objective is to achieve the highest level of economic return. In that regard, they may be no different than businesses anywhere else in the world.

But for the Chinese, businesses that offer a fair deal to everyone are perceived as leaving too much money on the table, and those that cheat indiscriminately risk losing their reputation. The ideal, from their perspective, is to provide a fair deal to customers that provide a key benefit to the business, such as a large volume of sales or a benefit to a business's reputation, while squeezing those that do not do so, mercilessly. In a sense, Chinese business owners treat customers not unlike cattle – distinguishing between those that are reserved for milking versus those that are destined for the slaughterhouse.[6]

Christianity's golden rule is to *do unto others as you would have them do unto you.* The Chinese version of this credo is more like, *whatever you do not want done to you, do not do to another.*[7] Chinese philosophy references the concept of the 'doctrine of the mean', which emphasizes the ideal of attempting to achieve mid-point solutions. As an example, when two parties have opposing points of view, under this doctrine, neither would be completely right or wrong, and an accurate truth would lay somewhere in the middle. By the same token, there can be no such thing under this doctrine as absolute loyalty to a person or organization, because fidelity is not viewed as a utility-maximizing proposition. Similarly, incrementalism in negotiations is seen as a core objective, with the goal of establishing a new foundation from which to negotiate to one's greater advantage.[8]

While Westerners tend to believe in the universal rule of law, the Chinese see it as little more than cultural precepts that may be used to manipulate foreigners. Whether in business or in international relations, the Chinese prefer the concept of mutual respect. *The Chinese do not generally believe in a universal set of values; the smartest ones come to the table believing in nothing at all. Ideologies are seen by them as inconvenient, because they tend to limit the range of options available at the negotiating table. The most strategically advantageous position is the one that ends up being the most adaptable in the end.* In international relations, Chinese negotiators balk when being accused of being expansionist or exercising hegemonic behavior because they view such terminology as Western in orientation and not applicable to them.[9]

Pretending to have a thin skin is common among Chinese when negotiating – with other individuals, with businesses, or with the Chinese government vis-à-vis other governments. Westerners often become convinced that their Chinese counterparts must be handled gently, which may turn out to have the opposite effect – inhibiting their success in negotiations.[10] *The Chinese presume that a system or set of rules must be rigged in someone else's favor. For this reason, the average person from China will inevitably seek to manipulate that system or set of rules.[11] This generates a general lack of trust – between the individual and businesses or the government, between businesses, and between governments.*

An illustrative example is China's used car market. In most developed nations, sales of second-hand cars outnumber new vehicle sales by a two-to-one margin. The opposite is true in China, where the used car market has failed to gain traction because of the widely held presumption among potential buyers that private sellers are only interested in unloading cars with problems. As a result, buyers generally offer less than a car may be worth, which discourages owners from selling their cars.[12]

The low-trust trap has manifest itself in numerous other ways throughout Chinese history. At the end of the nineteenth century, China wanted to build a railway system but lacked sufficient capital. Although China appeared to the outside world to be poor at the time, many families had actually accumulated large sums of capital, but the low-trust trap prevented them from investing in long-term projects that would have benefitted the country. As a result, the Qing government ended up asking foreign governments for assistance, which is why most of the railroad network that was built into the early 20th Century used foreign sources of capital.[13]

Little discussed in the literature is the fact that, following the overthrow of the Qing Dynasty in 1911, China was, arguably, a narco-state during much of the rule of the Kuomintang (KMT). During this period, a symbiotic relationship evolved between the sale of opium and the KMT's rise to power, particularly between 1924-1937. Despite attempts to identify other sources of income, the KMT became increasingly addicted to the tax revenues derived from the sale of opium, which many people in China were addicted to at all levels of society. Government policy vacillated between prohibition and legalization. The government ultimately sought to curtail the cultivation, sale, and consumption of opium through a government monopoly.[14]

The rest of the world has misunderstood or misread China in any number of ways throughout history. The Chinese are not by nature fighters but prefer whenever possible to deploy a 'cat's paw' strategy which entails getting others to intercede on their behalf. China rarely launches a direct attack, but, rather, prefers to hang back and assess (or take advantage) of the situation.[15] China's approach to the Iraq War is a good example of this. The Chinese did not fight in the War, sat quietly by the sidelines, and when it was over, swooped in to scoop up many of the oil contracts that the US and its coalition partners had fought so hard to earn.

China's Zero-Sum Vision of the World

The emergence of a new global power has often profoundly shifted an existing geopolitical landscape and caused considerable discomfort among the established order. China's economic and political resurgence is doing that, of course, but apart from the inevitable uncertainty and tension associated with any shift in global power, much of the angst generated in China's case stems from its failure to engage in behavior concomitant with the increased global responsibilities ordinarily associated with a becoming a global power – or even an acknowledgement of its obligation to do so.

China has ascended rapidly onto the global stage by virtue of its economic might, even as it retains characteristics of a developing country by GDP per capita (a function of its population size). *China seems to want it both ways – it plays geopolitical power games as a force to be reckoned with among equals, yet often declines to shoulder the burdens of a great power and even demands that it be afforded the benefits ordinarily due to a developing country.*

In this regard, China's leadership simultaneously nurses a profound grievance against 'colonialists' and 'aggressors' as it expands its direct political and economic influence across the globe. China's leaders show bravado when on the world stage but seem deeply paranoid that their rule at home could all fall apart at any time. Indeed, a preoccupation with maintaining social harmony and avoiding conflict at home is a primary driver of the government's policies.

While China's public pronouncements may at times appear mercurial, they are part of a well-conceived strategy. *China seeks to leverage benefits consistent with being a developing country, plays upon the West's historical guilt over colonialism, and exploits its continued belief that economic development will inexorably lead to pluralism. Yet Beijing does not hesitate to attempt to parlay its growing power into influence whenever and wherever it can. This Janus-like strategy gives China leeway and flexibility in crafting its international political and economic policy.*

At home, the CCP has established socialism with Chinese characteristics, or, less euphemistically, state capitalism, that necessitates state powers using markets to create wealth while ensuring the political survival of the ruling class. As a government that will soon preside over the world's largest economy – and one that depends intimately on flows of international goods and capital – the CCP no longer simply practices state capitalism at home: it applies it globally.

Although the West has long played mercantilist games, it gradually migrated toward the belief that liberalization of international markets is mutually beneficial for all countries. But China continues to see international economics as a zero-sum game. *It finds its developing status a convenient cloak and justification for the application of global state capitalism. Beijing engages in beggar-thy-neighbor policies it deems advantageous while distorting the world's markets according to the dictates of its political demands and dismissing criticism of such behavior as unfair to a developing country.* Similarly, on political issues, *China portrays naked self-interest as the reasonable demands of a developing country, and displays this behavior in nearly every arena in which it interacts with the world, from foreign aid and investment to multilateral institutions and international relations.*

Beijing's previous deliberate undervaluation of the yuan pointed to further distortions of international markets by China's state capitalism. But the yuan's undervaluation was just the tip of the iceberg. As importantly, Chinese banks receive a hidden subsidy: a wide spread between the rates paid on household deposits and the rates banks charge for loans. Many Chinese bankers, who are in effect state employees (given that the banking system is largely government run), funnel the artificially cheap money to state-owned enterprises (SOEs). Since households have no investment alternative to domestic banks, they in effect provide a huge subsidy to Chinese industry. The CCP's state capitalism mandates growth and employment through exports and investment at all costs, in order to ensure its political and economic supremacy.

Even as China increases its economic presence through investment and greater influence in multilateral institutions, it continues to reap benefits intended to accrue to the world's truly needy nations. By all rights, *China should be strictly a donor nation to MDBs, not a recipient of aid.* That China continues to be some of the development banks' largest recipient of funds really is scandalous, coming at the cost of the poorest of the poor, which truly need the resources. *At what point does China's absolute strength count for more than its per capita development? And, why do donor countries allow this double standard to continue to occur?*

China has arguably done more to advance global nuclear proliferation than any other state, having helped Pakistan develop its nuclear arsenal and ballistic missile technology to become what many intelligence analysts believe to be the world's most dangerous nuclear-capable power. The Chinese government sees nuclear power as a potentially powerful component of its Belt and Road Initiative (BRI), which aims to integrate China economically and politically with Europe, Africa, and the rest of Asia through the construction of major infrastructure projects, which include developing nuclear power in energy-dependent countries. The China National Nuclear Corporation has identified more than 40 countries within the BRI as potential future recipients of Chinese nuclear technology.[16]

The largest recipients of Chinese military aid have in the past been India's neighbors, including Myanmar, Pakistan, Nepal, Bangladesh, and Sri Lanka, in addition to Pakistan. India rightly fears that China is engaged in a concerted campaign to undermine and contain it. China continues developing its 'string of pearls' strategy in the Indian Ocean, investing significant resources to develop deep water ports in the Bay of Bengal, the Arabian Sea, Pakistan, Sri Lanka, and the Seychelles. These appear to be a basis for the projection of a powerful naval presence into what New Delhi considers its backyard.

China has in the past routinely blocked action against, or has actively supported, a rogue's gallery of nations, among them Iran, North Korea, and Sudan. It claims it has no influence over their actions, based on its policy of non-interference, but China's support clearly requires a quid pro quo, be it natural resource wealth, business ties, or geopolitical significance. China has avoided sanctions from the international community, partly due to this image it has cultivated of itself as a non-interfering developing country. While the West has also projected its power and has at times dealt with equally noxious states, domestic political constraints make such deals with the devil increasingly difficult to sell to electorates attuned to human rights, ethics, and governance, and who are provided with the freedom of speech to object to their governments' actions. No such freedom exists in China.

As long as the CCP continues to govern, China will continue to comport itself according to its zero-sum vision of the world: China Vision. At best, the West can hope the CCP's interests converge toward those of the larger globalized world.

Even as China speaks of a peaceful rise within the existing international structure, its behavior, which may at times be described as impertinent, belies the West's desire to have faith in its words. Indeed, many nations around the world appear to be running out of patience at China's uncompromising approach to the promotion of its own self-interest.[17]

The Century of Humiliation

To better understand China's frame of reference toward the rest of the world, bear in mind that China had been the world's largest economy for nearly two millennia. That position was significantly weakened by the slow rise of the US toward the end of the nineteenth century. China's GDP per capita was lower in 1952 than in 1820, and its share of world GDP fell from roughly a third to one twentieth. At the same time, its real per capita income fell from parity to a quarter of the world average.

A series of large scale nineteenth century rebellions caused a serious fall in living standards, from which China did not fully recover, resulting in a fall in per capita income from 1820 to 1890. In 1890, modern manufacturing and transport represented only 0.5% of GDP. The urban proportion of the total population of China was not much bigger at the end of the nineteenth century than it had been in 1820.[18]

In addition, rising domestic discontent was made worse by a series of foreign challenges to Chinese sovereignty from the 1840s onwards. China was totally unprepared to contest intrusions from the sea. It had virtually no naval forces or modern artillery to stand up to foreign intruders. For the better part of a century, China made humiliating concessions to foreign powers, chipping away at its own sovereignty and losing large territories.

China was unable to respond to, or even to comprehend, these new challenges. It had no foreign office, its capital city was located far inland, and the governing authorities had little interest in foreign trade. There was almost no knowledge of Western geography and technology, even less knowledge of Western languages; an education system that focused mostly on Chinese classics; and a power elite of bureaucrats who had no inclination to change the existing system of governance.

By the turn of the nineteenth century, China was a spent power, the US was rising fast, and, it would take generations for China to regain its footing. What is commonly referred to as *China's Century of Humiliation left a deep impression on China's leaders and much of its citizenry, which determined never again to be caught flat-footed in the face of internal and external challenges.*

From the British seizure of Hong Kong to the Taiping Rebellion (which affected 16 provinces, involved occupation of China's most prosperous areas, and was a major ideological challenge to Qing imperial authority and Confucian bureaucrats) to foreign interference during the Rebellion (including a joint attack by the British and French to expand their shipping and trading privileges, and Russian seizure of Eastern Siberia) to the war with Japan to the Boxer War and subsequent collapse of the Qing Dynasty, the rise of the KMT, and the creation of modern Taiwan – *the Chinese psyche has been filled with recurring memories of threats from within and from abroad, without the ability to meaningfully respond. That has shaped the frame of reference of China's current leaders and population, who are focused on regaining China's greatness.*

Pride and insecurity are common and underlying themes in the Chinese psyche. The Chinese are, understandably, a proud people, and the CCP's preoccupation with security and stability is deeply embedded in the modern Chinese psyche. The concept of national humiliation is similarly deeply embedded and is driven home through the country's national school system. "Never forget the national humiliation" is a well-worn slogan throughout China, so the Chinese are naturally sensitive on the subject. It was not lost on the Chinese that the date of the first implementation of President Trump's tariffs against China in 2018 coincided with the anniversary of the Japanese invasion of China.[19]

Doing unto Others

In seeking to recapture its greatness, China has opened itself up to being accused of doing something very similar to what it accuses colonial powers of doing to it for the past two centuries – exploiting the economies of developing countries in pursuit of natural resources. This begs the question, *is China trying to inflict a century of humiliation on the rest of the world?* It certainly looks and feels like that to a variety of developing countries that are playing host to hundreds of thousands of Chinese workers who are, with their, host governments' compliance, stripping them of a significant portion of their natural resources.[20]

Consider the sheer volume of ethnic Chinese living in natural resource-rich developing nations. As of 2017, an estimated 500,000 ethnic Chinese lived in South Africa and more than 250,000 were estimated to be living in Angola. In some of the least likely places on the continent of Africa, the Chinese are there in ample numbers. During the Arab Awakening in 2011, China evacuated 35,000 ethnic Chinese from Libya.[21] This will strike many as surprising, but not when one considers that the greatest single source of FDI into Africa is China. More than half of Chinese investment in Africa since 2005 has been in oil-rich Angola and Nigeria.[22]

Chinese influence in some developing nations is so great that there is question about just how willing host nation governments are to resist Chinese overtures. For example, in 2017 in Sri Lanka, the government agreed to a 99-year lease of the strategic southern port of Hambantota, in a deal that some government critics contended threatened the country's sovereignty. At the time, Sri Lanka's president was accused of playing geopolitics with national assets. Sri Lanka owed more than $8 billion to state-controlled Chinese firms – debt which cannot be repaid.

The Hambantota deal, valued at $1.1 billion, was necessary to reduce the size of the country's debt to China. Beijing now controls 70% of the port. While the Chinese and Sri Lankan governments referred to the port deal as a 'concession', such an arrangement comes perilously close to exactly the type of transactions China fought against during its own humiliation.

China's actions there have not gone unnoticed by India, an historically close ally of Sri Lanka. To attempt to reset the growing imbalance, India has partnered with Japan to develop a port on Sri Lanka's eastern coastline and has entered into talks to invest in an airport near Hambantota. Beijing's growing influence throughout Asia has prompted numerous Asian nations to realign their economic and political orientations. India and Japan have found common ground in a variety of areas.

While there have been some signs of pushback against Chinese investment, including the rejection of hydropower projects in Nepal, Pakistan, and Myanmar, many countries around the region and the world have already succumbed to China's unique approach to the utilization of loans to secure long-term strategic economic interests around the world.[23] By the time many of these countries' governments realized what China was doing, it had become too late to do much about it. They are, and will likely remain, in China's orbit and grip for decades to come.

Many of the resource-rich economies of Latin America have become inextricably linked to the Chinese economy by virtue of the fact that some of them sell up to 90% of their iron ore, copper, and other natural resources to China. That dependency has become a double-edged sword for exporting nations and China alike – a good thing for exporting nations when resource prices and demand are high and the reverse when prices and demand are low – making China's influence on economies half a world away hugely significant.

As a result, there is now a growing backlash against China as a foreign investor, among developing and developed countries alike. Numerous proposed investments by Chinese investors in sensitive sectors of the US economy have been blocked on national security grounds. Among the most recent examples are the high profile ZTE (the country's second largest telecommunications firm, which became the subject of direct discussion between Presidents Trump and Xi) and Jinhua Integrated Circuit (which had been accused of intellectual property theft). China's ambitious investment objectives, and the manner in which it sometimes goes about achieving them, have made Beijing a magnet for criticism.

China is the second largest trading partner with Latin America (the US remains its largest), and the number one partner of Brazil, Chile, and Peru. In Brazil, President Bolsonaro cast China as a menace during his 2018 election campaign, stating that China was not buying *in* Brazil, it was *buying* Brazil. Between 2000 and 2017, Chinese direct investment in Brazil reached nearly $50 billion. While countries such as Brazil are now regretting opening their doors to Chinese investment to such a degree, elsewhere, it is China that is having buyer's remorse. Beijing has lent Venezuela more than $60 billion since 2000,[24] now with little prospect of

14

being paid back more than a fraction of that amount without arranging a barter arrangement for oil over many years.

While many developing country leaders have a tolerance for (and may even welcome) overt backslapping, strong arming, and illegal transactions, their people increasingly do not. *China is playing a dangerous game by swooping in and laying claim to large swathes of other countries' economies.* It has laid itself open for criticism and long-term resentment on the part of populations who may not perceive much benefit from the arrangement and are saddled with tens of billions of dollars of debt once their leaders, who may have personally benefitted from such arrangements, leave office.

China's Dual Personality

China's emergence as a leader on the global political and economic stage may be best characterized as a combination of manifest destiny and a teenager taking his first test drive in a car. On one hand, China has ably influenced the course of global political affairs through deft diplomacy and its influence in multilateral institutions, as well as the course of the global economy through enormous FDI flows, bilateral trade agreements, and the disbursement of foreign aid. On the other hand, it has stumbled on a host of issues, such as attempts to project its power in blatant violation of international law (i.e. through the construction of military installations on the Spratly Islands) and numerous violations of its World Trade Organization (WTO) obligations.

Such a dichotomy may be expected of any country stepping on to the global stage, and there is no way that a nation the size and significance of China could flex its muscles without others noticing or objecting. But, as alluded to earlier, China's debut as a global player, particularly over the past decade, has been complicated by its chosen dual role as both a developed and developing nation. It is at once a major donor to poor nations and a recipient of multilateral aid from development banks – in essence, the 'poor' developing country that seeks to combat poverty at home and the global superpower that skillfully projects its power. China's leadership promotes this duality – wanting to be thought of as a country that must continually strive to 'develop' while at the same time acting like a superpower.

From the perspective of developed countries, this duality naturally makes it more difficult for China to achieve its international economic objectives, since Beijing can be accused of wanting to have its cake and eat it, too. It wants to have the benefits of multilateral development assistance normally afforded to 'developing' countries, while wanting to be able to robustly influence international fiscal and monetary affairs. Yet this 'dual personality' also makes it easier for China to establish relationships with developing countries by being able to both identify with the plight of poor countries while at the same time acting as a lender to them.

In a sense, *China has the best of both worlds, being at once a combination of kingmaker and 800-pound gorilla, while at the same time being a friend to countries that have few if any allies, and being willing to lend a helping financial hand when developed countries and MDB's fall short.*

Very soon, China will be forced to make up its mind about what it wants to be, because it cannot have it both ways indefinitely. It will either decide to embrace its 'destiny' as a global superpower and gradually discard its dual 'poor cousin' image, or it will fail in its efforts to try to be all things to all countries. More to the point, once China becomes the world's largest economy and perfects its diplomatic statecraft, it can no longer be seen as a developing country. Continuing its duality play becomes more and more disingenuous and less and less defensible with each passing year.

As noted earlier, that Beijing continues to suck up an enormous amount of multilateral development assistance is really becoming scandalous. Between 1986 and 2018, the ADB approved approximately $35 billion in sovereign loans and just over $4 billion for private sector operations (excluding B Loans) to China, accounting for just under 17% of the Bank's total loan portfolio.[25] Cumulative lending to China from the World Bank totaled $54 billion as of 2014[26] and the Bank lent another $2.5 billion to Beijing in 2017.[27] As of 2017, the World Bank's total cumulative lending portfolio since it began operations in 1944 was $681 billion[28], meaning that China has accounted for approximately 12% of the total, in an institution with 189-member countries.

According to the World Bank, more than 500 million people were lifted out of extreme poverty as China's poverty rate fell from 88% in 1981 to 6.5% in 2012.[29] Any legitimate

16

argument in favor of lending based on need from MDBs disappeared many years ago, yet the World Bank's former country director for China, Yukon Huang, has defended the Bank's continued lending to Beijing, arguing that provincial and local governments need the loans because structural impediments prevent domestic banks from providing sufficient credit to finance public projects.[30] In other words, he defended the practice on the basis that the Chinese government cannot seem to manage its banking sector sufficiently to get credit where it is needed in the Chinese economy. If every country in the world were to make such an argument, many developed countries would be lined up with their own hands stretched out just as China is doing.

There is another reason why the practice continues, however: the MDBs need China to continue to absorb billions of dollars of loans, grants, and technical assistance each year because many of the smaller and poorer countries do not have the capacity to absorb it. Without China, lending amounts would decline, which would call into question how these banks operate. That is a subject few in the management of these institutions are inclined to tackle seriously, even though doing so is long overdue. In 2017, the Trump administration was reluctant to endorse a capital increase at the World Bank, with US Treasury Secretary Mnuchin stating that "more capital is not the solution when existing capital is not allocated effectively."[31] This is what he was talking about.

For Beijing to continue to receive development assistance, given the strength and prominence of its economy, makes even less sense given that has taken specific action to assume a more substantial role lending to developing countries through the Chinese-led AIIB and its participation as a founding member of the New Development Bank. Beijing formed the AIIB to counter the absence of a more pronounced leadership role in other MDBs, as well as to help pick up the slack in infrastructure investment lending in Asia. *Why does it not recognize the incongruity in taking a prominent leadership role in infrastructure-related lending institutions while continuing to accept development assistance on a grand scale from the MDBs it is now competing with?*

China is naturally capable of getting to its desired finish line any way it desires to do so, but *it would ultimately be far preferable if it were to become the global power that it strives to be as a member of the community of nations that demonstrates that it acknowledges and plays by internationally accepted rules, standards, and norms.* It remains to be seen whether President Xi can transform China into a country that recognizes the longer-term benefits of playing on the same field by the same rules as most of the world's other nations.[32] If he were to become successful doing so, China's importance to the global economy would only grow, as would its ability to project its power politically and diplomatically.

Surely, he realizes that, but there is a larger question implied by such a statement: Can any Chinese leader successfully move the CCP in the direction of embracing international norms and standards while it maintains its paranoia about losing its grip on power at home? Opening one hand to the world while keeping the other fist clenched would appear to be an unrealistic and incongruous goal. The CCP will undoubtedly need to address this fundamental issue before it can make any meaningful and believable grand overtures to the rest of the world. That will probably never happen, for the supremacy and perpetuity of the CCP is what matters most to China's leadership.

2 Economic Considerations

China's Mythical Eternal Hard Landing

Almost every time China has entered a downward economic trajectory over the past couple of decades, many Western economic pundits have pontificated that China will experience a hard landing, even though its recent economic history has demonstrated that, in spite of global and national economic turmoil, China has not experienced a hard or soft landing, but rather, no landing at all. According to the International Monetary Fund (IMF), China has maintained blazing hot growth for decades. Astonishingly, between 1953 and 2017, China registered in excess of 5% GDP growth for all but 10 of those 65 years and, between 1983 and 2007, China registered GDP growth in excess of 10% for 14 of those 25 years.[1]

Economists have naturally been skeptical about the legitimacy of such statistics which, to many of them, seem fanciful, but the Chinese government claims to have been faithfully delivering sustained high growth year after year and decade after decade. It has to, because part of the implicit bargain it has made with the Chinese people is that it will continue to deliver economic growth and a better life for the average citizen in return for absolute allegiance to the CCP and everything that goes with it. The government believes it must keep all the plates spinning in perpetuity, for if one plate comes crashing down, they may all do so.

It has become increasingly difficult to maintain the type of growth necessary to accommodate tens of millions of new entrants into the national work force each year. One big reason that the government has been able to do so is that it has for decades been one of the world's largest exporting nations, but this has come at a price. Apart from the dependency it has created on the willingness of the world's countries to continue to manufacture in China and purchase all those exports, doing so has prevented China from being able to transition to an economy driven by domestic consumption – something that a country with a population of 1.4 billion people would naturally want to be able to do.

The erosion of some of China's largest export markets around the world, combined with cost push and wage inflation, has chipped away at the comparative advantage of China's manufacturing industry. At least four times since the Great Recession, China's Purchasing Manager Index – a widely watched indicator of the health of the manufacturing and service sectors – has dropped to below 50, meaning that the economy has contracted. This has occurred for a number of reasons, including the health of the global economy and trade disputes. But an additional reason why it has become a recurring theme in China's economy is that it has at times become difficult for small and medium-sized private businesses (SMBs) – the driving force behind China's manufacturing industry – to access credit.

More than 70% of China's banking market is controlled by the 'big four' banks – Bank of China, the China Construction Bank, the Industrial and Commercial Bank of China, and the Agricultural Bank of China. These state-owned commercial banks skew monetary resources towards state-owned enterprises or other privileged national corporations. This allocation deficiency in China's banking system has created a breeding ground for China's large and complicated shadow banking network, where most credit-starved private SMBs seek costly funding. The shadow banking system is little regulated or monitored and is awash with cash that earns negative real interest rates in commercial banks.

Monetary policy alone cannot fix the structural deficiencies of China's economy, whose well-being is highly leveraged, based on the consumption of European and US consumers. Like so many other countries around the world, China has an increasing wealth gap that has shackled domestic demand to such an extent that it fails to make up the difference left by the European and US markets. China has for years been saddled with a serious excess capacity problem, which forces down marginal returns on investment, making it more effective in causing inflationary pressures than propelling GDP and employment forward. This is a sign of serious over-investing and overheating.

Since 1999, China's exports and fixed investment have contributed nearly 70% of the country's GDP growth, while domestic consumption has contributed around 30%. Using export and investment to push the economy forward is what has become known as the Beijing Consensus, which works beautifully when the world is prospering but works poorly when it is not. Given that Europe and the US must transition from deficit-fueled consumption toward consumption based on fiscal surpluses in the long-term, they must increase their chronically low savings rate, produce more, and import less.

This means that the export-led growth that China has known for the past three decades will continue to gradually slow down. That said, China will likely continue to depend on an export-led economy for at least another 20 years, so something must change in the interim. A consumption-led economy is the only way out, unless the Chinese government chooses to fight for a greater share of overseas markets and is prepared for the possibility of recurring trade wars with its largest competitors.

In 2018, largely in response to China's trade war with the US, President Xi revealed his intention to start to refer to China as the world's largest importer. It is indeed the world's biggest importer of commodities and agricultural products, which also presents an ongoing cost-push inflation challenge. With negative real interest rates and diminishing marginal returns in industry pushing more and more money into asset investment and speculation, inflation will remain a persistent threat that must be carefully managed.

The Chinese government would be wise to unleash the big four banks and allow them to operate on a genuinely commercial basis, to allow for more efficient monetary allocation. China should transform its labor intensive, low value-added economy to a more high-value-added knowledge economy. And it should reform the wealth redistribution system to empower its broad consumer base and encourage a consumption-led economy. It is in the process of doing all this, but it will take many years to implement such broadly-based and ambitious economic objectives.

The US enjoys the luxury of continuing to have the dollar be the world's de facto currency and can link hands with its major trading partners to effectively export its liquidity issues and some of its inflation risk. China enjoys none of that. In this regard, the Beijing Consensus makes little sense. Pegging a country's growth to a certain set of policy tools or a reserve currency (the US dollar in this case) is equally dangerous. The world is changing fast. The battle between Keynes and Friedman has long proven that the only consensus that really makes sense in the long haul is to adapt and change. This is the consensus China should be embracing, or it may yet face what has until now been only a mythical hard landing.[2]

The Bubble Economy

The root cause of the decline in China's annual GDP – from double digits as recently as 2010 to the 6-7% range in the second decade of the twenty-first century – has a lot to do with the unsustainable economic bubbles that have been created by the government, and the collapsing demand that has accompanied it. Central Bank maneuvering can at best serve to sustain the over-leveraged economy and avoid a systematic short-circuit of debt financing on a temporary basis. An insufficient amount of liquidity has been invested in lending capacity or job creation, so the government's economic return on credit gradually deteriorates. If such structural deficiencies are not soon addressed by the government, the longer-term deterioration of the Chinese economy can only continue.

The Central Bank's ongoing aggressive actions, intended to enhance liquidity, at best serve to sustain the over-leveraged economy and avoid the systematic short-circuit of debt financing but, in the long term, this is unsustainable. A multi-year lending binge on the part of China's state-owned banks, encouraged by the central government to attempt to stimulate the economy, has put the banks in a precarious position. Their ballooning balance sheets – driven by the lending frenzy and strict capital requirements – have in reality made China's banks cash starved. China's credit-fueled economy is so over-leveraged that a great deleveraging is its only way out. The pyramid of debt and credit is cracking and will ultimately collapse, since underlying economic conditions are deteriorating and unsustainable. No amount of monetary band aids can change that.

Chinese businesses will need more and more credit to achieve the same economic result, so they will become more and more leveraged, less able to service their debt, and more prone to insolvency and bankruptcy. A turning point may arrive in which an increasing number of insolvencies and bankruptcies initiate an accelerating downward spiral for underlying asset prices and drive up the non-performing loan ratio of the banks. Should the over-stretched banking system implode, a full-blown economic crisis could arise. Rather than implement temporary stop gap measures to keep the economy from imploding, the Central Bank should be tackling the root causes of China's economic ills.

In 2010, China spent more than US $1 trillion on construction (including residential and non-residential real estate and infrastructure), representing around 20% of its nominal GDP – almost twice the world average. That year, the Chinese construction market surpassed that of the US and became the largest construction market in the world, accounting for approximately 15% of the global total. China's construction binge pushed its investment/GDP ratio to 48.5% in 2010, a record unprecedented in the recent history of China or any other major economy. China officially became a construction-led economy.

That year, China's cement consumption surpassed 1,800 metric tons, *about 55% of global consumption and around 25 times more than US consumption*. At the time, China constructed approximately 1.8 billion square meters of new residential floor space, the equivalent of Spain's entire housing floor space stock. This construction provided sufficient accommodation for 60 million people, but the urban population had only increased by around 20 million. Keeping that pace of construction for just five years would have resulted in 9 billion square meters of new housing stock-enough to provide accommodation for 300 million more people. The available floor space stock in China would have been able to accommodate an urbanized population of 65-70%, but the IMF did not expect China's urban population to reach that percentage until 2030.

For a glimpse of the position China has put itself in, consider what happened in Spain. For many years, Spain had a high consumption rate per capita before it crashed in the Great Recession. Spanish annual cement consumption reached nearly 1,300 kilograms per capita in 2007, just ahead of the financial crisis. Four years later, Spanish consumption stood at around 500 kilograms per capita, down more than 60%

from its peak. By contrast (and bearing in mind the size of China's population versus that of Spain), China's cement consumption per capita was 1,400 kilograms in 2010, and 1800 in 2014. Since 2014, China's cement consumption has plateaued at that high level.[3] Put another way, *by 2015, China had consumed more cement in 3 years than the US had consumed in the entire 20th century!*[4] Call it the new definition of what constitutes an economic bubble.

Does it Quack like a Duck?

If something looks like a duck, walks like a duck, and quacks like a duck, it is usually a duck – except in China. In China, you can have 30 billion square feet of unused office and residential capacity and, to the Chinese government, it is evidence of a permanent long-term boom. In most countries, that kind of excess would be called evidence of an imminent collapse, but not in China. Some Western pundits are divided about whether such statistics foretell the continuation of China's perma-boom or its imminent collapse. In a country that needs to grow 9% per annum just to keep up with the ranks of new entrants into the job market, the long-term boom prediction may just be right, even though official statistics may be suspect. *China is a country where market forces have less impact than the will of the government, so the boom will remain sustainable as long as the government says it will, and ensures that it is.*

If the world has learned anything about China since it adopted 'socialism with Chinese characteristics' in 1993, it is that the country has defied all conventional logic and reasonable predictions about how it would grow and come to impact the global economy. One benefit of being an authoritarian government is that it does not need to care what its people, or the rest of the world, think. Given all the economic headwinds the government has faced and continues to face – both domestic and international – *one could argue that it has done a stellar job of keeping the juggernaut that is the Chinese economy humming. Most economies would have collapsed under such weight.*

It has naturally made mistakes along the way, just as every other government has but, at the beginning of the Great Recession, the Chinese government acted like the bastion of fiscal conservatism when compared with the US Federal Reserve. Although the Chinese government can certainly be criticized for its heavy hand, it can also be argued that *the heavy hand is what has enabled China to weather crisis after crisis relatively unscathed, and what will probably enable it to continue to do so. The world has become dependent upon China to drive the global economy, so we should all wish the government well in its task.*

So is the duck that is the Chinese economy built on sustainable fundamentals or a pile of quicksand? There is much conventional evidence that the foundation of China's fantastic growth is unsustainable, but that has been the case for years and yet it continues to grow and grow. For example, bank lending nearly doubled between 2008 and 2009, the sale of residences rose by 44% that year, and two thirds of the country's GDP product consisted of fixed-asset investment, which is clearly unsustainable on a long-term basis. But these statistics mask some hidden strengths, such as, that most homes are paid for in cash, urban disposable income has risen an average of 7% per year since 2000, and real output per worker rises between 10% and 12% per year. It could, therefore, be argued that *there are checks and balances in place, whether deliberate or otherwise, that enable China's economy to maintain equilibrium.*

The flip side of China's lending binge is that China's banking system, which is dominated by those enormous state-owned banks, has almost unlimited access to low-cost credit, enabling it to engage in unbridled real estate speculation, and giving the banks an incentive to keep the seemingly endless cycle of high growth going. We know how that kind of behavior ended up in the US and elsewhere, but local governments depend on the tax revenue generated from such purchases, so they, too, have a vested interest in keeping the bubble growing.

Some pundits claim that there is no bubble, and that the amount of leverage typically used to purchase real estate around the world – which is the reason so many markets have gotten into trouble in the past – is simply not a major factor in China. Given that such a high proportion of homes are paid for in cash in China, most home buyers can actually afford to buy their homes. The government has imposed restrictions on the size and number of certain types of homes that can be purchased in order to erode some of the demand and, as a result of the housing and office space glut, rental prices have dropped, taking some steam out of the equation. So the Chinese government has a handle on the real estate market as only it can.

Can the Steamroller Continue?

When economic bubbles typically first start, the excess liquidity unleashed by central banks drives asset prices higher and higher. More and more people spend more and more money buying into the game, assuming that asset prices will only keep going up. At that point in time, leverage seems to have no ceiling, but when the great deleveraging begins, there is almost always a stampede toward the exit, which is when any Ponzi scheme eventually collapses. China's investment-fueled growth, including its construction binge, is just such a Ponzi scheme.

However, conventional wisdom only goes so far in explaining how the Chinese economy functions. What would decimate an ordinary economy becomes the Chinese economy's salvation, based on the country's economic and political fundamentals. China's financial system should be seen as a source of strength for the Chinese economy, however imperfect it may be, because of its ability to support the financing of infrastructure and other investments needed to sustain rapid growth. That the banking sector is dominated by state-owned banks that can lend at will at low cost certainly has its advantages, and is a prime reason why China's economy may be expected to continue to grow above 5% in the coming decade and beyond. Most other countries would kill to achieve that kind of growth rate.

Another reason is that China's population is becoming wealthier, and not just in the country's coastal cities. China's middle class has risen in size to become larger than the entire US population. It was estimated to be approximately 430 million in 2018 and projected to rise to as high as 780 million by the mid-2020s. That would be nearly more people than the US and EU *combined*. Consumer-driven domestic consumption already accounted for as much as 50% of GDP in 2015, a rise of 33% from 2014. That is a guarantee of high growth going forward.

Although tens of billions of square feet of completed real estate construction remains empty, one could argue that *a combination of government economic control, the high degree of liquidity, rising incomes and consumer spending, and the government's ongoing ability to tap on the brakes whenever the economy gets too hot should mean that the housing bubble that has developed may not actually burst any time soon.* If it were to, it can be controlled more meaningfully in China than in most other countries. The doomsayers and pessimists have been wrong *every time* they have predicted the Chinese economy's imminent demise. They will likely continue to be wrong.

China's biggest economic problem is that the state, SOEs, and crony capitalists wield too much power over the national economy, have too much control over wealth creation and income distribution, and much of the GDP growth and vested interest groups' economic progress are made at the expense of average consumers. Faster GDP growth will, in the end, not mean much when Chinese consumers are unable to support the overcapacity in the housing market and lending markets. China will try to create more export momentum in an effort to sustain its growth, but this is a vicious circle of imbalance that even a revaluation of the renminbi cannot break.

Those who argue that China's period of stellar performance might be coming to an end in the near future could be mistaken for two basic reasons: China's economy has great potential to continue to make progress in its productivity levels and eventually catch up with that of the most advanced countries, and it has, through a variety of domestic and global economic cycles, demonstrated its ability to generate sustainable rapid levels of growth.

However, as with Japan in the 1980s, the policies of ultra-high investment and rapid debt accumulation, which kept China growing so rapidly following the 2008 the Great Recession, make it vulnerable to sharp deceleration. China's investment rate of 44% of GDP in 2017 is unsustainably high. China's public capital stock per head is already far bigger than Japan's, at comparable incomes per head. Slowing urban household formation and an existing real estate bubble imply that fewer new homes now need to be built. Returns on investment in

China have recently collapsed. Investment-led growth must come to an early end.

Quite apart from its trade war with America, China has also hit a ceiling on export-driven growth, with a lower level of income per capita than other high-growth Asian economies. China's working-age population is also declining and, with government and corporate debt loads rising, sustaining fast growth will be prove difficult – at least in the near term. Future demand will increasingly depend on domestic-driven sources, yet, as of 2017, private consumption was only 39% of GDP.

Because the many distortions in China's economy, given that they are so large, and considering that the global economy is increasingly competitive, its ability to sustain the kinds of growth rates the Chinese government claims it has maintained over much of the past two decades will become increasingly difficult to achieve.[5]

China's Development Challenge

A lot of international companies have long believed that they must have a presence in China because they consider its 1.4 billion people to be potential consumers, implying a seemingly endless stream of future revenue. The existence of a robust middle class, upon which this vision is based, is clearly growing at an accelerated pace, but an increasing body of research raises question about who the country's middle class really are, and the true meaning of their disposable income.

Defining the middle class with accuracy is challenging at a time when China's economy has grown to be the world's second largest, yet 10% of the population remain classified by the World Bank as poverty stricken. Reputable sources disagree considerably about the size and scope of the Chinese middle class and its purchasing power implications, but there is little doubt that it is already a force to be reckoned with. As anyone who has walked down the main avenues of almost any major city in the world can attest, middle class Chinese tourists are everywhere.

The UN statistics division notes that the designations 'developed' and 'developing' countries are intended for statistical convenience and do not necessarily express a judgment about the stage reached by a particular country or area in the development process. The World Bank adds that classifying countries by incomes does not necessarily reflect their development status. The truth is, as previously noted, China possesses characteristics of both developed and developing countries, and has many things in common with a variety of countries.

Its recently unveiled sensitivity to the environment, for example, contrasts with a nouveau-riche mentality among China's powerful, notable for their lack of ethical codes commensurate with their status and wealth. This is a natural phase of development, akin to what the US experienced a century ago, as chronicled in Upton Sinclair's *The Jungle*. Sinclair showed how the presence of poverty, difficult living and working conditions, and hopelessness among the working class contrasted with deep-rooted corruption on the part of those in power at the beginning of the twentieth century, which perpetuated the status quo. It took the Depression to bring America to its senses and change its ways. Something similar will undoubtedly need to occur in China's case, for it cannot continue business as usual indefinitely. Or can it?

The Battle for China's Affection

Consistent with so much about China's thrust onto the global stage over the past decade, its outward foreign direct investment (OFDI) has grown far faster than OFDI from most other transitional economies. Chinese OFDI is largely politically driven, aimed at achieving specific nationalistic objectives, such as securing natural resources, acquiring strategic assets in key technologies and service industries, and creating national champion companies. China's approach to OFDI – which is often aggressive and brusque in nature – is increasingly coloring its relationship with recipient nations at all levels of development and income.

Until 2000, OFDI from China was negligible. That year, Premier Zhu Rongji officially announced that overseas investment would be one of the main objectives of the government's 10th Five-Year Plan (2001-05), giving birth to its 'go global' strategy. Premier Wen Jiabao then reinforced the importance of overseas investment in the 11th Five-Year Plan (2006-10). The government-led strategy proved to be effective. By 2006, yearly OFDI flow was 19 times that of 2000, growing at an average rate of 116% per year, dwarfing the average world OFDI growth of 6% over the same period. By 2016, China's OFDI had reached $196 billion but, in 2017, it dropped for the first time since 2001, by 19%, to $158 billion. Chinese investment in the US in 2017 was a little more than $6 billion, a decline of 62% from 2016. By contrast, Chinese OFDI in Europe exceeded $18 billion that year, up 73%.[6]

China has tailored its approach to OFDI based on the relative economic and political strength of the recipient country, in exchange for specific benefits. So, in heavily indebted poor countries (HIPCs), China tends to offer to build infrastructure in exchange for the right to access to raw materials. In developing countries, China may offer to help develop an indigenous industry; in emerging markets, it may grant greater access to the Chinese market. In developed countries, it may offer to expand reciprocal agreements related to cross-border investment. In each case, *China weighs the relative costs and benefits associated with expanding its relationship with a given country vis-à-vis what it will receive in return*.

China's overall strategy for SOEs is to 'grasp the large and let go of the small', aiming to create national champions from large SOEs through extensive government support while giving small and medium-sized SOEs greater exposure to the market. SOEs receive direct financial support from the government in the form of below market rate loans, direct payments, and other subsidies associated with official aid programs. The China Development Bank, China Export and Import Bank, and Sinosure (China's national political risk insurer) are the primary government organs that provide such support, although other state-owned banks and specially created funds also provide backing.

Chinese SOEs pursue OFDI in the primary sector, where investments are dominated by a few giant firms. A second strategic objective is to spur investment that acquires sophisticated, proprietary technology, technical skills, industry best practices, and established brand names and distribution networks. OFDI also serves as a strategic objective at the macroeconomic level, relieving some of the imbalances that have been built up by economic policy that distorts the marketplace. In the process, OFDI reduces the massive capital stock the government has accumulated while allowing for investment diversification, particularly away from US and other government bonds. Such investment often takes the form of merger and acquisition activity. Lenovo's purchase of International Business Machine's (IBM's) computer unit and Huaneng Group's acquisition of InterGen are good examples of this. These were accomplished before the US more closely scrutinized Chinese OFDI from a national security perspective. Such transactions in the sensitive high-tech sector in the US and elsewhere have become more difficult for the Chinese to achieve.

Some governments remain wary that such investment will lead to the 'development trap': a flood of cash that results in heightened corruption and largesse without building indigenous capacity, knowledge, management skills, or that allows movement up the global economic value chain. The blowback China has received from some African countries objecting to its one-size-fits-all approach to OFDI has prompted China to reconsider its approach. An increasing number of countries are no longer simply rolling out the red carpet. Natural resource export earnings must now be deposited into off-shore escrow accounts, with the value of the exports determined at the time of export, rather than in advance, for example.

This is a far cry from how Chinese OFDI started in some of these countries, with the Chinese simply dictating the rules of engagement. *Developing countries accounted for 95% of Chinese OFDI stock by the end of 2006, with a significant percentage in countries with weak governance and rule of law. Many of these countries subsequently experienced the classic 'resource curse' in which valuable reserves of minerals or fossil fuels enhanced corruption and conflict rather than promoting economic development.* Chinese SOEs have typically stepped into this environment with the advantages of political backing and government subsidized and insured investment, and China has typically used significant sweeteners to win contracts.

To secure investment deals, the Chinese government typically offers infrastructure projects, soft loans, and grant programs as a package deal with a proposed natural resource investment. With government financing and political support, Chinese SOEs avoid risks that often plague investments in resource-rich, economically poor countries. Political and reputational risks are therefore usually minimized and financing uncertainty is eliminated. Such risks hinder Western multinational enterprises (MNEs) that must respect the bottom line but tend to be of little concern to Chinese SOEs.

China's relationship with other emerging markets can be more complex. Subsidized Chinese OFDI may crowd out less substantial or unsubsidized OFDI or investment from other emerging market countries. At the same time, many emerging markets view Chinese investment into their countries – particularly in infrastructure and industrial projects – as a valuable resource for economic development, especially since it comes with few strings attached. China's strategy has been to negotiate such investment through diplomatic channels, with investments taking the form of partnerships and quid pro quo loans, as opposed to being exclusively under Chinese control. Emerging markets have more negotiating power than HIPCs, and the Chinese know it.

Using such sweeteners as diplomacy, ideology, and camaraderie tends not to work in developed countries, where China finds it is playing on a more even field. When placed in a competitive environment with a formidable opposite number, *China tends to use a sledgehammer to get what it wants – crossing a line, retreating, then doing so again, until a new line of been established and Beijing gets what it wants* (this is a strategy Beijing has deployed in a number of contexts, whether in economic negotiations or in a military context such as the South China Sea).

Points of conflict with developed countries tend to occur in three areas:

- OFDI by Chinese SOEs is seen as unfairly competitive vis-a-vis private sector companies. By virtue of government ownership and backing, Chinese SOEs often operate investments in risky environments where Western multinationals may prefer not to operate, and at reduced cost, thereby outmaneuvering Western firms. As Western multinationals generally operate based on market conditions, albeit with advantages from established reputations, technology, and industry best practices, they and their home countries come to believe that the playing field is no longer level. China's growing non-commercially motivated OFDI has the potential to distort global markets, leading to long-term loss of productivity and efficiency.

- Chinese official aid to unsavory governments in order to lubricate OFDI contracts raises governance and humanitarian concerns and, therefore, hackles among developed country governments. China's general willingness to befriend rogue or unsavory governments – funding projects in countries such as Sudan, Iran, and Venezuela – creates tension with the developed world. Some of this tension may actually stem from the fact that the exercise of realpolitik by China puts it on top and outwits Western firms that have had their activities circumscribed in such countries due to sanctions, reputational, or political risk.
- Chinese SOEs' attempts to acquire ownership interest in, or assets of, large developed country MNEs operating under market conditions have unnerved some developed country governments, which fear losing market access to strategic resources, as well as their technological and advanced practices edge.

If it were not for the West's preoccupation with achieving a higher moral standard and adherence to international standards of acceptable behavior, China would not have been as successful as it has been in fostering OFDI in the developing world. China is in the process of beating the West at its own game – identifying what it sees as the West's 'weakness' on the grand chess board and filling in the gaps. If the West played the game the same way, China's investment ambitions would be more restricted, or at least more expensive. But the West is not going to change its stripes any more than China will be changing its own.[7]

In some ways, China is better at achieving capitalist nirvana than the countries that invented it. China is quickly learning the benefits of establishing more equitable and mutually beneficial bilateral economic relationships. Soon enough, it will master that game, too. Once that occurs, China will be able to truly demonstrate why this is the Chinese century. Until then, the developing world will have to figure out a way to encourage China to leave something other than a football stadium behind.[8]

All Aboard?

When Li Keqiang, China's premier, in 2015 took 16 European leaders on a high-speed train ride in China, the trip revealed more than an enthusiasm for rolling stock. It was also Beijing's push for an engineering technology that it hoped would spearhead the launch of a grand geo-strategic ambition. China's ability to build high-speed railways more cheaply than its competitors gave the technology a central place in the BRI. Mr. Li left his central and eastern European guests in no doubt about the link between smooth diplomatic relations and securing Chinese infrastructure. He predicted that railway technology would become China's 'golden business card'.

Less than two years later, China's high-speed rail ambitions were already running off the tracks. Several of the projects had already been abandoned or postponed. Such failed schemes have raised suspicion and public animosity among many of the countries that Beijing had intended to target in the BRI. China had put a lot of emphasis on high-speed rail, but the effectiveness of 'high-speed rail diplomacy' has proven to be limited. The total estimated value of 18 Chinese overseas high-speed rail schemes – including the completed Ankara-Istanbul service, five that were under way as of 2018, and another dozen that had been announced at that time – was estimated to be approximately $143 billion.

To put the enormity of that number in context, the Marshall Plan, which helped revive Europe after the Second World War, was completed with $13 billion of American funding, equivalent to approximately $130 billion in current dollars. The combined value of cancelled projects in Libya, Mexico, Myanmar, the US, and Venezuela was estimated at the time to be about $48 billion, nearly double the $25 billion of total value for five projects that were under way in Laos, Saudi Arabia, Turkey and Iran.

Some of the cancellations resulted from factors well beyond Beijing's control. In Libya, for example, the outbreak of civil war in 2011 resulted in the cancellation of a $2.6 billion project to build a line from Tripoli to Sirte. In other cases, some of the schemes appear to have unraveled amid criticism of China's approach to lending for the projects. Mexico's 2014 decision to cancel a $3.7 billion contract was made to ensure clarity, legitimacy, and transparency. In the case of Venezuela, a project once touted to bring 'socialism on rails' to the country became what locals ending up referring to as a 'red elephant'.

Why did so many projects meet such an early demise? The first reason is an issue familiar to multilateral lenders: the divergent capacities of countries to assume and absorb debt. At home, China's method of lending allows state-owned companies to benefit from government guarantees on loans and operate at a continual loss. The China Railway Corporation, the state-owned rail operator and investor in the country's high-speed networks, had debts to the state in 2018 in excess of $550 billion, significantly more than the national debt of entire countries.

A country the size of China, with its strong sovereign credit rating and in excess of $3 trillion in foreign exchange reserves, can support such absurd debt loads. But a country such as Laos, with a GDP just under $17 billion in 2017, is much less able to absorb the cost of a high-speed railway that was estimated to cost nearly $6 billion. Doubts about the viability of the project were expressed well before the deal was formally agreed between the two governments.

In 2013, the ADB called the project's proposals unaffordable, while the World Bank questioned the implications for debt sustainability. Chinese rail companies were reluctant to invest in the project, so Beijing suggested that Laos should be the main investor in the project, and recommended financing it by borrowing from China's Ex-Im Bank. Beijing's goal was to create a land route to move goods from western China to mainland Southeast Asia. Given Laos' small population and economy, little of this trade would ever have remained in Laos, so any potential justification on the basis of domestic benefit was hollow. Beijing was quite happy to ensure an enormous debt burden for Laos, with very little in the way of Laotian economic benefit, so that it could achieve its goal.

In the case of Indonesia, the mismatch was not so much one of debt capacities but of political systems. In China, state-owned rail companies face few obstacles securing land and construction permits. By contrast, Indonesia has strong land tenure laws. More than a year after an official groundbreaking ceremony for the $5.5 billion Jakarta to Bandung rail line was held in 2016, construction had yet to start in earnest. As Jakarta recalculated the cost of the 140-kilometer project amid expectations of considerable overruns, Indonesian President

Widodo remained committed to the project, having told the Chinese government that their fates were bound together on it. At issue was Widodo's reputation, which apparently mattered more to him than basic project economics. *Chinese state-owned companies are accustomed to sealing backroom deals with government officials without enduring any private or public scrutiny.*[9] *For some reason, Beijing seems to believe that such a modus operandi applies everywhere in the world.*

The Sad Case of Ecuador

Located in the Amazon Basin, the 1500-megawatt Coca Codo Sinclair hydroelectric facility is the largest energy project in Ecuador's history. It was designed to produce an average of 8.6 gigawatt hours of electricity per year, supplying approximately 44% of the country's electricity needs. A country as poor as Ecuador could clearly not finance a project of such magnitude on its own, so it turned to the Export-Import Bank of China, which financed 85% of the project cost via an approximately $1.7 billion loan, with high rates of interest, payable over 15 years, and requiring that Chinese construction companies build it.

Only 2 years after it became operational in 2016, more than 7,000 cracks had appeared in the dam's machinery because of substandard steel and inadequate welding by Sinohydro. In addition, the dam's reservoir became clogged with silt, sand, and trees and, the only time engineers attempted to run the facility at full power, it shook violently and shorted the national electricity grid. The dam was intended to solve the country's energy needs but it has instead become a national scandal, serving to highlight Ecuador's endemic corruption and tether its financial future to Beijing. Almost every top Ecuadorean official involved in the dam's construction has either been imprisoned or sentenced on bribery charges, including a former vice president, a former electricity minister, and the former anti-corruption official monitoring the project, who was caught on tape talking about Chinese bribes.

Chinese loans were earmarked not only for the dam, but for bridges, highways, irrigation, schools, health clinics, and a half dozen other dams the country could not afford. In return, Beijing gets to keep 80% of Ecuador's most valuable export-oil – since many of the contracts are to be repaid in oil rather than dollars. And the Ecuadoran government agreed to sell China the oil at a discount, which it can then re-sell at a profit. The government is drowning in debt; it slashed social spending, gasoline subsidies, several government agencies, and more than 1,000 public jobs by 2018. Most economists expect the country to slide into recession.

Over the past decade, China has become South America's top trading partner. As noted earlier, some Latin American countries have become so beholden to Beijing that up to 90% of their exports go to China. Many of them are now so accustomed to turning to Beijing as the natural destination for funding in times of need that they may bypass MDBs or their previous preferred destination, Washington. In Ecuador's case, Beijing did not take much risk regarding repayment; most of the financial risk became Quito's. Ecuador's president at the time even flew to Beijing in 2018 to attempt to renegotiate his country's debt to Beijing while borrowing another $900 million.

Coca Codo Sinclair was built even though previous Ecuadorian governments had rejected the idea because a volcano was located nearby and a major earthquake had decimated oil infrastructure in the area in 1987. In fact, the volcano had been erupting with some regularity since the sixteenth century. An independent review of the project in 2010 warned that the amount of water in the region to power the dam had not been studied for nearly 30 years. A Chinese diplomat in Ecuador admitted that the Chinese government had doubts about the project and failed to pay sufficient attention to environmental concerns, but neither Beijing nor Quito chose to address these issues because it would have caused a multi-year delay in commencing the project. Inadequate safety measures led to the deaths of more than 100 workers, the dam displaced more than a million people, and the resulting environmental damage was considerable.

China knew that Ecuador would play along. Its president at the time the dam was negotiated, Rafael Correa, was a fiery left-wing politician who succeeded in effectively alienating Western governments. The country needed new sources of funding and, even though it was experiencing a severe drought at the time, Correa chose to double down on hydro power and turned to Beijing, which was only too happy to 'help'. As of 2018, the dam typically ran at half capacity and, given the country's wet and dry seasons, could only generate electricity at full capacity a few hours a day, perhaps six months out of the year, if everything worked perfectly.

The $1.7 billion loan, based on 7% per annum interest (extremely high for a power project loan to a developing country), means that Quito owes Beijing approximately $125 million per year in interest. The government had promised that electricity prices would decline after the dam was operational, but the average citizen is paying more per month since the dam became operational. China made some concessions to Ecuador, such as paying 92 cents more per barrel of oil, but the government remains billions short of the funding it needs to service its foreign debt.[10] Where will that money come from? Probably Beijing.

Buyer Beware

While China may be the poster child and most visible manifestation of some of the structural defects in the global economy, it could easily be argued that it is merely a symptom, rather than the cause. China certainly did not invent greed, lax risk management, inadequate regulatory enforcement, or short memories – all of which precipitated the Great Recession (which of course originated in the US). These basic ingredients, which got the world into trouble in 2008 and in countless other economic crises that preceded it, remain at play. Although risk management procedures and regulatory enforcement mechanisms have definitely improved around the world, the propensity to water them down has gained momentum as time has passed.

China also did not create global supply chains, electronic money flows, and instant communication, which have accentuated the speed with which markets can rise and have heightened our collective vulnerability to economic downturns. China became the 'drug' that the world's 'addicts' (commodity producers, goods importers, and seekers of cheap labor) needed. *The world happily accepted China's invitation, rushing like lemmings into the Chinese marketplace to establish their manufacturing facilities.*

Many of them also failed to recognize that the Chinese joint venture partners they selected would prove to be more than a headache; many of them would actively conspire to suck their Western partners dry of technological prowess and managerial know-how before finding a way to either buy out their share and take control of the venture entirely or have them kicked out of the country through the country's courts. Who is to blame for that? The Chinese or their Western partners who failed to do proper due diligence and who allowed their greed for profit to cloud their judgement?

Too many global investors and lenders have learned relatively little since 2008, creating more bubbles, ignoring more warning signs, and continuing to party like it's 1999. Then, as now, we are at times our own worst enemy. The bankers remain greedy, lobbyists continue to find ways to dilute rules that restrict the freedom of movement of their constituents, and risk managers have been busy trying to figure out how they can remain in compliance with the latest regulations but at the very edge of new rules. Voters around the world also continue to elect lawmakers who have a vested interest in perpetuating the system. The result is a global polity that is rotten to the core. China is certainly not to blame for that.

If the Great Recession was not enough to change the hearts and minds of the bankers, legislators, lobbyists and voters, what would be? We bear collective responsibility for perpetuating a terribly broken system. Since the market is clearly not self-regulating, ever greater restrictions should be put in place regarding how investors may invest and lenders may lend. Regulators need to do a better job of enforcement, risk managers must focus on managing risk rather than skirting rules, and since greed is part of the human condition, we should all do something to remember the lessons of the past. Pointing the finger at China will not achieve that, any more than blaming America did in 2008.[11]

The Stage is Set

That said, China will remain an easy target for criticism on a whole host of issues, but it should not be forgotten that, as a nation, it is doing what many other nations do to project its power and enhance its influence. Beijing just goes about doing so somewhat differently than most other countries. Should it only be criticized for that, particularly if some good comes of it? China is in a unique position to influence the global economy and the future course of globalization. The question is whether it will do so responsibly, and at what cost for other countries.

Although China's ambitious BRI is seen by some as a blatant attempt to exert Hard Power in 65 nations that require new or upgraded infrastructure, while the program will enhance Beijing's economic and political influence, it will also greatly enhance transportation systems, power projects, and other essential construction in a lot of countries that badly need it. No other country is willing to lead such an effort, or devote such financial, engineering, and construction resources to that task, so China should be given credit where credit is due.

If another country were to undertake such an endeavor, it would also undoubtedly seek to garner some form of influence in the recipient nations. It would be disingenuous to suggest otherwise. More good could ultimately come from the BRI than harm, but expectations and impacts should be managed by host countries. After all, they are not being forced to accept Beijing's offer of assistance. Only India has overtly criticized the BRI and refused to participate in the program.

Sometimes China does not get credit where credit is due. Anyone who has visited any large city in China is aware of how dirty its air can be. It is often difficult to see across the street when the air is at its worst. The country that has for decades been addicted to coal-fired power plants and was for years building a new plant every week is, surprisingly, on its way to becoming a global green powerhouse. Although it is not yet in a position be claim that title, by 2025, most new cars in China will be fully electric vehicles, putting it well ahead of the targets set by a variety of developed nations to do the same. China already accounts for more than 60% of the world's high-speed rail and has committed to achieving blue skies in all of its major cities early in the next decade. The Western press does not spend much time reporting on such facts.

China has also become a leader in the digital economy, including cashless payments. In major cities, as many as 90% of all commercial and retail transactions occur through digital payment systems such as Alipay and WeChat. Through Alibaba, e-commerce delivery in large Chinese cities is the fastest in the world. The company consistently breaks records for single day sales. A number of Chinese universities have become among the top ranked in the world[12], with dozens more expected to join their ranks in the coming years. While Western universities continue to dominate the rankings, students from around the world already attend Chinese universities.

These are examples of some things that China is doing right, and very well. *China Vision is not only about projecting the country's power and influence in a uniquely Chinese way, it is also about having foresight and a willingness to act on what it sees as its, and the world's, future, in a decisive way.* One great benefit of being an authoritarian government is that there is no need for a lot of debate about what to do and how to do it. Of course, that has pluses and minuses attached, but the Chinese can build a convention center or complete a toll road in the time it can take some municipal authorities in the US to repair an escalator at a metro stop. In fairness, much of what goes on in China gets little press outside its borders, including on many of the initiatives it is undertaking to try to correct past mistakes.

There is no question that China will play a major role in the globalization process going forward. The question is how it will choose to do so. Will it become a leader in providing foreign assistance and alter the manner in which is distributes foreign aid? Will it continue to demand repayment of loans that cannot be repaid by HIPCs? Will it continue to demonstrate leadership in some of the world's most pressing environmental challenges? These are among the issues that Beijing must consider if it wishes to be perceived as a net positive force in the global economy.

The Chinese perception of the country's impact on the world can be very different from that of the rest of the world. To date, China Vision has a mixed record of net pluses and minuses from the perspective of the global community. Beijing is uniquely positioned to act as an interlocutor of the world's emerging and advanced economies. Since the turn of the century, it has notably ramped up its engagement in regional and multilateral agreements and pursued deep engagement with developing countries in trade, investment, and security. It now has the ability to enhance such efforts with greater credibility. The AIIB and New Development Bank are poised to become leaders among the international financial institutions and China is well positioned to flex its economic muscle through these, the BRI, and its growing influence among the MDBs and other global organizations.

It is also in the process of resetting its economic and political relationships with countries as diverse as Russia, Saudi Arabia, and the US. Just as it is pursuing even deeper engagement with Africa, China is building ties throughout the world via investment, educational and cultural exchanges, and research collaborations. But Beijing can do much more in terms of taking corporate governance more seriously, adhering to global legal norms and abiding by rulings from international bodies. The Chinese government can and should take a more enlightened approach toward shaping the direction that continued globalization will ultimately take. However, as its economy continues to be buffeted by trade conflicts and the government finds it increasingly difficult to generate sustained levels of GDP growth above 6%, it appears less and less likely to place a priority on revamping its image in the international arena.

3 Asia and the South China Sea

China has become a master at pushing right up to the boundary of internationally acceptable behavior, then crossing over the line, retreating, and doing the same again, until it establishes a new normal for what is deemed to be acceptable. This has been seen for some time in a variety of contexts, whether vis-à-vis compliance with WTO rules, other applications of international law, or in its dealings with foreign governments and companies. Given the saber rattling between China and Vietnam over national maritime boundaries regarding the Paracel Islands, as well as the muscle flexing that has occurred between Beijing and Manila (in particular) over the Spratly Island archipelago, it appears that China is incapable of speaking the vernacular of international diplomacy in a manner commensurate with established international law and the expectations the global community has of responsible leading nations.

The Spratly Island group has long been a source of conflict between Brunei, China, Malaysia, the Philippines, Taiwan, and Vietnam. They comprise 100-plus islands, atolls, and shoals in the southern part of the South China Sea. Not only are the Spratlys at the heart of one of the world's busiest sea lanes, they are known to hold rich oil and natural gas reserves – so much so that, in 2002, a Declaration of Conduct of Parties was agreed between China and the Association of Southeast Asian Nations (ASEAN) to demilitarize the Islands, maintain the status quo, and to pave the way for joint deep sea oil exploration.

Among the six claimants, China, the Philippines, and Vietnam have been the most assertive. The Philippines predicated its claim against China at The Hague (an award for which was granted to Manila in 2016) under the theory of occupation and discovery since 1947, and Vietnam through a broader (and less particularized) French title in the 1920s. At first, China attempted to lay claim to the entire South China Sea – forming what on a map looks like a long tongue – extending hundreds of miles outside the country's exclusive economic zone, and tracing its title, according to the Chinese, back to the Han Dynasty in the 200 B.C. era. It was only in 1992 that China first attempted to occupy one of the eight islands in the Spratlys – an odd way of addressing a sacred right, given that China is not known for simply ignoring its historical land claims.

Beijing expected to be able to wave its flag, whip up nationalistic fervor, and lay claim to the entire South China Sea simply because China's name is on a map. India would not dare do the same with the Indian Ocean, nor Japan with the Sea of Japan, nor Saudi Arabia with the Arabian Sea. Yet, the international legal framework governing the world's bodies of water – the UN Convention on the Law of the Seas (or UNCLOS) – which entered into force in 1994, has been criticized as controversial, and its own grievance machinery as being ill-equipped. The US has still not ratified it.

Since at least six Asian states are jockeying for a piece of the Spratlys, ownership of the Islands is an issue ripe for adjudication under international law. The Spratly issue is ultimately a litmus test for if, and when, China may act as a responsible member of the international community that exercises discretion and judiciousness in its actions.[1] The opposite has been true.

China's Nine-Dash Line and its Misplaced National Pride

Beijing has mastered the art of playing the international system against itself. Nowhere is this better exemplified, nor is China's frame of reference vis-à-vis Asia best illustrated, than by its territorial and governance claims over the South China Sea. China's government argues that its 'nine-dash line' of sovereignty over the entire Sea is based on centuries of maritime history, and that China's claim is air tight. The Chinese Foreign Ministry has even asserted that ample historical documents and literature demonstrate that China was the first country to discover, name, develop, and exercise continuous, effective jurisdiction over the South China Sea islands.[2] The Chinese government has beaten this drum so

44

hard and for so long that the Chinese people believe it. The nine-dash line has appeared in school room maps throughout China for decades, in conjunction with the narrative of national humiliation that resulted from the previously noted tales of imperialist plundering of China, its interests, and its assets, by foreign powers.

However, as noted in the book *The South China Sea,*[3] the first Chinese official documented to set foot on one of the Spratly Islands was a Nationalist naval officer in 1946, the year after Japan's defeat in World War II and its own loss of control of the Sea. *He did so from an American ship crewed by Chinese sailors who were trained in Miami.* As for the story of the nine-dash line, it began a decade earlier via a Chinese government naming commission. China was not even the first to name the islands; the naming commission borrowed and translated wholesale from British charts and pilots.[4] It is unclear how the Chinese government translated all this into the bill of goods it has sold to the Chinese people but, by now, it is a source of national pride, however misplaced it may be.

The Chinese government and its people have essentially backed themselves into a corner. They have been drinking the nine-dash line Kool-Aid for so long that even despite the 2016 Hague ruling that there is no legal basis for China's claim over the Sea, and even though the Chinese government has failed to produce evidence of its declaration to back up its version of the facts, national pride will not allow it to admit that what the government is doing in the South China Sea is illegal under the very international maritime law (UNCLOS) to which it first subscribed on the very day in 1982 when the Convention became a legal instrument.

Although China formally ratified UNCLOS in 1996, in 2006 the Chinese government filed a statement with UNCLOS saying that it did not accept certain provisions of the Convention that refer to Compulsory Procedures Entailing Binding Decisions as issued by at least four venues: the International Tribunal on the Law of the Sea, the International Court of Justice (ICJ), an 'arbitral tribunal' which may refer to the Permanent Court of Arbitration (PCA), and a 'special arbitral tribunal'. While there are venues available for the resolution of disputes under the UNCLOS regime, China does not wish to be bound by its compulsory processes – the ICJ and PCA included. In essence, *it wants to be able to pick and choose which of the statutes of the treaties it has voluntarily signed that it wishes to adhere to, and be free to ignore those that it finds inconvenient.*

Can a state remain a party to a treaty or convention without being bound by its rules? Can contracting states adhere to an international legal regime and simultaneously opt out of any binding force required or to be required by that regime? A state can be found to be in violation of a substantive legal norm even without a coercive or compulsory judgment in a given venue, provided, of course, that there is truth to the argument supporting a violation and that it is appreciated by the alternative venue.

When Manila took Beijing to The Hague, China accused the Philippines of violating the 2002 ASEAN Code of Conduct, which states that unilateral initiation of arbitration is a violation because parties to the Code are supposed to resolve their differences over their overlapping territorial claims on a bilateral basis via negotiation.[5] Curiously, however, *it was through the same ASEAN Code of Conduct that the parties reaffirmed their commitment to UNCLOS as well as to the purposes and principles of the UN Charter.* UNCLOS is clearly adverse to the Chinese position. Since there is some authority under international law holding that a state's avowed reliance on a source of law preempts a retraction of this reliance, by invoking the ASEAN code (which invokes UNCLOS), China admitted to the binding force of that code. Under the law, this is the case especially when a state's admission will be an admission against its own interests.

While China disavowed UNCLOS vis-à-vis the Philippines, it expressly *invoked* UNCLOS provisions in its own legal claims against Japan – so it wants to have its cake and eat it, too. In 2009, China submitted a claim over the Senkaku Islands (which, like the Scarborough Shoal and the Spratlys, are believed to be natural resource rich) and turned to UNCLOS rules in defining and delineating its continental shelf beyond the 200 nautical mile exclusive economic zone – again within the meaning of UNCLOS. There is some international legal doctrine supporting the view that a state's acts in one place can be used as an admission and adversely bind that state in another set of circumstances.

The larger point is that China has not personified the Rule of Law in the Philippine case, or in others related to maritime borders, and wants to be able to cherry pick which provisions of international treaties it will willingly comply with, and which it will not. That is behavior unbecoming of a rising global power and will make states which are signatories to treaties with China wonder if its signature is worth the paper it is printed on. This cannot be in China's long-term interest.

The Chinese government had an opportunity to pivot after The Hague ruling but it chose not to do so, even though *its pride is based on a doubtful historical record*. In the absence of proof to the contrary, the only conclusion to be drawn is that the government has been drinking its own Kool-Aid for so long that it cannot reverse itself without losing face and credibility with its own people.[6]

The Scarborough Shoal

The Scarborough Shoal is a triangular-shaped island group of 150 square kilometers located 124 nautical miles off Zambales in the Philippines. Named after the ill-fated East India Company trade ship *Scarborough*, which was wrecked on the rocks of the shoal in 1784, the Shoal forms part of a larger dispute over who really 'owns' the South China Sea (or the West Philippine Sea, as Filipinos refer to it). The Scarborough Shoal is known under Filipino vernacular as Panatag Shoal, and to China as Huangyan Island. While only 124 nautical miles from Zambales, Scarborough is 550 nautical miles from Hainan Island (the closest Chinese port), which, by itself, raises serious question as to the legal validity of the Chinese claim over the territory.

The dispute over Scarborough arises from conflicting territorial and maritime claims between China and the Philippines on grounds of discovery and occupation. Beijing has argued that it first discovered and mapped the entire South China Sea during the Yuan Dynasty (1271-1368 AD), and that it was again mapped in 1279 AD by Chinese astronomer Guo Shoujing in a survey of islands surrounding China. The Philippines likewise claims historical ties to the territory, the earliest being the *Carta Hydrographical y Chorographics De Las Yslas Filipinas* (Hydrographic and Chorographic Map of the Philippine Islands). Published in 1734, Velarde's map identified the Shoal as part of Zambales. Later expeditions,

47

such as Alejandro Malaspina's 1808 survey, likewise identified the territory as part of the Philippines.

Given its proximity to the Philippines, common sense dictates, and territorial law concurs, that the Shoal resides within Philippine territorial waters – not that of China – and international law is on the side of the Philippines. The Treaty of Paris of 1898, The Treaty of Washington of 1900, and the Treaty with Great Britain of 1930 all state that the westernmost limit of Philippines territory is the 118th degree meridian of longitude east of Greenwich, arguably excluding Scarborough. But even as the 1935 Philippine Constitution (and, by definition, all subsequent Philippine constitutions) affirms the legality or legitimacy of these treaties, constitutional provisions assert that Philippine national territory is comprised of the "Philippine archipelago, with all the islands and waters embraced therein, and all other territories over which the Philippines has sovereignty or jurisdiction."[7]

UNCLOS provides for a 200 nautical mile exclusive economic zone and continental shelf, which effectively places Scarborough within Philippine sovereignty or jurisdiction. China predicates its nine-dash line claim over most of the South China Sea despite the fact that UNCLOS prevents a state from invoking historical rights, save for areas which are "internal waters". Internal waters and territorial waters do not extend beyond 12 nautical miles from a coastline for any coastal state.

The Philippine claim at The Hague was further strengthened by Republic Act No. 9522 (known as the Philippine Archipelagic Baselines Law). Said to be compliant with UNCLOS, the Law defined Philippine territory by connecting straight lines from the outermost points of the outermost islands of the Philippine archipelago. Even in the face of such evidence, China's Foreign Ministry has denied it all and said that the only way the Scarborough issue can be resolved is for the Philippines to surrender all sovereignty over it to China.

While the Philippines 1951 Mutual Defense Treaty with the US is considered to be the most vital military alliance pact entered into by the Philippines, it has also signed a variety of other military cooperation agreements with leading military powers, such as South Korea (1994), Germany (1974), France (1994), Italy (2004), and Russia (2009). In ASEAN, the

Philippines has defense pacts with Malaysia (1994), Thailand (1997), Indonesia (1997), Vietnam (1998), and Brunei (2001) – so Manila is well positioned should it ever wish to escalate perceived breaches of its territorial sovereignty against China. The question becomes whether any of these other states would choose to engage China on the Philippines' behalf. Clearly, the breach would need to be perceived to be serious for the Philippines to call upon any of the signatories to act on its behalf.[8] China, of course, knows this and has been very careful not to breach Philippine territory in an overtly military manner.

The South China Sea/West Philippine Sea issue has become a litmus test for whether China will engage other contestants in a rules-based regime in accordance with established norms of diplomacy. With China maintaining an adversarial approach to its well overstretched claim to the South China Sea, the Philippines and many other countries in the region believe they have little choice but to strengthen alliances with the US, Australia, Japan, South Korea, and Singapore.[9] The message to China is simple: the South China Sea is not Beijing's bathtub to do as it pleases. China must decide whether it wishes to maintain an antagonistic approach to territorial claims outside its legal and territorial reach, or stubbornly continue on the path it has embarked on.

The South China Sea Challenge

In spite of The Hague ruling, the question remains whether the arbitral award turns out to be little more than a paper judgment, given China's intransigence and non-recognition of the case, and given the Philippines' reluctance to take the issue any further by invoking any of its defense treaties. This will remain the post-arbitration challenge for the Philippines and all the other nations bordering the South China Sea in the years to come.

Yet, *even Manila has been seduced by the prospect of Beijing's money and resources. Ignoring the Philippines' own judicial victory, President Duterte, who had a history of telling leaders the world over exactly what he thought about them, essentially capitulated to President Xi in 2018 in order to secure Chinese money and cooperation in developing natural resources in its own exclusive economic zone.* With the US having essentially taken a back seat on the South China Sea issue, and with US influence waning in the region in recent years, it is not unreasonable to expect that other claimants to the South China Sea's riches may capitulate in their own way. Even though neighboring claimants were not parties to the arbitration between the Philippines and China, all claimants indirectly benefitted from The Hague ruling. Do any of the other claimants see it that way?

In the absence of formal military engagement to prevent it (which is highly unlikely – and Beijing knows it), there appears to be little doubt that China will maintain its now entrenched stance, despite the ruling and the ongoing 'freedom of navigation' naval operations being led by the US. China's approach is to attempt to convince other nations that lawfare is neither a necessary nor sufficient condition to end disputes, and that no outcome of litigation can deter the practical effects of its 'cabbage strategy' – that of surrounding contested islands with as many civilian and military ships as it can, so that each island is wrapped layer by layer, like a cabbage.

The quality of international consensus on this subject will also matter. Immediately following the arbitral award, more than 40 countries voiced support for the binding nature of the arbitral award or called on China to respect it. Many of them score high in transparency perception and rule of law indices. While China claims to have garnered more than 60 countries in favor of its view, very few issued explicit statements of support. The Washington-based Center for Strategic and International Studies could only confirm official statements from Afghanistan, Gambia, Kenya, Lesotho, Niger, Sudan, Togo and Vanuatu. Of these, six are in Africa, many of them are landlocked, distant from the disputes, and all are in some way beholden to China for military, development, or financial aid.

The Philippines continues to benefit on this subject from the US's 'ironclad commitment' to mutual defense, as well as from declarations of support for the arbitration outcome from the G7 and a number of other countries known for their respect for the rule of law. If the PCA or other legal body had ruled in China's favor, Beijing would surely be praising 'the process', but, given the outcome, that was never going to happen. While Beijing presumably does not want to be seen as an international outlaw, since that would undermine its narrative- that it is a responsible, peace loving rising power, and that it deserves a greater role in the international order – its continued intransigence will make other countries wary of Chinese objectives and will continue to drive neighboring states even closer to Japan and the US. In an international legal order that has no centralized system of enforcement, international pressure has always been, and will remain, the sole enforcement mechanism for international legal decisions.[10]

China is not waiting for the pieces on the chess board to be more formally arranged before proceeding to reinforce its now established geostrategic position and military presence in the South China Sea. In 2018, President Xi commenced plans to create the world's first deep sea base for unmanned submarine exploration in the Sea. The base would be located in the deepest part of the ocean, some 6,000 meters below the surface, which means scientists will need to develop new technology and materials to withstand pressure at that depth. President Xi's intention is to install an undersea base controlled by AI, where unmanned exploration vehicles could dock and robots could carry out scientific research.

Of course, President Xi *could* have suggested this be established in any part of the world's oceans but has specifically chosen the South China Sea. The potential location identified by scientists is the Manila Trench, where the Eurasian plate meets the Pacific plate, which happens to be claimed by the Philippines, near the Scarborough Shoal.[11] Given that Manila has become ever closer with Beijing since The Hague ruling, and given that President Xi's declared intention to construct the deep sea base occurred without strenuous objection from Washington, there is every reason to believe that China will do exactly as President Xi has described – establishing yet another new benchmark in terms of what is deemed acceptable behavior in the international arena and under international law.

Meddling in domestic politics can come with a price

Although Beijing has become accustomed to getting its way with its Asian neighbors, some of them are schooling China in the consequences of meddling in their domestic politics. As previously noted, Chinese OFDI is largely politically driven, aimed at achieving specific national objectives, such as securing natural resources, acquiring strategic assets in key technologies and service industries, and creating national champion companies. As an extension of state power, China's approach to OFDI has had a profound impact on its relationship with recipient nations at all levels of development and income. Not unlike any variety of other nations, China weighs the relative costs and benefits associated with expanding its relationship with a given county vis-à-vis what it will receive in return.

As a result of government financing and political support, Chinese SOEs are generally able to avoid a plethora of risks that often plague investments in resource-rich poor countries. By virtue of being Chinese state enterprises, political and reputational risks are sometimes automatically mitigated, and the uncertainty that often accompanies project finance is effectively eliminated. Still, points of conflict with recipient countries do occur and realpolitik can bite back. China is learning some hard lessons about the way the world works, and how a unidimensional approach to OFDI may not be in its own best long-term interests.

For example, in 2011, the government of Myanmar halted the construction of the Myitsone Dam in the country's north, a large hydroelectric project that was under construction along the Irrawaddy River and was to be completed in 2017. It was to generate up to 6,000 megawatts of power for Yunnan Province in China. However, the project had been highly controversial, largely because of the environmental damage it would cause and the thousands of people in Myanmar who would have needed to be displaced to build it.

A broad range of interests and organizations opposed construction of the Dam, which was being was being built by the China Power Investment Corporation – one of China's largest power producers – and Sinohydro – one of the world's largest hydropower contractors. Cancellation of the Dam raised a whole host of issues which China had never before had to address in public. It was extremely rare for a developing country government with a long history of friendly relations with China to publicly challenge the Chinese government in such a manner. Even more interestingly, it was one of the first instances when major Chinese government-owned companies had been forced to deal with issues related to contract cancellation and de facto expropriation of Chinese assets related to OFDI.[12] As a result, the Chinese government learned that it is ultimately as powerless as any other government on those rare occasions when its contracts are canceled in another country.

Environmentalists say the dam site has some of the highest biodiversity in the world and warned that the project would both destroy the natural beauty of the Irrawaddy River and disrupt water flow, contending that it could potentially flood an area the size of Singapore, displace more than 10,000 people, and destroy livelihoods. It is hard to imagine that such objections would ever result in the cancellation of a similar project in China, of course. As of 2018, Beijing was still trying to find a way to restart construction, having invested up to $800 million in the project. If Myanmar proceeds with the cancellation, it could owe the Chinese government that money; if it decided to proceed, it stood to gain up to $500 million per year in revenue.[13]

And that is the dilemma. Accepting Beijing's money and its companies comes at a price, and its investment is always, by definition, self-serving (then again, whose investment is not?), but it generally also results in economic development and significant revenue generation for the host country. Beijing is not generally accustomed to having to jump through too many hoops to get its OFDI approved and it is certainly outside the norm for one of its mega-investments to be canceled outright. The irony, in the Myitsone Dam case, is that the cancellation occurred at a time when Myanmar's military dictatorship – itself unaccustomed to bowing to domestic pressure – was unable to avoid overwhelming domestic opposition to the Dam. The cancellation was maintained even after the Aung San Suu Kyi's National League for Democracy assumed power in 2016.

China and Myanmar have had a mixed postwar relationship, ranging from warm to hostile, with Burma having been the first non-communist country to recognize China in 1949; it then expelled much of its Chinese population following anti-Chinese riots in the 1960s. Since the pro-democracy riots in 1988, Myanmar has generally sought a closer relationship with China, as the government wished to strengthen itself in the process. The relationship is characterized by strong bilateral trade and investment but also a similar sensitivity as other Southeast Asian nations to China's growing strength and influence in the region.

The acquisition of energy has become a dominant influence in China's foreign policy orientation generally and has been a driving force in its relationship with Myanmar in recent years. Myanmar is resource-rich, was one of the world's first oil exporters, and has noteworthy gas reserves. In addition, because of its geostrategic position, the country has punched above its weight in perceived significance to China. Beijing also views Myanmar as important to its own strategic objective of having access to more ports in the Andaman Sea and Indian Ocean.

The Shwe Gas Pipeline (otherwise known as the Myanmar-China Oil and Gas Pipeline), which commenced operation in 2013, certainly symbolizes China's willingness to invest in Myanmar in order to achieve its energy acquisition objectives. Although built by a consortium that includes India and South Korea, the pipeline is an important component of China's ability to deliver oil and gas to southwest China. The 478-mile long crude oil pipeline the runs the length of Myanmar and transports oil from the Middle East and Africa to southwest China. Not surprisingly, China's National Petroleum Corporation owns 50.9% of the venture, which included the construction of a new deep-water port and oil storage facilities on Myanmar's Maday Island.

The completion of the port was also a long-held strategic ambition of China in terms of its ability to project its military power in the region. So, apart from the Dam, bilateral economic relations remain strong between the two countries. Myanmar's economic significance to China has never been higher.[14] So the country represents an uncharacteristic dichotomy for Beijing. Given the military's continued behind-the-scenes influence in Myanmar, and the strong economic relationship its generals have had with Beijing for decades, it remains possible that the Dam could be restarted at some point in time in the future. China wields considerable clout in Naypyidaw and the country needs both the energy and the money, so, in the end, Beijing may get its way.

Malaysian Backlash

Of all the countries participating in the BRI, Malaysia was at the heart of China's efforts to gain enhanced influence in the region. That was until Mahathir Mohamad unseated Najib

Razak as Prime Minister in 2018 and unceremoniously canceled several Chinese-financed projects that had been previously approved by the Malaysian government. In its quest to control the South China Sea, Beijing viewed Putrajaya as central to that effort, because it presides over the region's most vital maritime chokepoint, through which much of Asia's trade passes. A Chinese power company had been investing in a deep-water port large enough to host an aircraft carrier, and other Chinese entities were busy revamping a harbor and financing a railway network to speed Chinese goods along what will effectively be the new Silk Road. One Chinese developer was even creating four artificial islands that could become home to nearly three-quarters of a million people, which was being heavily marketed to Chinese citizens.

While Malaysia was once at the forefront in Beijing's plans to gain global influence, it is now leading the Asian pack in pushing back against Beijing, as even middle-income nations fear becoming overly indebted by projects that are being deemed neither viable nor necessary, except in their strategic value to China. Shortly after assuming office, Mohamad canceled two major Chinese-linked projects, worth more than $22 billion, amid accusations that Razak's government deliberately signed bad deals with China to bail out a graft-plagued state investment fund (One Malaysia Development Berhad (1MDB)) and generate funds to extend his time in office. In his comments delivered in Beijing at the Great Hall of the People shortly after assuming office, Mahathir took a swipe at the Chinese government, stating that he did not want to support China's new version of colonialism.

Mahathir was voted into office in part with a mandate that is familiar to poorer countries: relieving Malaysia's burden of suffocating under Chinese and other forms of debt. A significant percentage of Malaysia's $250 billion in debt was owed to Chinese companies. He halted a contract for the China Communications Construction Company to build the East Coast Rail Link, thought to have cost the government about $20 billion, along with a $2.5 billion agreement for a Chinese energy company to construct gas pipelines.

Mahathir was of the view that Beijing was well aware that when it lends large sums of money to a poor country it knows that, in the end, it will end up having to assume responsibility for the repayment of the project itself. Having been forced to itself cope with unequal treaties imposed upon China by Western powers after its defeat in the opium wars, the Chinese leadership must understand that many of these loans will undoubtedly never be repaid.

The Portuguese, Dutch, and British have all gravitated toward Malaysia in the past, by virtue of its geostrategic location; China is only the latest power to do so. Kuantan, a Malaysian city nestled on the South China Sea coast, had never previously been a sought-out prize, but Beijing's aspirations along its nine-dash line changed all that. Chinese financing began appearing in Kuantan around 2013. Guangxi Beibu Gulf International Port Group, a state-owned firm from an obscure Chinese autonomous region, won a contract supported by the Malaysian government to build a deep-water terminal and industrial park. Nearby was a planned stop on the East Coast Rail Link that would mostly be financed by the Export-Import Bank of China. At the time, Razak had claimed that Malaysia was ahead of the curve, but local residents worried even then about presiding over a white elephant, echoing concerns of Sri Lankans that their sovereignty had been sold to the highest bidder.

Upon taking office, Mahathir's administration discovered that billions of dollars in inflated Chinese contracts were used to relieve debts associated with a Malaysian state investment fund at the heart of the 1MDB scandal that led to Razak's downfall. When the indebted fund began a fire sale of assets, two Chinese state-owned giants – the China General Nuclear Power Corporation and the China Railway Engineering Corporation – suddenly arrived on the scene, insinuating that Beijing was happy to keep Razak's government afloat indefinitely.

Mahathir uncovered a proposal from a Malaysian construction company containing evidence that the East Coast Rail Link could have been developed by a Malaysian company for less than half of the $13.4 billion contract won by the China Communications Construction Company. Not surprisingly, the bidding process for the rail contract was neither open nor transparent. Malaysia's finance minister subsequently told Parliament that their country would not be able to cover the operational cost of the railway, much less the capital expenditure. It turned out that not all the money was used to build the railway line; a large portion had simply been stolen, and no construction work had been completed.

Forest City, a new metropolis being built at the tail end of the Malaysian peninsula, was being designed specifically for Chinese clientele, from the layout of the luxury apartments to the signage in Mandarin. The development, four artificial islands covering eight square miles, was to be large enough to accommodate about 700,000 people. It was created by Country Garden, one of the largest private Chinese property developers, in cooperation with an investment entity whose largest shareholder was the local sultan. Part of the sales pitch was an electronic display highlighting Forest City's strategic location, placing it at the center of a map of Beijing's BRI projects.

More than any other BRI project in Malaysia, Forest City helped turn local sentiment against Chinese cash amid suspicions that a private Chinese property developer was plotting to reshape Malaysia's delicate ethnic balance (being a primary combination of Malay and Chinese), designed to dilute the Malaysian national identity. Mahathir knew a thing or two about that, having instituted the program of Bumiputra during his first term in office, designed to ensure that Malays maintain an edge over ethnic Chinese Malaysians. That makes Chinese intentions and actions a particularly sensitive topic in Malaysia.[15] It appears that Beijing did not have the presence of mind to consider that before diving in head first into the ethnic mosaic of Malaysia.

Taiwan

One of President Xi's first acts in 2019 was to issue a new threat to use military force in Taiwan as Beijing intensified its efforts to achieve unification, using China's relationship with Hong Kong as a model for Taipei. As was the case when Beijing reassumed its rule over Hong Kong, President Xi proposed that the peaceful reunification with Taipei would protect Taiwan's freedoms, as was supposed to be the case under the Hong Kong model of 'one country, two systems', but in the more than 2 decades since that 'reunification' occurred, Hong Kong's freedoms have gradually been chipped away. President Xi reiterated Beijing's willingness to use its military power to achieve its objectives, including in the case of Taiwan, which it sees as a renegade province.

Since 2016, Beijing has sought to further isolate Taiwan by successfully persuading a number of countries to cut ties with Taipei. As of 2019, only 16 countries and the Vatican maintained formal relations with Taipei. President Xi's comments were the first instance of a Chinese leader so openly expressing China's will and determination for unification, even though the vast majority of the Taiwanese oppose the Hong Kong model.[16] President Xi was attempting to be conciliatory but did not renounce the possible use of military force to accomplish its objectives – a lingering threat which has been a prominent background component of the reunification debate.[17] Given Washington's historical and ongoing military support of Taiwan, forced reunification seems as unlikely as ever, but the threat of the use of military force will continue to be part of Beijing's lexicon on the Taiwan issue.

China and India's Battle for Influence in Asia

While being historically suspicious of Indian intentions, Southeast Asia holds a much stronger dislike of China than of India. Chinese machinations in the region are still prominent in popular memory, given China's 1979 invasion of Vietnam, its support of the Pol Pot regime in Cambodia (1976-1979), accusations of involvement in Indonesia's 1965 coup, and being North Korea's only real ally in the region. Furthermore, China still has unresolved border disputes with several nations in the region, including Bhutan, Taiwan, Japan, Vietnam, the Philippines, and Malaysia, as well as claiming a sizeable chunk of the Indian state of Arunachal Pradesh. Tibet, of course, remains a sore bone of contention in Sino-Indian relations.

India's diplomacy has been heavily focused on East and Southeast Asia for more than 20 years. India's Look East policy aims to improve economic and political ties with the region and attempts to carve out a place for India in the larger Asia-Pacific dynamic[18]. One factor helping India in this regard is its democratic political system, prompting many countries in the region to view India's own economic rise to be relatively benign, and something to be welcomed. Being the world's largest democracy lends a certain degree of transparency to India's foreign policy motives, something that is worryingly absent from relations with China. A regional order dominated over the past two decades by open markets, international cooperation, and an evolving democratic community backed by Washington's diplomatic and security ties, has also facilitated India's growing stature among its regional neighbors.

The stark difference in political systems has at times appeared to be both sides' Achilles heel, however. For India, adherence to democratic norms, checks, and balances has hindered its ability to achieve its larger regional goals. For example, for decades India refused to have any relationship with Myanmar, leaving an opening for China, and long-held political tension with Sri Lanka hindered closer ties between the two countries – a gap that China since has fully exploited. For China, whose leaders have no qualms with benefiting from economic opportunities in countries with distasteful human rights records, opaque decision-making has bred mistrust amongst its regional neighbors. Almost every country in the region has a sizeable Chinese minority population – another factor that has encouraged governments to befriend India as a counterbalance to Chinese influence.[19]

Economic Counter-Weights

India and Japan have for many years been concerned about the rising power and influence of China. Apart from that, there are clear economic benefits to be gained by India and Japan by forging closer ties. Japan is keen to enhance its accessibility to rare earth metals, which are vital to the high-tech Japanese economy, and for which China controls an estimated 95% of the global market. Maritime conflicts with China and prior disruption in the supply of rare earth metals has placed diversification of supply firmly on the Japanese agenda. For India, the removal of Japanese tariffs on agricultural products is expected to be of enormous benefit, while India eyes Japanese contractors to invest in and upgrade its poor infrastructure network.

In addition to enhanced bilateral trade agreements with Japan, India has in recent years signed bilateral or comprehensive Free Trade Agreements with Nepal, South Korea, and the ten-member ASEAN (including Brunei, Cambodia, Indonesia, Laos, Malaysia, Myanmar, the Philippines, Singapore, Thailand and Vietnam). Given an existing agreement with Sri Lanka and ongoing negotiations with Bangladesh, the agreements cover the majority of Asian economies. China has been equally busy negotiating or signing agreements with ASEAN, Australia, New Zealand, Pakistan, and South Korea.

China's economic and political presence in Asia, Africa, and Latin America, its financing of large construction and infrastructure projects, and its voracious appetite for natural resources, has worried India, which fears being marginalized in its own backyard. New Delhi is effectively reinforcing the concept of Japanese centrality in Asian affairs, while engaging in ongoing security talks with countries such as Malaysia, South Korea, and the region's foremost naval power, Indonesia. Jakarta has been keen to forge partnerships with India's defense sector, while India sees Indonesia as an important strategic partner in constraining the growing Chinese presence from the Bay of Bengal to the Malacca Straits.

Long viewed by India as firmly within its sphere of influence, New Delhi has been concerned by Colombo's active solicitation of Chinese aid and investment, with China now Sri Lanka's number one aid donor, largest trading partner, and majority supplier of more than half the country's construction and development loans. China financed 85% of the Hambantota Development Zone, home to an international container port, oil refinery and international airport, as well being used as a refueling center for both countries' navies. India claims the Zone has increased China's intelligence-gathering capabilities vis-a-vis India, but both Sri Lanka and China have dismissed such concerns, claiming the site is a purely commercial venture.

Sri Lanka is merely one front in a broader battle for control of the Indian Ocean. China has steadily built Indian Ocean ports in Bangladesh (Chittagong), Burma (Kyaukphyu) and Pakistan (Gwadar), while also steadily assisting Pakistan's naval expansion, much to the chagrin of India. India has referred to Sino-Pakistani cooperation as detrimental to regional peace.[20]

Since the BRI commenced in 2013, Pakistan has been the program's leading participant, with some $62 billion in projects planned in the China-Pakistan Economic Corridor. Pakistan naturally pivoted to Beijing as bilateral relations with the US have gradually deteriorated during the Obama, and especially the Trump, years. With President Trump having ended hundreds of millions of dollars in economic and military aid with Islamabad since 2017, Beijing was only too happy to fill the void. Some of China's biggest projects in Pakistan have geostrategic implications, such as the Chinese-built seaport and special economic zone in Gwadar, establishing a faster route to sells Chinese goods via the Arabian Sea. The port also gives Beijing a strategic card to play against India and the US in the future.

The prospect of the sale or sharing of advanced military technology under the BRI is the biggest potential threat to the West in the future. One of the less discussed aspects of the BRI is the central role Pakistan has played in China's Beidou satellite navigation system. Pakistan is the only country that has been granted access to the system's military service, which allows for more precise guidance of missiles, ships, and aircraft. The close cooperation between Beijing and Islamabad is intended to become a blueprint for Beidou's expansion to other BRI recipient nations.

The construction of the Gwadar port included an $800 million development plan that benefitted Chinese companies with a special economic zone and a 2,000-mile network of highways and rails through resource-rich Baluchistan Province, ostensibly to ship natural resources obtained from the Province back to China. Military analysts predict that China could also use Gwadar to expand the naval footprint of its attack submarines, after agreeing to sell 8 submarines to Pakistan for up to $6 billion in 2015. China could use the equipment it sells to Islamabad to refuel its own submarines, extending its navy's regional reach.

That kind of relationship with China naturally comes at a cost. Pakistan could end up owing China as much as $90 billion (including interest), if all the BRI's proposed programs for the country come to fruition. Pakistan's first debt repayments to China under the BRI begin in 2020, starting at approximately $300 million and gradually increasing to reach about $3.2 billion by 2026. Not surprisingly, Pakistan was already having trouble paying what it owes to Chinese companies as of 2018. The stakes are high, for both countries. In 2019, a special economic zone was to be created in Pakistan to produce a new generation of fighter jets. For the first time, navigation systems, radar systems, and onboard weapons would be jointly built at factories in Pakistan, expanding the two countries' existing cooperation on the JF-17 fighter jet, which is assembled at Pakistan's military-run Kamra Aeronautical Complex in Punjab Province. The Chinese-designed jets have given Pakistan an alternative to the US-built F-16 fighters that have become difficult to obtain, given its relationship with Washington.

Islamabad hopes that Beijing will become a permanent counterweight to Washington while Beijing hopes that Islamabad will become a showcase for other countries seeking to shift their militaries and alliances away from the US and toward China. Since Beijing is not averse to selling advanced weaponry such as ballistic missiles to countries throughout the region, Pakistan could become a steppingstone to a larger market for Chinese weapons in the Muslim world. By 2020, it is estimated that all 35 satellites that will comprise the Beidou system will be launched in collaboration with other BRI recipient nations. Any rocket launch using Beidou – whether for satellite launches or offensive missiles – will of course be tracked by China once the system becomes fully operational[21]. Doing so will open a new potential pathway toward long-term military relationships with a host of countries throughout the Muslim world.

India has, until recently, kept pace with China's naval modernization program, but China's aggressive expansion of its navy implies that whatever maritime advantage India had in the past will soon be gone. India is not in a position to keep pace with China in that regard, given China's superior satellites, missile systems, and production cost advantages.[22] India and China will likely continue their respective economic and political ascent relatively harmoniously, as there is plenty of scope for both countries to flex their muscles in their own neighborhood.

India has aligned itself with countries where it appears to have more to gain than lose (Japan, Indonesia, and Vietnam, among others). New Delhi also appears to be making more headway than Beijing in the battle for hearts and minds, which bodes well for the long-term future of Indian relations throughout the region. This suggests that India has the upper hand in the medium-term. However, anyone who underestimates China's ability to learn quick lessons and adapt to dynamic investment climates will be disappointed. China has proven itself to be a shrewd and cunning competitor in the global economic and political arena, and its ability and willingness to hurl money at countries yearning for assistance will continue to enhance its influence throughout the region and beyond for many years to come.[23]

Asia is China's to Lose

While the cases of Myanmar and Malaysia cited herein are good examples of how China has experienced substantial blowback in some of its efforts to promote the BRI and flex its muscles in Asia, it is, and will remain, *the* force to be reckoned with in the region. *Experiencing a few setbacks has not, and will not, deter Beijing in its mission to steamroll through the political and economic crosscurrents that lie in its path toward implementing China Vision.* And just as it will continue to have some setbacks, it will also continue to have many successes along the way.

As noted earlier, despite the long and hard-fought battle Manila had with Beijing in The Hague and the court of public opinion vis-à-vis maritime and territorial rights in the South China Sea, *President Duterte handed China a substantial victory during President Xi's visit to Manila in 2018. This is likely to weigh heavily on the psyche of the Filipino people, and people throughout Asia, for, if someone like Duterte essentially just rolled over, is there any potential leader – in Asia or anywhere else in the world – who may not ultimately do so?*

Both presidents agreed to a joint oil and gas exploration deal – one of 29 deals that were signed at the time to bolster bilateral cooperation, trade, and investment. The two nations also signed a memorandum of understanding sealing the Philippines' agreement to participate in the BRI Initiative and to invest 2 billion dollars in a 500-hectare industrial and high technology estate located at Clark, the home of a major US military base for almost 7 decades. The irony that China has supplanted the US to become one of the Philippines' largest aid donors and sources of investment should not be underemphasized.

President Xi played his hand well. He managed to strengthen bilateral political and economic ties with Manila as The Hague ruling remains in effect, while getting the two nations to agree to find a way to jointly explore oil and gas deposits in the very disputed waters that The Hague ruling addresses. Duterte was loudly criticized, accused of putting the Philippines' sovereignty up for sale by choosing to set aside The Hague ruling in favor of courting Chinese investment.[24] Yet Duterte came to the realization that, in the end, in spite of its numerous bilateral military defense treaties, the Philippines had no practicable way to defend its border and economic interests against the goliath that is China. Once Beijing had seized the Spratly and Paracel Islands and built military bases on them, that moment had passed. *Duterte came to the conclusion that it would be better to work with Beijing, rather than against it, and that is exactly the conclusion virtually every other smaller and poorer country in Asia has arrived at.*

Central to Beijing's strategy in crafting the BRI, in more freely distributing aid throughout the region, and in not hesitating to unapologetically flex its military and diplomatic muscles, is the knowledge that, just as the US is the unrivaled power of the Americas, China is the unrivaled power of Asia. No amount of protestation by the US, Australia, India, Japan, or any other Asian nation is going to change that. 800-pound gorillas do as they please for a reason.

With the South China Sea issue a fait accompli – thanks to Beijing's de facto expropriation of the Spratlys and Paracels – and with the majority of Asian nations on board with the BRI, the stage is clearly set for Beijing to continue to distribute significant sums of aid and roll out a diplomatic charm offensive to emphasize that it, too, rules with both carrots and sticks. Most of the region's countries are small and poor, so they naturally prefer carrots. While there will be more blowback to the BRI, and more protestations from the US and the region's larger, richer nations, there is no viable alternative to an omnipotent China. Beijing knows it, and so does the rest of Asia.

4 The United States

Realistic Expectations

Deng Xiaoping said that "the China-US relationship can never be too good or too bad"[1] because it is too important, meaning both countries' leaders and people should be realistic about how close their bilateral relationship can be at any given point in time and they should never let their disagreements get so out of hand that they threaten their general peace and prosperity. While seemingly simplistic, the quote accurately encapsulates the general nature of relations between the two nations since Richard Nixon and Mao Zedong commenced the modern bilateral relationship in 1972.

While China recognizes America's unique position as the world's sole superpower (for the time being, at least), its political orientation and national pride dictate that it pursue its own political and developmental path, and an independent foreign policy that it believes (and would like the rest of the world to believe) is ultimately aimed at achieving peace in Asia and elsewhere. Many countries in Asia, and the world, are highly skeptical about this so-called 'peaceful development', pointing to China's unilateral actions in the South China Sea as directly contrary to that objective. As previously noted, in spite of The Hague ruling against China, the Chinese government and most of its people believe that the country's actions are consistent with both recent regional history and current international law, based on their own unique perspective of history and international relations.

Part of the reason for the vastly different perspectives on this issue is a genuine belief on the part of both sides that each is right. China points to previous maps and maritime practices, which were at the time unopposed by other nations. The US (and other nations) see this as inconsistent with modern international maritime law as defined by UNCLOS, which, ironically, China has signed and ratified while the US has not. China views itself and the US as 'different, but not distant' because Confucian philosophy advocates 'accommodating divergent views'. *President Xi has repeatedly said that the Pacific Ocean is vast enough to accommodate both China and the US and has proposed a new model of international relations aimed at avoiding confrontation and conflict, and respecting one another's political systems and national interests, while pursuing joint win-win cooperation.*

That all sounds good on paper. The question becomes whether and how Confucian philosophy may become more consistent with current international law, whether both sides can reach an understanding about how China's rise may coincide with America's gradual decline as a global power, and how China's neighbors will view ongoing territorial disputes in the future. We stand at a critical juncture, given The Hague ruling, China's decision to continue its aggressive posture in the South China Sea, and uncertainty about the possibility of future military conflict. Therefore, much will depend on how far all sides are willing to reach across the table and genuinely compromise.

China's dual strategy of claiming to want to pursue diplomatic negotiations on the South China Sea dispute while simultaneously continuing its unilateral construction activities on its islands creates an environment that is not conducive to honest and meaningful negotiation. Maintaining equilibrium between China and its neighbors, as well as China and the US, will remain of paramount importance. Sino-US relations will remain the world's most important bilateral relationship for many years to come, with implications for the entire world. Both nations' people have much more to gain by maintaining a friendly and cooperative relationship with each other, rather than the other way around. It will clearly take a great degree of wisdom, an appreciation of history, and a willingness by all sides to compromise, in order to maintain mutual peace and prosperity.[2]

So, what should constitute a realistic set of expectations to govern the bilateral relationship? Should Beijing be expected to succumb to Washington's demands? In the end, *Washington is really looking for three things from Beijing:*

- *Play by the same set of rules everyone else is expected to play by;*

- *Level the playing field with respect to a more equal trading relationship; and*

- *Act as a responsible global leader and do its part to promote global development and maintain peace.*

On its face, there is nothing unreasonable about any of this, but from the Chinese perspective, it is merely acting in accordance with China Vision: doing things the Chinese way. For this, it sees no reason for any other nation to object. *Beijing, in turn, wants Washington to:*

- *Mind its own business and not interfere in what it considers to be Chinese domestic issues;*

- *Practice what it preaches and stop being hypocritical about its own rhetoric versus its own actions around the world; and*

- *Stop trying to impede China's inevitable rise.*

There is clearly incongruity between what both are seeking and what either may be prepared to deliver. What differentiates this challenge from that of any other two nations is that both countries need each other in order to prosper and either of them is capable of causing insurmountable problems politically, economically, and militarily for the other.

An Asymmetric Battleground

As a result of China's de facto expropriation of the Paracel and Spratly Islands, a significant portion of Asia's navigable waterways are once again contested territory. Yet, to prevail in the South China Sea, Beijing knows that it need not defeat the US (or any other military power) outright, but merely make potential intervention so costly (economically, politically, and militarily) that no power will directly challenge

China to control the Islands and, therefore, the South China Sea. So far, that approach has worked very well, despite coinciding with former US president Obama's 'pivot' to Asia (wherein some 60% of America's naval power was redirected there). It also happens to have concurred with a more isolationist America under both Presidents Obama and Trump.

That China achieved this as the US was officially reinforcing how important Asia was to Washington (in every respect), without firing a shot, and while the US was strenuously objecting to what Beijing was doing (but utterly failed to do anything meaningful about it), speaks volumes to both how cunning and driven Beijing can be, and how comparatively meek Washington can be. President Xi must have known that the US would not send warships to prevent its acquisition of the Paracels and Spratlys – at a time when the US had the world's largest and strongest navy, and while China possessed a single aircraft carrier. In power politics among the biggest players there is an unwritten code of conduct which basically says: I will let you do what you want in your backyard, and you will do the same. History is filled with such examples; this is one of them.

To accomplish what it did while anticipating possible military action against it, Beijing developed 'anti-access' military capabilities that use radar, satellites, and missiles to neutralize the comparative advantage that America's aircraft carrier strike groups possessed. It also rapidly expanded its naval forces to quickly develop a blue water navy that would allow it to defend its interests beyond its own coastal waters. As a result, China became capable of controlling the South China Sea in any scenario short of war with the US. Even if a war were to erupt, some in America's military establishment believe there is no guarantee the US will prevail.

In 2017, the Chinese Navy became the world's largest, with more warships and submarines than the US, and it continues to build new ships at a blistering rate. Though the American fleet remains superior qualitatively, it is spread over a much broader geography than China's, making China Asia's supreme naval power. Chinese warships and aircraft now regularly operate in the waters near Japan, Taiwan, and throughout the South China Sea. China's naval expansion began in 2000 but accelerated sharply after Xi became president in 2013. Since then, the People's Liberation Army

(PLA) has been reduced in size in order to generate resources for a more modern fighting force. While every branch of China's armed forces lags behind the US in terms of experience and firepower, China has made significant gains in *asymmetrical weaponry* to counter America's advantages.

One focus has been in what American military planners call A2/AD, or 'anti-access/area denial' – what the Chinese call 'counter-intervention'. Since Beijing cannot match Washington in terms of quality, it is doing so with the quantity of weapons at its disposal. The Pentagon is bloated and supremely bureaucratic, ensuring that its procurement process takes much longer than should be necessary. China's military makes up for this by doing what China does best – getting things done quickly.

A centerpiece of this strategy is an arsenal of high-speed ballistic missiles designed to strike moving ships. The latest versions, the DF-21D and (since 2016) the DF-26, are known as 'carrier killers', since they can threaten the most powerful vessels in the American fleet well before they would ever approach China. *These missiles are almost impossible to detect or intercept, being directed at moving targets by an increasingly sophisticated network of radar and satellites.* Neutralizing them could require launching an attack deep inside China, which would be unimaginable except in the most dire of circumstances, and Beijing knows it. *The American Navy has never faced such a threat before, and it has caught the attention of US military leaders.* The establishment of weapons such as the YJ-12B anti-ship cruise missile by China on its bases in the South China Sea has the capability to target most of the waters between the Philippines and Vietnam.

Since at least 2013, the Chinese military has been preparing for a limited military conflict from the sea. As of 2017, China had 317 warships and submarines in active service, compared with 283 by the US, which has had unrivaled access to the world's oceans and seas since the collapse of the Soviet Union in 1991. *Beijing's defense budget now ranks second only to the US.* In 1995, China built just 3 new submarines to begin replacing an older fleet totaling 83. Since 2014, China has launched naval vessels with a total tonnage greater than that of the entire French, German, Indian, Italian, South Korean, Spanish, or Taiwanese navies. As of 2018, it had almost 60 new submarines, with plans for at least 20 more in the near future. And Beijing has plans to build nuclear-powered carriers. What they all lack is experience in battle.

While Washington sees such a military buildup as competition and a potential threat, Beijing views the buildup as an attempt to achieve parity with the US and protect its interests. The truth probably resides somewhere in the middle. *It is disingenuous of Beijing to maintain that it is merely protecting its interests in doing so, for this is clearly also about projecting its power.* For example, in 2017, it opened its first overseas military base in Djibouti, declaring that it will be used to support its participation in multinational antipiracy patrols off Somalia. Beijing has also ramped up its participation in peacekeeping efforts around the world. Soon enough, it will have the ability to deploy a squadron anywhere in the world, as it did in 2015 when Chinese warships evacuated 629 Chinese and 279 foreigners from Yemen.[3]

Yet Washington has something Beijing does not have: a lot of friends who are happy to share intelligence and for which it has numerous military alliances. The 'Five Eyes' intelligence alliance is a good example. The US, Canada, UK, Australia, and New Zealand freely share the fruits of their eavesdropping on China and have redoubled their efforts to track China's interference in foreign countries. Many other of Washington's allies are only too ready to work more closely with Washington to give Beijing something to think about. America, Japan, and India hold annual military exercises that grow more ambitious by the year, and an intelligence-sharing agreement between America and India, which Indian leaders had resisted for years, was executed in 2018, opening the door for more advanced weaponry to flow to India's armed forces. The US and Australia are also actively pursuing the prospect of new military bases in the southern Pacific.[4]

Economic Brinksmanship

When the Xi government launched its Made in China 2025 policy in 2015, it said the objective was to enhance the strength and competitiveness of domestic manufacturing by increasing the domestic content of core materials to reach 70% by 2025, in line with its WTO obligations. The US Government (USG), and many of its businesses operating in China, saw the policy as an attempt to dominate key industries while forcing

American companies to give Chinese competitors US technology and, eventually, remove the need for Chinese firms to be forced to rely on American and other foreign businesses in order to remain competitive in the global arena. So, what China portrayed as a perfectly innocent effort to enhance Chinese manufacturing and competitiveness did not appear that way to foreign business interests.

The escalating brinkmanship between Washington and Beijing is forcing other nations to choose sides. Both China and the US are jockeying to build or enhance alliances at the expense of the other. In spite of the commencement of the trade war by Washington against Beijing in 2018, a report issued by the Office of the US Trade Representative at the end of that year stated that China had not fundamentally altered its acts, policies, or practices related to technology transfer, intellectual property, and innovation, and appeared to have taken further unreasonable actions in recent months.[5] Beijing subsequently said that it was perfectly normal for countries to have trade friction. *Both countries have become lost in their respective narratives and risk becoming so entrenched in their positions that a middle ground becomes increasingly difficult to achieve.*

The USG has attempted to deter nations from accepting Chinese loans while speaking ominously about Beijing's 'debt trap diplomacy', and has created new government-sponsored lending and insurance programs to support private sector investment throughout the world. In its first two years in office, the Trump administration produced a variety of new regulations on export controls, intended to protect such industries as AI and quantum robotics against the theft of intellectual property by Beijing, and implemented an even more aggressive system for policing foreign investment through the expanded powers of the Committee on Foreign Investment in the US (CFIUS). The administration also embarked on bilateral trade deals specifically intended to exert pressure on Beijing.[6]

The battle lines have clearly been drawn between those nations that choose to side with China versus those that choose to side with the US. *China's range of allies is primarily based on bilateral trading relationships, and occasionally on common geopolitical interests; only rarely are its relationships based on shared ideological interests.* There are very few communist countries still in existence and the world ceased being divided along Cold War grounds decades ago. That said, North Korea is a special case (based on geographic and historical ties) and a few countries, such as Pakistan, have had a long military relationship with Beijing based on their common animus vis-à-vis India.

By contrast, Washington's list of allies is broad and deep, based on a range of shared economic, military, and ideological interests. Many of them share Washington's concern with China Vision. While they may have a deep trade-based relationship with Beijing, they, too, want a level playing field with China with respect to bilateral trade, and they share significant concern with how China is rising and flexing its muscles. While, publicly, many of them may not like President Trump's tactics in terms of his rhetoric or the imposition of unilateral sanctions against Beijing, privately, they applaud that an American president is at last doing what many of them have thought for decades should be done. They are just happy they did not have to do it themselves.

Theft of Intellectual Property

In 2018, the Trump administration and more than a dozen US allies formally objected to China's persistent efforts to steal other countries' intellectual property (IP). The unprecedented mass condemnation marked a significant effort to at last hold China to account for its acts, representing a growing consensus that Beijing is flouting international norms of fair play in order to become the world's predominant economic and technological power. The countries taking part in the joint announcement included Britain, Australia, Canada, Japan, and Germany.[7]

China's theft of US IP and commercial secrets is well documented, ranging from computer chips and genetically modified rice to aircraft design and jet engines. Beijing's approach to this subject has rewritten the rules about how industrial espionage is 'supposed' to be done. Rather than being an isolated incident or occasional pursuit, *China has turned its IP theft into a state-sponsored industry and art form, wherein the ends justify the means.* Beijing has deployed an army of domestic computer hackers, overseas spies, and corrupt corporate insiders in the US and around the world to procure trade secrets in order to make China more competitive and self-reliant.

That there has been a surge in IP theft in recent years by China against the US, despite China having been indisputably identified as being the culprit, helped propel Donald Trump to the US presidency and prompted his administration to initiate its trade war against Beijing. The USG contends that the Chinese theft of US commercial software and technology has been relentless, expanding, and impactful against multiple industries in the US, with Chinese hackers having successfully penetrated corporate and government email and corporate computer and Internet networks. Chinese spies have successfully recruited US executives and engineers, and have accomplished a general level of intrusion that has also impacted ordinary US citizens through the theft of their most personal identification information.

In a comprehensive 2018 report issued by the White House Office of Trade and Manufacturing Policy[8], the USG outlined how China has meticulously and methodically sought to steal IP from the USG and US businesses. It claimed that Chinese industrial policy seeks to introduce, digest, absorb, and re-innovate technologies and IP in the US and around the world through a combination of:

- State-sponsored physical theft, cyber-enabled espionage and theft, the evasion of US export control laws, and counterfeiting and piracy;

- Coercive and intrusive regulatory policies designed to force technology transfer from foreign companies, typically in exchange for limited access to the Chinese market;

- Economic coercion via export restraints on critical raw materials and monopsony purchasing power;

- Methods of information harvesting that include open source collection, placement of non-traditional information collectors at US universities, national laboratories (and other centers of innovation), and talent recruitment of business, finance, science, and technology experts; and State-backed, technology-seeking Chinese investment.[9]

The report concluded that China's instruments of coercion to force the transfer of foreign technologies and IP to Chinese competitors include:

(1) Foreign ownership restrictions (such as forced joint ventures and partnerships) that explicitly or tacitly require or facilitate technology transfers;

(2) Adverse administrative approvals and licensing processes;

(3) Discriminatory patent and other IP rights restrictions;

(4) Security reviews;

(5) Secure and controllable technology standards;

(6) Data localization;

(7) Burdensome and intrusive testing;

(8) Discriminatory catalogues and lists;

(9) Government procurement restrictions;

(10) The imposition of indigenous technology standards that deviate significantly from international norms and that may provide back door Chinese access to source codes;

(11) Forced research and development;

(12) Antimonopoly laws;

(13) Expert Review Panels;

(14) CCP committees that influence corporate governance; and

(15) The placement of Chinese employees at foreign joint ventures.[10]

Taken in whole or even in part, this represents a truly significant threat to the national security of the US, which is why a partisan US Congress has found common ground in agreeing that something must finally be done to counter Beijing's efforts.

China has a commanding share of a wide range of critical raw materials that are essential to the global supply chain and production of high-technology and high value-added products. For example, China is the world's dominant producer of rare earths, tungsten, and molybdenum, and has used export restraints including export quotas and duties to restrict access to critical raw materials to the rest of the world. China's export restraints affect US and other foreign producers of a wide range of downstream products, such as steel, chemicals, hybrid and electric cars, energy efficient light bulbs, wind turbines, hard-disk drives, magnets, lasers, ceramics, semiconductor chips, refrigerants, medical imagery, aircraft, refined petroleum products, fiber optic cables, and catalytic converters.

These restraints can create serious disadvantages for foreign producers of these products by artificially increasing China's export prices for their raw material inputs, which also, of course, drives up the price for consumers. Such export restraints can also create pressure on foreign downstream producers to move their operations, technologies, and jobs to China.[11] The report concludes that China's information harvesting, economic coercion, and state-sponsored investment, combined with the extent of its market-distorting policies and stated intention to dominate the industries of the future, targets the technologies and IP of the world and threatens the global system of innovation.

The Cyber Arena

Chapter 6 is devoted to China's capabilities and escapades in the cyber arena. For now, suffice it to say that China and the US have also become competitors in the cyber sphere, where both countries exhibit cutting edge skills and capabilities. Chinese cyberattacks on US government and commercial interests have become so frequent and serious that they have morphed from being an annoyance to being of critical importance to the national security of the US. *Although, in 2015, Presidents Xi and Obama agreed that neither government would conduct or knowingly support cyber-enabled theft of IP, the USG believes that China undoubtedly entered the accord to avoid threatened sanctions and enhanced legal pressure at the time*, which included the indictment of five Chinese military hackers on economic espionage charges in 2014.

Chinese commercial hacks plummeted as much as 90% in the months after the agreement was reached, but that reversal did not last very long. Since 2016, Beijing has dramatically increased its hacking of US businesses and grown far more aggressive in its economic espionage. China's military no longer appears to be directing the bulk of the attacks. Rather, China's chief civilian intelligence agency, the Ministry of State Security (MSS), has replaced it, and then some.

The Ministry employs more sophisticated and experienced hackers than the military, making it harder to attribute the digital sabotage and thefts. The USG maintains that China has also boosted its efforts, since 2015, to recruit corporate insiders to provide trade secrets. One of the highest profile examples was the arrest of Yanjun Xu, a senior officer of the Ministry, who was charged with attempting to commit economic espionage from multiple US aerospace companies, including GE Aviation. His was the first known extradition of a Chinese spy (in this case, from Belgium) to face US charges. Yet, the scope of the problem makes it doubly difficult to effectively combat[12]; for every case that is successfully prosecuted there are thousands more that either go unreported or for which no suspect is either identified, successfully apprehended, or prosecuted.

The US Trade Representative's 2018 investigation of China's policies and practices related to tech transfer and IP[13] concluded that *cyber intrusions into US commercial networks consistent with Chinese industrial policy goals had continued since 2015, and that Beijing's cyber espionage against US companies persisted and evolved.* Chinese policymakers apparently believe that they have reached a new equilibrium with the US. Shifting industrial cyber espionage to the MSS and deploying a higher level of tradecraft have created an equivalent of the hacking conducted by the US National Security Agency (NSA).

Beijing never truly accepted the distinction that Washington had promoted between 'acceptable' hacking (which all cyber-capable nations do) and unacceptable hacking (such as theft to support the competitiveness of Chinese industry and military espionage). Instead, Chinese policymakers saw the issue in terms of the level of relatively 'noisy' activity generated (i.e. for which they were likely to get caught and be called out on). Bringing cyber intrusions more in line with what it believed the NSA conducts – a smaller number of attacks that gave the US large-scale access to Chinese assets – has, in Beijing's view, resolved the issue. *China appears to have come to the conclusion that the combination of improved techniques and more focused efforts have reduced Western frustration to levels that will be tolerated.*[14] There is, therefore, no real reason to believe that China will modify its behavior.

The list of alleged cyberattacks by China is long, but three, in particular, stand out: the US OPM, healthcare provider Anthem, and Marriott hotels. There is no publicly available evidence that any of the sensitive personal information acquired in these attacks was sold on the dark web or to or among criminal enterprises. The conclusion is that *Beijing is embarked on a mission to uncover as much highly sensitive information about Americans as it can and piece together information about how important individuals in government and business live, work, and travel, so that the Chinese government may attempt to either obtain information from them (without their knowledge) or turn them into spies.*

The 2014 OPM breach gave Beijing access to extensive files on every US individual with a security clearance, the 2015 Anthem breach gave China the Social Security numbers of 80 million Americans, and the 2018 Marriott breach gave the Chinese information on hundreds of millions of hotel guests (including passport information in some cases). These hacks provide raw data for China's MSS to build data sets on US (and other) citizens, enabling China to build dossiers on US citizens of interest, but also to be able to spoof their identities in cyberspace.

When the US Defense Advanced Research Projects Agency (DARPA) attempted to do something similar in the previous decade, with its prototype "Total Information Awareness" program, the US Congress stopped it.[15] That is not to imply that the USG is an angel in that regard. Former president Obama famously said that anything any other government can do in the cyber arena, the USG can do better. The new normal is for massive databases of sensitive information to be compiled by any government capable of doing so. Not much appears in the Western press about what the US does in terms of information gathering in other countries but it is presumed to do much the same as the Chinese are accused of doing.

Huawei

Since 2018, the USG has embarked on a global campaign to prevent Huawei and other Chinese telecommunications firms from participating in the most dramatic and ambitious upgrading of the Internet since it came into existence more than a quarter century ago. Acknowledging that the world is engaged in a new arms race to reign supreme in 5G (fifth generation) telecommunications technology, the Trump administration is focused on its potential national security implications, for, whichever country (or countries) dominate(s) 5G will gain an economic, intelligence, and military advantage for the foreseeable future. Through the use of AI and virtual reality, the 5G networks of the future will consist of sensors, robots, autonomous vehicles, and other devices that will continuously feed each other vast amounts of data, allowing factories, construction sites, and even entire cities to be run with less human intervention.

Whoever controls the networks ultimately controls the information flow and may be able to change, reroute, or copy data without users' knowledge. 5G's potential has prompted the Trump administration to seek to ban US companies from using Chinese equipment in critical telecommunications networks, which goes well beyond existing rules that ban such equipment only from government networks. Mindful that Chinese technology has penetrated the length and breadth of the US, the administration is motivated by the fear that the Chinese could insert a "back door" into telecom and computing networks that would allow Chinese security services to intercept military, government, and corporate communications.

It is worth recalling that China's 2017 National Intelligence Law requires Chinese companies to support, provide assistance to, and cooperate with China's national intelligence work in any jurisdiction where they operate.

This is an economic competitiveness, national security, and balance of power issue, which should incentivize the USG and US companies to work together for a common cause. Countries have already begun to auction off the rights to install 5G cellphone networks and the multibillion-dollar contracts to build the switching systems that will support them. In 2019, the US Federal Communications Commission announced that it had concluded its first high-band 5G spectrum auction. It should therefore come as no surprise that Chinese electronics giant Huawei has garnered the Trump administration's special attention.[16]

The 2018 arrest and detention of Meng Wanzhou, the CFO of Huawei, in response to the company's alleged violation of US-imposed sanctions on Iran, attempting to steal trade secrets from competitor T-Mobile, and promising bonuses to employees who collected confidential information on competitors[17], proved to be a watershed moment in Sino-US relations. The company sells smartphones and telecommunications equipment around the world and had faced increased scrutiny in the US and other countries where government officials had warned of potential national security risks specifically associated with using Huawei products. The USG had for some time been concerned that the Chinese government could be using Huawei's networking technology to spy on Americans.

Earlier that year, the Pentagon had ordered stores on American military bases to stop selling smartphones manufactured by Huawei and its Chinese rival, ZTE. The USG also blocked ZTE from buying US parts, stating that the company had lied to US officials about punishing employees who violated US sanctions against North Korea and Iran. It later lifted the ZTE sanctions after coming to 'an understanding' with the company, which was highly controversial at the time and deemed to be in response to a personal request from President Xi to President Trump. It then ordered the cessation of the purchase and use of software from the Russian manufacturer Kaspersky Labs, citing similar concerns.

The Trump administration subsequently urged America's allies to stop using Huawei telecommunications equipment. Australia and New Zealand then prevented its telecommunications companies from using Huawei equipment for their 5G mobile networks. British Telecom then said it would no longer purchase equipment from Huawei for the core of its next generation wireless network and that it would remove existing Huawei technology from the heart of its 4G network.[18]

To put this into perspective, the trade war should really be considered a skirmish in a larger technology war, which is itself a component of a long struggle between the US (to maintain its dominance) and China, the ascending challenger. It is not a cold war, but rather, *a race for political, economic, military, and geostrategic superiority. Put another way, it is a battle for control of the future*.

The Trump administration's ultimate goal is to end China's state-directed industrial policy, which enables Beijing to compete on an uneven battlefield. The US, and most other countries, have distinct lines drawn between their public and private sectors. Since that is not the case in China, it is able to integrate the best of both into a unified game plan, which also permits for rapid and effective policy execution. On that basis, and with the application of its own set of rules, it could bury the West if left unchecked.

China/US Collaboration

The bilateral relationship is primarily about competition, of course, but, occasionally, China and the US collaborate on issues of mutual interest and importance. In 2018, a team of American, British, Norwegian, and Chinese experts assembled to remove highly enriched uranium from a research reactor in Kaduna, Nigeria, that nonproliferation experts had long warned could be a target for the Boko Haram terrorist organization, which had for years been active in the area. China played a central role in transporting and storing the plutonium, the operation occurring only hours after President Trump had made an explicit threat to China about enhancing America's nuclear arsenal.

In the mid-1990s, China had helped Nigeria commence work on what would become Nigerian Research Reactor 1 (NIRR-1), located at Ahmadu Bello University in Kaduna.

Opened in 2004, NIRR-1 was classified as a miniature neutron source reactor, designed for scientific research, neutron activation analysis, education, and training. The reactor powers scientific experiments, not the local power grid, but the design used highly enriched uranium (HEU), otherwise known as weapons-grade uranium, which forms the core of any nuclear weapons material. The Nigerian material had been more than 90% enriched, making it an attractive target for terrorists to create a dirty bomb.

While virtually all of the cost of the $5.5 million operation was borne by the US, the final destination for the HEU was China, making its role critical. The Antonov plane carrying the HEU (and American inspectors and security) arrived at Shijiazhuang airport just as the arrest of Huawei's Meng Wanzhou had inflamed fears of a formal bilateral trade conflict between Beijing and Washington. Beijing carried right on with the operation, with the Chinese National Nuclear Corporation noting at the time that China's role was evidence of its commitment to the peaceful use of nuclear energy. It remains a mystery what happened to the HEU after that, but it is presumed that China put it to good (civilian) use.[19]

The episode was an excellent example of how China can, and does, at times step up to the plate and make meaningful contributions to international operations, from peacekeeping to anti-terrorist operations. China's role is becoming increasingly important and the USG recognizes this fact. It is reasonable to expect that Beijing will most definitely wish to contribute to future such efforts, not only as a responsible global leader, but also to raise its global profile and footprint. It is similarly reasonable to presume that bilateral relationships may indeed prove to be an obstacle to such actions going forward.

A Thucydides Trap?

For much of the past 50 years, the US engaged China in the belief that attempts to achieve political and economic integration would encourage the Chinese government to become more liberal and pluralistic. Armed with the right set of incentives and given sufficient time, American policymakers continued to believe that, eventually, Beijing would gradually move toward a more democratic form of government and become an increasingly responsible stakeholder. Few among

US policymakers, thought leaders, or observers of China would say that approach has worked.

The USG, which was always leery of what China was, and skeptical about what it might become, now clearly views China as a strategic rival, a malevolent actor, and a rule-breaker. Socialism with Chinese characteristics, which has been a work-in-progress since the days of Mao, has now morphed into President Xi Jinping Thought, whose 14 points[20] (with some caveats) basically boil down to the following precepts: *enforce the rule of law, strengthen national security, and ensure the perpetual omnipotence of the CCP.*

President Xi is under no illusions about what he wants China to become – an even more entrenched authoritarian state where making money is just fine as long as the omnipotence of the CCP is neither questioned nor challenged. Peaceful coexistence with the rest of the world and a common destiny is fine just as long as it occurs based on China's rules and objectives. The USG now understands what China and President Xi are all about, and is acting accordingly – calling Beijing out on its decades-long theft of American intellectual property, intensive spying, and a deeply unbalanced trading relationship.

Not since the late 1940s has there been such unanimity of opinion among American law makers, the military, businesses, and citizens about who America's number one rival is. For a short time, during the 2016 presidential election, many believed it was Russia, but that has changed. Similarly, *Chinese strategists have long suspected that America was mostly interested in preventing China from reaching its true potential and surpassing the US in both economic size and power. Many Chinese see America as a hypocrite that commits all the sins it accuses China of, while poisoning the atmosphere that would otherwise give Beijing a clear path toward its destiny.*

History has shown that hegemons such as the US and rising powers like China can become locked into a cycle of belligerent rivalry. *According to the Thucydides Trap theory, a rising power threatens to displace the supremacy of an established power, and war is often the result.* Some may be inclined to characterize the Sino-US trade war in such terms, but military conflict is unlikely to be the outcome of this spat. The central importance of the bilateral relationship – for the global economy and in terms of future regional stability – will prevent this economic dispute from turning into a military dispute.

Since the establishment of diplomatic relations in 1979, China and the US have experienced numerous tense episodes, such as the US arms sales to Taiwan in 1981, the Belgrade Chinese embassy bombing in 1999, and the military aircraft collision of 2001. These incidents did not result in escalatory military conflict. Bilateral relations not only survived, they thrived thereafter. Decades ago, when the two countries' economic relationship was not nearly as entrenched as it is today, the leadership of both nations desired to ratchet down tension and preserve the relationship, which has proven to be the cornerstone of bilateral relations ever since.

The foundation of the trade war is the imbalance between both countries' trading relationship; it is not, at its core, about a desire for trade supremacy. America's merchandise trade deficit surged by 12% to US $566 billion in 2017, the highest since 2008, of which 66% (US $375 billion) was attributable to China. From the US perspective, this is, of course, unsustainable, even if it has itself partly to blame. US manufacturers, in search of inexpensive labor and access to China's marketplace helped make China the economic engine of the world. And it was the US that agreed to the terms of bilateral and multilateral trading relationships that may have been to its own disadvantage in the long-term.

That said, while China has been a party to numerous trade agreements (including the WTO), it imposes, and maintains, some strict conditions on foreign investors, which many foreign investors view as both unfair and lopsided in favor of Beijing. For example, foreign investors cannot have access to Chinese foreign exchange reserves when transferring currency and must generate their own foreign exchange. No one forces investors to invest in China, of course, but the lure of access to the Chinese marketplace has prompted many foreign companies to agree to terms they may not have agreed to anywhere else in the world.

Indeed, China is accustomed to being seen as, and treated as, separate, distinct, and special by the foreign investment community, and Beijing has maximized that to its advantage. According to the US Trade Representative's exhaustive Section 301 Report for 2018, "the Chinese government uses its administrative licensing and approvals processes to force technology transfer in exchange for the numerous administrative approvals needed to establish and operate a business in China."[21] Although China has repeatedly rebutted such accusations, many foreign investors contend that it continues to utilize so-called 'state capitalism' to its advantage.

From China's perspective, America's trade imbalance is a long-standing structural problem more related to Washington's inability to effectively compete in the global marketplace and should be resolved through bilateral negotiations. However, the Trump administration's credo is that there is no longer any time for 'consultation' and 'political correctness'. It sees Beijing as having skillfully manipulated the bilateral and global trade regime to its distinct benefit, and it blames countless previous US administrations for pandering to Beijing while the US trade relationship with China became more and more imbalanced.

President Trump is seeking nothing less than a reordering of the global trade regime so that it is not tipped so much in Beijing's favor but levels the import and export playing field for America, and for the rest of the world in the process. President Trump sees this escalating trade war with Beijing, and the trade war he initiated with the rest of the world, as an effort to tip the balance before it is too late. It may already be too late, however. America's trade imbalances did not occur overnight but rather over the course of many decades. If the balance is to be readjusted, it will take many years – perhaps decades – for it to occur.

The Chinese government and many Chinese people believe that Trump's trade war and other investment restrictions placed on Chinese companies are ultimately aimed at curbing China's technological development – particularly in light of its 'Made in China 2025' strategy – to attempt to contain China's rise as a great power. This is indeed a consideration in President Trump's strategy, as the race for supremacy in 5G, AI, and enhanced cyber technology heats up. The stakes are extremely high in that regard.

At its outset, the US was perceived as aggressive and offensive in the trade war, while China was seen as reactive, defensive, and reciprocal. Based on this, it would appear that Beijing wanted to avoid the Thucydides Trap. Similarly, there was no reason to believe that President Trump desired military conflict with China. On the contrary, both countries' leadership realized what was at stake, and neither ultimately desired to derail the mutually beneficial economic relationship that forms the foundation of their economies.

In postwar history, there have been many opportunities for both countries to escalate tension and trigger military conflict. Beijing and Washington have always understood that this is a line that neither should cross, and there is every reason to presume that neither desires to cross that line in the future. It is ultimately the degree of economic pain both countries can endure, and the length of time it can be endured, that determines the economic outcome of such trade conflicts. Mutual respect and benefit is the long-term objective. What is unknown is how long it will take to arrive at an equilibrium and at what cost for both countries.[22]

Time may be on China's side, however, for its economy is growing at more than twice the rate of the US and has been significantly outpacing the growth of America's 'mature' economy for decades. As Beijing continues to pour massive amounts of money into advanced technologies such as AI, quantum computing, and biotechnology, the USG and many other governments are only starting to lace up their shoes and determine a course of action. Many of the new norms governing how the world's leading nations will behave in the future are only just being established.

Do America and China have any real hope of achieving a genuinely peaceful and possibly a collaborative existence in the decades to come? To accomplish that, both nations must believe that they are sufficiently strong – militarily, economically, and politically – to *want* to strive toward achieving such objectives. Clearly, Washington has ramped up its game against China and raised the ante for Beijing. Given the inherent inequity in the two nations' trading relationship, and Beijing's ongoing insistence on continuing with its theft of IP and high level cyberattacks, it is up to President Xi to *demonstrate* that China is willing to modify its behavior. Many in the USG will believe that when they see it, on a sustained and unwavering basis.

That appears unlikely. What appears to be more likely is that Beijing will continue doing what it has been doing – getting away with whatever it can get away with. *The US will continue to object and attempt to give President Xi a taste of his own medicine. But with China as the ascendant power and the US as a power in gradual decline, President Xi has little real incentive to change the Chinese playbook on a wholesale basis. That means that the US should reset its expectations about future Chinese behavior.* The modern trading system does not and cannot prevent China's state-owned enterprises from blurring the line between commercial interests and national interest. Chinese government funds subsidize and protect Chinese companies as they purchase dual-use technology or distort international markets.

To effectively counter more of the same from China in the future, the US needs a strategy, not merely tactics. This would ideally be executed in conjunction with the other largest and strongest countries opposed to Chinese tactics in the West. The Trump administration's disdain for collaboration with America's historical allies, and the institutions it was central to creating in the postwar era, should be replaced with a global alliance of the willing. This is not merely America's issue or battle, for the same bones of contention Washington has with Beijing are shared, to a greater or lesser degree, by countries around the world. The disarray and fractious nature of America's existing relationship with much of the rest of the world should be replaced by an approach more consistent with Washington's historical norm. That is the only way Beijing will become incentivized to change its behavior. *When America competes with China as a guardian of a rules-based order, it starts from a position of strength, but any Western democracy foolhardy enough to enter a race to the bottom with China will – and should – lose.*

It should also not be forgotten that, as a result of the connectivity between the American and Chinese economies, the two countries ultimately need to find a way to cooperate. As the world's largest economies and most powerful nations, they also share responsibilities, to set the stage for peace and prosperity for the rest of the world. Although there is some degree of inevitability in the notion that Beijing and Washington will end up as rivals, that is not inevitable, nor is it inevitable, as previously stated, that such rivalry must lead to war.[23]

Henry Kissinger has opined that the Sino-US relationship should not be considered a zero-sum game, nor that a prosperous and powerful China should, in and of itself, be considered an American strategic defeat. Both countries are compelled to interact; the question is whether they will do so as collaborators or adversaries. China's greatest strategic fear is that an external power will establish a periphery capable of encroaching on Chinese territory (which helps explain Beijing's actions vis-à-vis the South China Sea). America's greatest strategic fear in Asia is that its interests and military capability will become overwhelmed by another power. That has not been an issue, previously, but it is now. Washington's pivot to Asia during the Obama administration was an acknowledgement of that.[24]

The gradual rise of China coincides with the gradual decline of America's preeminence in global affairs, but it should be remembered that the USG was long ago relieved of the need to be preoccupied with satisfying its population's food, energy, manufacturing, and technology needs, for it has done that very well over the course of decades. By contrast, *when China becomes the world's largest economy in the coming decade, the Chinese government will still be preoccupied with satisfying the domestic needs of a population 4 times the size of the US. Washington would be wise to recognize this, recognizing that Beijing's distinct set of domestic and international challenges are quite different from America's.*[25] Washington should not expect that Beijing will go about meeting its nation's requirements the same way Washington did.

A strategy that presumes confrontation in the future might be completely justifiable in the business, military, and cyber arenas, but that does not necessarily imply confrontation if Beijing comes to understand that the gloves are now off and modifies its behavior so that the US will eventually arrive at a more equal footing in the trade arena. By the same token, *Washington must understand that China's rise is inevitable, just as is America's eventual decline as the world's leading power.* The question is whether superpower rivalry will succumb to historical precedent.

5 Africa and The Middle East

The New Face of Neocolonialism in Africa?

Many analysts contend that China has become the new face of neocolonialism in Africa, having loaned tens of billions of dollars to the continent's governments while knowing that, in all likelihood, many of those debts will never be repaid. Beijing proceeded on the presumption that its access to Africa's markets, enhanced influence, and ability to exploit the continent's rich deposits of natural resources would compensate it for any unpaid loans.

Chinese investment in Africa has a long history, dating back to the Ming Dynasty, but it was not until the late twentieth century when China pursued what is now commonly referred to as 'debt trap diplomacy' in order to have its way with Africa. In countries such as resource-rich Angola, China offered to build infrastructure in return for a guaranteed percentage of oil production. The loans that were made for the infrastructure were to be paid back with oil production, but Chinese investment in the continent has grown far beyond that original purpose, particularly among the continent's poorest of the poor countries.

In 2000, China's official loans to Africa were just in the millions of dollars. Johns Hopkins University has estimated that between 2000 and 2015, the Chinese government, banks and contractors loaned $94 *billion* to African governments and state-owned enterprises. Many countries welcomed Chinese investment because it did not come with strings attached, such as a requirement for free elections, gender equality, anti-corruption programs, or government accountability.

In Djibouti, for example, Chinese funding has resulted in dozens of posh apartment blocks having been built amidst a rising standard of living for some inhabitants. However, many African leaders' willingness to agree to Chinese funding – whether for natural resource extraction, infrastructure building, or for commercial purposes – has come at a cost. Some of the apartment blocks and related investment associated with that Chinese investment now resemble the 'ghost cities' so prevalent in many places in China, where over-investment in real estate has resulted in a credit bubble and a pending economic disaster when that bubble finally bursts.

Many people in Africa have complained that workers are not treated fairly, the environment has not been well considered, and much of the Chinese-built construction is shoddy and dangerous. Some highways that have been built began to crumble just a year or two after construction, leaving host governments to foot the bill. Regardless of the quality of the construction, the loans must, at least in theory, be repaid to China, adding to governments' debt burden. Two HIPCs – the Democratic Republic of Congo and Zambia ---have particularly high levels of Chinese government debt, raising questions about how those loans may ultimately be repaid, at what cost, and what sacrifices the governments may have to make to repay those loans. This has led some analysts to suggest that the relationship between China and Africa has become toxic.

Much of the debt of the HIPCs was written off by lenders just after the millennium. As a result of China's aggressive lending throughout the developing world in the second decade of the twenty-first century, particularly in Africa, *countries such as Zambia have accumulated almost as much debt as they had before the previous generation of national debt was written off.* Between 2013 and 2018, Zambia's national debt tripled as a percentage of national income. Most of it was owed to China.

Some NGOs consider the accumulation of debt unnecessary and reckless on the part of African governments, which, they maintain, certainly share the blame for the continent's predicament vis-à-vis China. After all, no one forced them to accept the loans. Some projects were considered 'vanity' spending, to help get politicians elected or re-elected. In Zambia, for example, Chinese loans paid for two new airports and a variety of 'roads to nowhere', while the country still lacked so many basic needs. While it takes two to tango (a lender and a borrower), development loans are often difficult to obtain, so free-spending Beijing had an obligation to ensure that the borrowers understood the implications of accepting its money, yet responsible long-term lending has often taken a back seat to near-term objectives, such as resource extraction.

The impact of Zambia's debt burden was certainly felt among its people. Basic services such as education and the provision of water suffered in the interim, and new taxes ended up being imposed to help the government repay the Chinese debt. It was even alleged that some state-owned assets – such as the state broadcasting corporation and the national power company – were being held as security by Chinese companies to ensure that their loans were repaid, a charge Beijing denied. No one in Zambia believed China was simply going to forgive its debt.

In 2018, Kenya's public debt first surpassed the $50 billion mark. At that time, China was Kenya's largest lender by far, accounting for 72% of bilateral debt – a 15% increase from 2016. Kenya's debt to China was also 8 times more than what it had received from its next largest lender, France. Overall, China accounted for more than 21% of Kenya's external debt that year, coinciding with Moody's downgrading of Kenya's credit rating because of its rising debt levels and what the agency saw as deteriorating debt affordability. That same year, the IMF ceased Kenya's access to a $1.5 billion standby credit facility due to non-compliance with fiscal targets, urging Nairobi to lower its deficits and put the country's debt onto a sustainable path.[1]

That same year, Kenya was forced to relinquish control of its largest and most lucrative port in Mombasa to Chinese control as a result of Nairobi's inability to repay its debts to Beijing. Other assets related to the inland shipment of goods from the port, including the Inland Container Depot in Nairobi and the Standard Gauge Railway (SGR), were at the time threatened with being compromised in the event of a Chinese port takeover. Kenya has accepted large loans from Beijing to develop some major highways and the SGR, which forms a crucial transport link to and from Nairobi for the import and export of goods through Mombasa.

It was suggested by local media at the time that the SGR, which was operated by the Chinese, may have been designed to be a loss-making venture. With a reported loss of KES 10 billion (US $98 million) in its first year of operation, it was clearly impossible to repay the loans taken for its construction in the allotted time. Kenya reportedly accepted loans of KES 500 billion (US $4.9 billion) for the SGR's construction. Kenya agreed to the deal with the understanding that any investment disputes would be subject to Chinese law and occur in China. Should default occur, China's Exim Bank would take possession of the assets from Kenya's Port Authority. At the same time, Zambia was slated to lose its international airport and national electricity grid to Beijing because of defaults on Chinese loans.[2]

Perhaps in response, in 2018, China froze its funding for Africa for the first time. Had Beijing developed a sudden conscience about the nature of its lending to Africa, a concern about whether its enormous level of lending would actually be fully repaid, or both? Some would argue that China is learning to better understand its African partners and their needs. The Chinese government and its companies certainly have much more knowledge and insight about the continent and its plethora of needs following so many years of intensive lending. Similarly, African countries understand much better the implied costs and benefits of agreeing to accept Chinese loans in exchange for natural resources.

The Chinese know that Africa is going to be a smarter clientele continent going forward, and a more difficult and demanding negotiator in the future. The Angolans, for example, began specifying exactly the number of schools and railroad lines they would like the Chinese to build, and what they hoped to achieve as a result. The relationship was in essence being rebalanced out of necessity. African leaders were perhaps afraid to stand up to China, or were simply greedy, and feared that the money would not flow in the end. Many of them did not consider the consequences; nor did the Chinese.

As the world's natural resources become increasingly scarce, African countries have come to realize just how many cards they hold, and they have finally decided to stand up to China. Should African countries successfully manage the transition from nations that merely possess natural resources to manufacturing powers that can actually compete with China, the nature of their relationship with Beijing will change even further. That said, both sides know they ultimately need each other. The challenge will be to find the right balance between China's wealth, power, and money, and African countries' resources and vast potential.[3]

Two Sides to the Story

While the neocolonialism narrative in Africa is a familiar one, there is another side to the story. The existence of such large-scale lending to public sector entities throughout the continent is well understood, but the avalanche of *private* Chinese businesses that have become established in Africa is less known. In 2017, McKinsey estimated, based on extensive fieldwork, that more than 10,000 Chinese owned firms operate across Africa, almost four times what the Chinese Ministry of Commerce had indicated at the time.

Many Chinese businesses have found it increasingly difficult to compete in China, which is becoming a mature economy in some ways. As is the case with businesses elsewhere in the world, an increasing number of Chinese businesses have sought to expand globally. When they expand into Africa, many of these businesses operate there with a purposely low profile, since local media often publish negative reports of rule breaking and maltreatment of workers. The Chinese owners of these businesses have remained almost completely out of sight to the local population. Of course, some Chinese businesses have become incredibly successful in Africa, such as the Nigeria-based Tung family, who operate a billion-dollar steel business and sit on the board of the Africa Finance Corporation, and the Lee family, whose Lee Group produces everything from bottled water to bread, producing more than one million pairs of flip-flops each day.[4]

It turns out that about 90% of Chinese firms in Africa are actually privately owned, which sheds a different light on the more commonly held view of 'China Inc.' on the continent. Nearly a third are involved in manufacturing, a quarter in services, and about a fifth each in either trade, construction, or real estate. McKinsey estimated that, as of 2017, approximately 12% of Africa's industrial production (valued at some $500 billion per year) was already attributable to Chinese firms. In infrastructure, almost 50% of Africa's internationally contracted construction market belonged to the Chinese at the time. Up to 90% of employees among these firms were believed to be African, creating millions of jobs and generating a lot of skilled labor, salaries, and tax revenue. That said, fewer than half of these firms sourced inputs or had African management.[5]

Yet, for every horror story (and there are many), there are plenty of other stories of knowledge sharing, skill development, and mutually beneficial success. Africans tend to think of China in mixed terms, but surprisingly positively. While some of the allegations made against China in Africa are indisputable – such as that Chinese investment exacerbates corruption and that many governments fall into a debt trap as a result of Beijing's approach to funding and lending – some of the allegations made against China in Africa simply are not true. Among them, an oft-repeated criticism is that Chinese companies employ primarily Chinese workers. China actually creates more jobs in Africa than any other foreign investor, and surveys of employment on Chinese projects there have repeatedly found that three-quarters or more of workers are locals. While early-stage projects, particularly in countries where China has had little experience, tend to be staffed primarily by Chinese employees, that pattern has tended to be reversed over time.

And while, on an individual country basis, Chinese foreign direct investment has accounted for a significant portion of national debt, it is worth noting that, from 2000 to 2016, despite all that lending, Chinese loans only accounted for just 1.8% of Africa's foreign debts, and most of that had been invested in infrastructure."[6] Chinese loans tend to either be competitive with, or of lower interest, than most of the MDBs. Some of the debt is eventually written off, since it cannot be repaid. It is also worth noting that the 2018 Forum on China-Africa Cooperation (FOCAC) Summit included $15 billion of grants, interest-free loans, and concessional loans.

Regarding numerous allegations that China is in the process of sending millions of peasants to Africa in order to grow food for China, and that Beijing is grabbing land, there is no evidence to support the claim. According to the United Nations (UN) Commodity Trade database, China has been sending food to Africa. While this will eventually change, the only significant food exports sent from Africa to China as of 2018 were sesame seeds and cocoa, produced by African farmers.[7]

In 2015, Afrobarometer issued some surprising results in its survey of 54,000 people in 36 African countries. China ranked number two in terms of favorable views, following the US. In three of five regions of the continent, China either matched or surpassed the US in popularity vis-à-vis its approach to development. Public perceptions not only confirmed China's perceived economic and political importance to Africa but also generally portrayed its influence as beneficial.[8]

China Vision has not created a black and white chess board in Africa but, rather, a rich mosaic of color. Debt trap diplomacy is creating some distinct casualties, but Chinese loans are also powering a vibrant Africa. While the jury will be out for some time on whether China's experiment with Africa was a net-plus or minus, its impact on African business and society is casting a wide net.

China's View

At the 2018 Beijing FOCAC Summit (first established in 2000), President Xi declared that China follows a 'five-nos' approach to its relations with African nations:

- No interference in the development paths of individual countries;

- No interference in their internal affairs;

- No imposition of China's will;

- No attachment of political strings regarding assistance; and

- No seeking of selfish political gains in investment and financing cooperation.

He said that "China follows the principle of giving more and taking less, giving before taking, and giving without asking in return."[9] Not everyone in the audience agreed with his assessment. Some might even have been tempted to burst out laughing, but the fact that President Xi said this with a straight face serves to emphasize that he and the CCP believe that China is approaching Africa in a manner consistent with these precepts.

Given the generally beneficial experience tens of thousands of Africans have had with China, as noted in the Afrobarometer poll, many Africans would actually agree with President Xi's statement. Rwandan President Paul Kagame said at the time that China's engagement in Africa had been "deeply transformational, both internally and with respect to Africa's global position,"[10] and that China had "proven to be a win-win partner and sincere friend."[11] Djibouti President Ismail Omar Guelleh said that his country's relationship had been "based on win-win cooperation and mutual benefit,"[12] and that "Africa had found in China a partner that believes in the continent's ability to lift its people out of poverty and achieve economic independence and self-sufficiency."[13] Such sentiment is clearly not an aberration, any more than the debt diplomacy narrative.

At the summit, President Xi announced 8 initiatives to bolster bilateral cooperation through 2021, including promoting industrial cooperation, developing infrastructure connectivity, facilitating trade, protecting the environment, and upgrading health aid programs. Beijing backed the initiatives up with a financing package of $60 billion, in addition to the $60 billion in funding support it had pledged to provide Africa at the 2015 Johannesburg Summit.[14] So, President Xi is delivering what Africans are expecting in terms of financial support. A shame that so much of it, the methods deployed, and the end result, often stand in stark contrast with the "five-nos".

A Rising Nigeria

Bilateral relations between China and Nigeria, Africa's most populous country, will likely take one of two paths in the long term: either China will remain the overwhelmingly dominant actor or Nigeria will become a regional superpower, leveling out the playing field. If China remains the stronger player, it will shape Nigeria in its own interests (commonly referred to as 'Chinese Imperialism'). If, however, Nigeria rises to reach its economic and political potential, Beijing may one day find Abuja a potential rival in Africa.

China has only recently started to play an important role in Nigeria. During the first eleven years of its independence, Nigeria and China had no diplomatic relations. The Nigerian government's view of China grew especially sour after Mao had officially supported the secessionist state in Biafra by supplying the Biafran administration with weapons. Throughout the 1970s and 1980s, China was not a significant trading partner of Nigeria, as its international trade was conducted primarily with Europe and North America.

During the period of General Abacha's military rule (1993-1998), Beijing's no-strings-attached development projects were increasingly well received. Nigeria's leaders grew resentful of Western conditions for aid and investment, and many Nigerians began to question what a generation of economic dependence on the West had achieved for Nigeria. Abuja subsequently adopted a new approach to international trade, balancing traditional Western partners with China. The evolution of Nigerian-Chinese relations mirrors that of China's relationship with other African states (such as Angola, Sudan, and Zimbabwe) that sought alternative forms of aid and development packages following the imposition of sanctions by Western nations, based on alleged human rights violations.

Between 2000 and 2010, annual Nigerian-Chinese trade increased nine-fold, from $2 billion to $18 billion. Ten major bilateral agreements concerning commerce, agriculture, tourism, and security were signed during that period. Nigeria imported more goods from China in 2012 than it did from the US and India combined (Nigeria's number two and three import partners, respectively). Today, hundreds of Chinese firms operate in Nigeria and China is the country's top source of imports.[15]

During the presidency of Ọbasanjọ (1999-2007), many 'oil-for-infrastructure' contracts were implemented. When his successor (Yar'Adua) came to power, some of these were canceled or suspended, as the two administrations pursued different approaches toward Beijing. While many Nigerians consider China's growing presence to be nothing short of a godsend, others have raised concerns about the sanctity of Nigerian sovereignty, bearing in mind the impact Chinese trade and investment has had on other African countries. The Chinese model of importing many of its own workers to build infrastructure projects, for example, does not sit well with many Nigerians.

A number of Nigerians have also voiced objections to labor conditions in Chinese-operated factories across Nigeria. Attention was first brought to these conditions when 37

Nigerian workers died after being trapped inside a locked Chinese-owned factory that caught fire in 2002. Nigeria's trade unions have similarly complained that the notable rise in Chinese imports resulted in the elimination of hundreds of thousands of manufacturing jobs, primarily in the textile sector. Much of the bilateral trade is also 'off the record', given that many Chinese imports arrive in Nigeria via the porous borders the country shares with its neighbors, which exacerbates the problematic level of corruption in Nigeria.

In spite of all this, Nigerian-Chinese economic ties can be expected to continue to grow. After agreeing to a 3-year, $2.5 billion currency swap with China in 2018 (to boost its reserves and promote bilateral trade), Nigeria began selling the Chinese yuan to local traders and businesses. An underlying motive was to help ease pressure on the naira, which had endured a long slide against the US dollar. Abuja intends to increase the use of the yuan as an alternative trading currency; direct trade using yuan will avoid the need to first convert naira into dollars, making it easier for local businesses to conduct business with Chinese counterparts.[16]

China's dependency on Middle Eastern oil and gas is a grave concern for Beijing, given the rising political uncertainty in the region and the number of perceived political risks for foreign investors. In this context, a deeper partnership with Nigeria, the world's 6th largest producer of crude oil,[17] provides China with a more diverse set of options for acquiring oil and gas.

Despite all the concerns voiced by a variety of constituencies within Nigeria, most Nigerians recognize that China's growing presence is likely more beneficial than harmful. Western powers that claim a desire to help Nigeria develop are often perceived as insincere, with their own aid being viewed as an infringement on Nigeria's sovereignty, since it often comes with strings attached. In this respect, China is not viewed as hypocritical and is thought of as more respectful of African aspirations to manage their own affairs without fear of meddling by a foreign power.

The Nigerian government also understands that China's growing presence in the country will not inevitably provide solutions to the plethora of domestic challenges Nigeria faces, from grinding poverty to indigenous violent political movements. In the end, *it accepts that China's number one objective is meeting China's strategic interests. At least China is up front about saying so.* The bilateral relationship between the two may yet serve as a model for China's growing influence throughout Africa.[18]

Why China is Betting on Africa

As China is in essence running circles around the rest of the cross-border investment world vis-à-vis diving into Africa and making long-term commitments to the continent, the US, major European nations, and much of the rest of the world are looking in awe at what Beijing is doing there. *Long believed to be the world's last 'frontier' investment destination, to China's credit, it is not waiting to see what other of the world's powers will do in Africa but is instead leading the way.* While the Americans and Europeans agonize about human rights concerns and environmental considerations, Beijing has set its sights on its, and the continent's, future.

In addition to Africa's incredibly rich vein of natural resources, one of the most important considerations driving China forward there has to do with population growth. With few exceptions, sub-Saharan Africa is one of the few places in the world where citizens continue to have large families. Though family sizes will decrease as the continent becomes wealthier, Africa is still expected to continue to experience much more population growth than just about anywhere else.

By the end of this century a third of the world's population, and a greater fraction of its young people, will be African. The future of Africa is therefore synonymous with the future of the human race. As the continent becomes more populous, those companies with an established presence there will be better positioned to sell into African markets, which will continue to grow.

Several other trends contribute to making investment in Africa a tempting prospect. Literacy rates and the percentage of citizens with access to the Internet have increased rapidly, which should unleash vast pools of previously hidden talent. In addition, democracy is proliferating, governance is improving, and local business environments are becoming more competitive, with each other and other parts of the world. Part of that is due to the cumulative transformative impact of Chinese investment there. The hundreds of millions of young, wealthier Africans of the future will all need places to live, energy to power their homes, and they will have rapidly increasing infrastructure requirements.[19] China is ensuring that it is extremely well positioned to provide all of it.

Military Footprint

Coinciding with its growing political and economic footprint in Africa, in 2018, China hosted the inaugural China-Africa Defense and Security Forum, designed to address regional security issues, the financing and upgrading of Africa's security capacities, and enhanced defense cooperation. The Forum is consistent with Beijing's positive image of itself on the global stage and serves to re-emphasize its win-win approach to bilateral and multilateral relations. The Forum is, of course, also consistent with Beijing's intention to further secure its strategic interests abroad and with being perceived as an active participant in global peacekeeping operations.

Over the past decade, China has actually become among the world's largest contributors of troops to UN peacekeeping missions, some of which dovetails nicely with countries in which it has substantial interests in natural resources, such as South Sudan (for oil) and the Democratic Republic of Congo (for cobalt and copper). Providing logistical and defense support to African countries is also in sync with Beijing's portrayal of itself as being in solidarity with developing nations. Beijing operates its first overseas military base in Djibouti, which gives it a meaningful way to project its military power in Africa and the Middle East and has made Washington wary that Djibouti's allegiances could be vulnerable to the highest bidder.[20] For Beijing, it is merely a natural progression on the path toward achieving eventual military parity with the US.

China's Bold Moves on the Middle Eastern Chess Board

China long ago mastered the art of casually sitting on the sidelines while regional and global economic and political forces clash, then swiftly swooping in to scoop up the spoils. That was best exemplified when Chinese oil companies won a variety of contracts from the Iraqi government following the end of the Iraq War. China did not fight in that war, but that did not stop Beijing from seeking to benefit from it, nor did it stop the Iraqi government from awarding the contracts to Chinese firms at the expense of firms from the US and other coalition members. China's geostrategic positioning vis-à-vis the Middle East has been deliberately and carefully choreographed to ensure that its oil and gas purchasing power is well spent.

China's relationship with the Middle East dates back to the Rashidun Caliphate, following the death of Muhammad in 632, and China has had diplomatic and trade relations with the region in one form or another since that time. Jiang Zemin became the first modern Chinese leader to visit the Arab League in 1996; the Sino-Arab Cooperation Forum was first established in 2004. Chinese leaders have regularly visited the region's capitals for many years. President Xi made his first visit to the Middle East and Pakistan in 2015, setting the stage for other tours through the region.

China clearly sees the region's shifting political sands as an opportunity to enhance its economic and political role, particularly as America's power and influence continues to decline. President Xi visited Tehran in 2016 just days after global sanctions were officially lifted (Beijing literally did not waste a single day in attempting to establish a foothold with Iran), which resulted in some $600 billion worth of contracts for Chinese firms. China had already become Iran's number one export partner. *By visiting both Iran and Saudi Arabia in the same trip, President Xi attempted to play off of both countries' proxy regional conflicts for Beijing's own benefit, keeping both sides in its camp.*

China has clearly established itself as the future growth market for Saudi petroleum. Saudi oil exports to China exceeded those to the US for the first time in 2009, and the kingdom exports in excess of three times more to five Asian countries (China, Japan, South Korea, India, and Singapore) than to Europe and North America combined. *By 2030, Chinese demand for oil is expected to reach more than 16 million barrels per day, while US oil imports are expected to continue to dwindle in the era of fracking.* In shifting its oil export focus, Saudi Arabia is joining the world's major Muslim powers (Egypt, Indonesia, Iran, Iraq, Kazakhstan, Malaysia, Mauritania, Nigeria, Pakistan, Sudan, and Turkey) that have also deepened their economic ties with China over the past decade.

Given its ongoing economic crisis as a result of the chronically depressed price of oil, the Saudis need the Chinese to continue to buy as much of its crude as possible. The House of Saud wishes to maintain its historical relationship with Washington, while giving themselves the freedom to pursue alternative economic and political relationships. China's military lacks the capacity to police the Persian Gulf and safeguard shipping, and no country other than the US has the capacity to provide a security umbrella to countries in the region. The Saudis will therefore remain dependent on the US in that regard, which also suits Beijing's interests. China has been content not to be seen as actively promoting regional stability, but rather to ride the coat tails of the US militarily.

China, Saudi Arabia, and the US are likely to continue to practice a rather awkward triangular balance of power in the Persian Gulf, reflective of an understanding of their interwoven dependencies, which limits their mutual capacity to deny each other a preeminent role in the region. Beijing and Riyadh realize that, with US military bases in all of Saudi Arabia's fellow Gulf Cooperation Council (GCC) member states, neither Beijing nor Riyadh is capable of removing Washington from its position as the most dominant military actor in the Persian Gulf. Of course, neither China nor Saudi Arabia would benefit from a change in the US role, as America continues to bear the burden and cost of policing the region.

The path China is blazing in the Middle East is rewriting the rule book on how to become important and influential- economically, politically, and diplomatically, without using military force to either project power or as a bargaining chip. No other country in the world would dare to visit Riyadh and Tehran in the same trip and hope to maintain favorable relations with both, yet China has done just that. Beijing has also become masterful at using a variety of approaches to get what it wants.[21]

That said, only so much can be achieved by waiting in the background for the right moment to pounce. That model has worked reasonably well for China up to now, but regional and global geopolitical dynamics are shifting at an accelerated pace. President Xi has an opportunity to up the ante by catapulting Beijing to the forefront of geopolitical diplomacy and crisis management. That is an objective worthy of a country which has already assumed leadership roles in so many other aspects of the global chess board.[22]

The Maturing Saudi-Chinese Alliance

No country in the Middle East is more important to China than Saudi Arabia. Energy security lies at the heart of its bilateral relationship with the kingdom, as has been the case with many of Beijing's most important strategic relationships over the past two decades. China has adopted a multi-tiered foreign policy designed to acquire and secure long-term energy supplies by diversifying its sources of oil and gas, engaging in 'energy diplomacy', and establishing energy reserves.

The kingdom demonstrated its intention to adopt an independent approach to global affairs more than 20 years ago by holding talks between the former Soviet Union and Afghan rebels in 1988. Beijing and Riyadh signed a Memorandum of Understanding and opened commercial offices in each other's countries that year as well, which led to the formal establishment of diplomatic bilateral ties. Their relationship has steadily grown since then. Just as China has been vociferous in its pursuit of a deeper relationship with the region, Saudi Arabia has been the most assiduous in the region in cultivating a stronger relationship with China. King Abdullah's first foreign visit upon assuming the throne was to China; then President Hu paid two subsequent visits to the kingdom in the span of three years.

Saudi Arabia has cast its eye on Asia with greater fervor over the past two decades, recognizing that Japan's thirst for oil, combined with China's and India's economic growth and increasing influence in the global economy, meant that Asia will eventually replace North America and Europe as the largest consumer of Saudi oil. In 2009, Saudi oil exports to the US fell to 989,000 barrels per day – the lowest level in 22 years, and down by a third from 2008. By contrast, Saudi oil exports to China doubled between 2008 and 2009, to more than a million barrels per day. And the kingdom will export as much as 1.7 million barrels per day to China in 2019,[23] surpassing Russia to once again become China's top source of crude oil. China is Saudi Arabia's second-largest importer and largest exporter in general.[24] Chinese industrial products are increasingly replacing western goods in Saudi markets, which is impacting

Saudi attitudes regarding the relative importance of China, and therefore the West, in long-term strategic relations.

The truth is that many in the GCC have grown tired of US pressure on fighting terrorism and of perceived American interference in domestic affairs. Many Gulf states find their burgeoning relationship with China refreshing, in that China tends not to meddle in the affairs of its trading partners. But Beijing's cordial relationship with Gulf States is not without its sensitivities. In particular, China's repression of Muslims in Xinjiang Province has complicated its political dialogue with states in the region. Religious activists in the Gulf are bound to draw parallels between Xinjiang, Gaza, and Kashmir. Ultimately, the strength of the region's economic relations with China will dominate its political relations with Beijing, and any disagreements over political policy will take a back seat to ensuring that regional and bilateral relations remain cordial and on the right track.

It will not be long before China will want to take its relationship with Saudi Arabia to another level. To do so, it must choose between working within the confines of the postwar diplomatic landscape crafted by the US or challenging that order in bold fashion. Doing so would enable China to begin to mold its bilateral and regional relations in its own image. But would this be something Beijing actually seeks? Breaking the status quo ante and undoing a century of history and influence would entail enormous effort in terms of persuasion, fiscal largesse, influence peddling, and relationship building. Africa was a relatively easy nut to crack by comparison, since most African nations need China's money and the enhanced infrastructure it has provided. But the Gulf does not need China's money, or its infrastructure, and is not generally so easily accommodating to such overtures.

So what would China need to do to accomplish a similar feat in the Gulf? *It would need to replace the security umbrella the US has so carefully crafted over the past 60 years*. Beijing has projected its military power in the Gulf since the 1980s, through missile proliferation and arms sales. Saudi Arabia purchased intermediate range CSS-2 missiles from China in 1988, raising suspicion at the time about the kingdom's nuclear ambitions. China met an important strategic need for the kingdom at the time that America would not agree to meet. The US continues to measure its military support for the kingdom with its strategic imperatives for Israel – something Beijing has not and will not do.

Chinese behavior in the Gulf is primarily driven by two potentially contradictory factors. One is China's newly-found status as a stakeholder state favoring regime stability. But this is somewhat inconsistent with China's tendency to elbow its way into relationships it deems important, and its history of dictating the terms on which it will address topics of critical perceived importance. China is also still finding its footing on the global stage and, at times, continues to clumsily manage bilateral relations. *The other is the Chinese quest for energy in light of its economic explosion, the opportunistic pursuit of which may lead Beijing to have a destabilizing influence in the Gulf.* Saudi Arabia has hinted that it may increase oil shipments to China in times of military crisis, which could prompt Beijing to overstep its reach in the Gulf, and elsewhere.

For the foreseeable future, Saudi Arabia will keep a foot in both the American and Chinese camps, judging that its own long-term interests are well served by maintaining the comparative advantages offered by both nations. That said, the pendulum is clearly shifting toward the Chinese camp. In time, as Riyadh's economic ties grow firmer with Beijing, their military relationship will expand. *As China's military power comes to match its political and economic power globally, it could well become Saudi Arabia's strongest military ally.* However, a potential roadblock stands in the way – the Shanghai Cooperation Organization (SCO). If the SCO were to change Iran from observer to member status, the calculus may change, as Beijing (and Moscow) could then arrive at the Gulf's doorstep through a Persian doorway.[25] That seems unlikely, however.

A Pivoting Egypt

Another country that Beijing has set its sights on in the region is Egypt. Ties between Egypt and China date back to the 1955 Bandung Conference of Asian and African countries, which laid the groundwork for the creation of the Non-Aligned Movement. At the conference, Egyptian President Nasser and Chinese Premier Zhou Enlai first met. Nasser, who expressed Egypt's support for revolutionary movements throughout Asia and Africa and a vision of a strong and independent Egypt, ensured that Egypt became the first Arab or African state to establish diplomatic relations with China.

After the US declined to sell Nasser arms, he quickly turned to Beijing, which supported Cairo's position during the Suez crisis of 1956. Nasser was, in turn, supportive after China first detonated a nuclear weapon in 1964. However, Egypt's support for Moscow in Sino-Soviet disputes, Nasser's subsequent criticism of Chinese policies in Tibet, and China's inability to influence the Middle Eastern war of 1967 to the Arabs' favor, limited the degree to which the two states perceived the other as a durable and reliable strategic partner.

Nonetheless, bilateral relations continued throughout the course of subsequent decades – even when President Sadat aligned Egypt with the US during the 1970s. China's commitment to non-interference in the affairs of foreign states was well received by the Mubarak regime. At the UN, Egypt and China have been aligned on a variety of issues, including Taiwan's status, resolution of the Arab-Israeli conflict, the invasion of Iraq in 2003, and Western efforts to impose sanctions on Sudan in response to the humanitarian crisis in Darfur. China's reputation on the Arab Street suffered as a consequence of Beijing's firm diplomatic and military support for the Assad regime in Damascus, but China perceived the cultivation of the Egyptian-Sino alliance as a means of counter-balancing this.

Between 1989 and 2008, Egypt was China's largest market for arms sales on the African continent, purchasing more weapons from China than Sudan and Zimbabwe combined. Today, China is Egypt's largest source of imports and one of its largest exporting partner nations.[26] China views deeper ties with Egypt as part of an agenda of expanding Chinese influence and commercial ties globally. Given its geostrategic significance, open economy, and relatively cheap labor force, Egypt offers China opportunities to increase exports of low-cost consumer goods throughout European, African, Arab, and sub-continental markets.

The establishment of deeper Egyptian/Sino ties will not constitute the end of US influence in Egypt. Washington has deep ties with Cairo and will retain leverage over Egypt well into the future. For China to truly supplant the US militarily in Egypt, it will need to become its top military supplier, and that is unlikely to happen any time soon. *As is the case vis-à-vis*

Saudi Arabia, China's foreign policy in Egypt is being shaped by Beijing's desire to fill the vacuum created by Washington's declining influence. Given how low Washington is regarded by the average person in Egypt and the Arab Street, Beijing should not have too much difficulty inserting itself as a wedge between them going forward.[27]

What the examples of both Egypt and Saudi Arabia show is that Beijing is not afraid to enter into the swirling waters of the Middle East or to target the most historically important and trusted partners of Washington. It can do so because it is a valued trading partner, but also because few see Beijing becoming less important and Washington becoming more important to the region in the future. The Middle East is no longer Washington's de facto sphere of influence; China and Russia are swiftly taking the reins.

Whether Africa or the Middle East, Beijing has already proven itself to be a worthy competitor (or adversary, depending on one's point of view). Washington, Europe, and the rest of the world could learn a lot from the manner in which Beijing has acted, and continues to act, with bravado, swiftness, and resolve in pursuing its political, economic, and military ambitions. The question is not whether Beijing will continue its bold push onto the global stage, but rather, what, if anything, can be done to stop it.

6 Cyber Warfare

The cyber era has changed the manner in which individuals interact with organizations and their governments. Not surprisingly, the Chinese government has been one of the most prominent government actors lurking, probing, and stealing information without the knowledge of either its citizens or the citizens of the world. As any Chinese citizen or visitor to China knows well, the Chinese government's attempted control of the Internet within China is legendary. Knowledgeable people inside China believe that the Chinese government has ambitions to govern the Internet on a global scale.

From the time he assumed power in 2012, President Xi made it clear how important a role he believed the Internet would play in China's future. To his credit, he recognized that the future is digital, and that those countries that can get ahead and stay ahead in the race for digital supremacy would hold a natural advantage in global economic competition. He set China on a path that would help ensure its future economic competitive by harnessing the power of the Internet. Based on the manner in which he has unleashed China's participation in that race, the Xi era will be remembered for putting an end to the West's naive optimism about the potential of the Internet to liberalize global polities.[1]

In 2016, China founded its first national nonprofit organization for cybersecurity, the Cybersecurity Association of China (CSAC). Led by Fang Binxing, who helped build the CCP's system for censoring the Internet, the Great Firewall, the CSAC had 275 founding member organizations, including major Internet firms, cybersecurity companies, scientific research institutions, the National University of Defense Technology, Alibaba, Baidu, and many others. The organization's declared goal is to organize and mobilize forces in all aspects of society to participate in building China's cybersecurity.

This ties back to a push that was brought to the surface in 2014, when the CCP hosted its first World Internet Conference, which had the slogan "An Interconnected World Shared and Governed by All." At the time, the US had already announced its plans to relinquish federal control over the Internet through the Internet Corporation for Assigned Names and Numbers. The Great Firewall's secretary-general was Li Yu Xiao, a research fellow at the Chinese Academy of Cyberspace and a major proponent of Chinese governance of the global Internet. Li publicly questioned who will take the baton from the US and how the Internet will be run in the future. He sees China as transitioning from merely being a participant in the Internet to playing a dominant role in it. He believes China has a right, as the country with the most netizens, to make the international rules of cyberspace governance.

The CSAP carries the same overall message. The Association is not so much about *cybersecurity* as it is about *cybergovernance* and about extending law to the Internet (and if Li has his way, specifically, the laws of China). The CCP would like to impose its approach to cybergovernance globally, with its model of strict government control over all facets of the Internet, including all companies involved in the Internet.

For the CCP, the word 'cybercrime' refers to more than just hackers; it is also about an ongoing crackdown on online rumors, pornography, gambling, and other 'crimes', which tend to be a major focus of the CCP's systems for Internet control – which include suppression of free speech, religion, and the promotion of democracy in China. The 2015, 2016, 2017, and 2018 assessment of global Internet freedom from Freedom House[2] ranked China dead last.

The Council on Foreign Relations also reported in 2015[3] that the CCP would likely do more to gain influence over the UN's International Telecommunications Union (ITU) in its quest to gain more power over the global Internet. As two of the permanent members of the UN Security Council, China and Russia have pushed major programs in the past designed to direct the ITU's role in global Internet governance in their favor. Some of the authoritarian programs proposed for global Internet governance through the ITU were outlined by the Center for Democracy and Technology while the ITU was holding its meeting on rules for the Internet in 2012, which included programs to decrypt information passing through the Internet.[4] *The CSAC appears to be a continuation of these efforts but is using the term 'cybersecurity' to give Chinese ambitions a more benign appearance.*[5]

Unrestricted Warfare

Chinese military doctrine has long articulated the use of a wide spectrum of warfare against its adversaries. Much of what is known outside of China about its approach to asymmetric warfare is contained in a book first published in 1999 and translated with the title *Unrestricted Warfare. The first rule of unrestricted warfare is that there are no rules and nothing is forbidden*. The book advocates tactics known as *shashou-jian* (Assassin's Mace), the concept of taking advantage of an adversary's seemingly superior conventional capabilities by "fighting the fight that fits one's own weapons"[6] and "making the weapons to fit the fight.[7] It proposes ignoring traditional rules of conflict and advocates such tactics as manipulating foreign media, flooding enemy countries with drugs, controlling the markets for natural resources, joining international bodies so as to be in a position to bend them to one's will, and engaging in cyberwarfare (the doctrine was quite ahead of its time, given that it was written in the early days of the advent of the Internet).

Having had nearly two decades to develop this philosophy, Chinese military strategists are, of course, prepared to use conventional weapons to fight their enemies, but, especially where it lacks a competitive advantage – such as not having a large or effective blue water navy – *one of its tactics is to use cyberwarfare to make up the difference*. Since the turn of the century, China has set in place an impressive cyberwarfare infrastructure that includes citizen hacker groups, military units. and an extensive cyberespionage network around the world. This includes an aggressive effort to obtain advanced Internet network technology.

Noteworthy in that regard was China's threat to ban government procurement of Microsoft software, hardware, and technology unless Bill Gates agreed to provide China with a copy of its proprietary operating code, which he had refused to reveal to Microsoft's largest US commercial clients. *After Gates agreed to provide it, China then copied the Cisco network router found on almost all US networks and most Internet service providers. China then sold counterfeit routers at cut-rate discounts around the world. The buyers apparently included the Pentagon and a host of other US federal agencies.* A subsequent report by the FBI concluded that the routers could be used by foreign intelligence agencies to take down networks and weaken cryptographic systems.

Armed with intimate knowledge of the flaws in Microsoft's and Cisco's software and hardware, China's hackers had the ability to stop most of the world's networks from operating. Chinese networks would also have been vulnerable but, *as part of its deal with Microsoft, the Chinese modified the version of Microsoft software sold in China to include a secure component using their own encryption. They also developed their own operating system (Kylin) and secure microprocessors for use on servers and Huawei routers.*

By 2003, the Chinese government had created cyberwarfare units with defensive and offensive capabilities with weapons that had never been seen before, including the ability to plant information mines, conduct information reconnaissance, change network data, release information bombs, dump information garbage, disseminate propaganda, apply information deception, release clone information, and establish network spy stations. By 2007, China was penetrating US and European networks, successfully copying and exporting huge volumes of data.[8] *China has since developed its cyberwarfare capabilities into a finely tuned and largely unrivaled machine.*

The CCP, PLA, and GSD

China is extremely adept at waging economic warfare. One way to estimate the damage done in this war is by the cost of intellectual property theft. The Commission on the Theft of Intellectual Property has estimated that such theft costs the US $300 billion and 1.2 million jobs per year. Other organizations believe the cost is closer to $500 billion worth of raw innovation that is stolen from US companies annually, which would otherwise generate revenue, profits, and jobs. *The Chinese government's theft of intellectual property for economic gain is just one piece of a larger strategy to fight a war while avoiding troop-to-troop combat.*

China's spy and cyberoperations are orchestrated under the PLA General Staff Department (GSD), the Chinese military's highest-level department dedicated to warfighting. Under the GSD, three departments work on its spy campaigns for unconventional warfare. The Second Department focuses on human spies and intelligence (HUMINT), the Third Department focuses on cyberespionage and signals intelligence (SIGINT), and the Fourth Department focuses on electronic warfare, intercepting satellite data, and electronics intelligence (ELINT). The GSD also oversees China's military regions, the army, navy, and air force, and the Second Artillery (the home for China's nuclear weapons).

The Chinese government's applications of Hybrid Warfare (a military strategy that employs political warfare and blends conventional warfare, irregular warfare and cyber-warfare with other influencing methods, such as fake news, diplomacy, lawfare, and foreign electoral intervention[9]) are broad, enabling it to deploy a large array of tactics and methods to achieve its objectives. This includes capabilities in areas as all-encompassing as trade, finance, ecology, psychology, smuggling, media, drugs, Internet networks, technology, economic aid, culture, and international law.

Estimates on the number of soldiers in each GSD varies; most only focus on cyberspies. The Project 2049 Institute estimated, in 2011, that there were 130,000 personnel in the Third Department, while the Wall Street Journal estimated, in July of that year, that the Department had 100,000 hackers, linguists, and analysts in 12 operational bureaus. Others have estimated that there are 20 operational bureaus with between 250,000 and 300,000 soldiers dedicated to cyberespionage (the *New York Times* has also reported 20 bureaus). Under the Second Department, between 30,000 and 50,000 spies are believed to be working on insider operations targeting US and other foreign companies. No estimate is publicly available on the number of operatives in the Fourth Department.

According to a report from the US Congressional Research Service, the PLA is not a national army belonging to the state, but serves as the Party's armed wing. The soldiers deployed in the GSD's spy departments are used to further the financial and political ambitions of the CCP. *The PLA is, in essence, a state within a state, completely devoted to the survival of the CCP, which provides the PLA with financial and material resources.* State-run cyberattacks and China's use of more conventional spies are part of a larger, coordinated effort under the GSD that answers to China's top leaders in the Central Committee of the CCP.

The orders governing China's spy departments are derived from the CCP's Five-Year Plans, which often include targeted industries and economic goals of the Party. One of the clearest links between the Five-Year Plans and the campaigns of economic theft by the Chinese military is Project 863, set in motion by former leader Deng Xiaoping in 1986, which mandated theft of intellectual property from foreign businesses. The Project was emblematic of the CCP's drive to "catch up fast and surpass"[10] the West, according to a 2011 report from the US Office of the National Counterintelligence Executive. It provided funding and guidance for efforts to clandestinely acquire US technology and sensitive economic information.

Originally, an Attempt to Maintain Control

China's first publicly known cyberattacks began in 1999. The media was under the CCP's control, the Internet was already tightly censored, and the Party's history of campaigns against its own people, and its use of pervasive surveillance, left a residual environment of fear that ensured a level of self-censorship among the masses. However, the Party wanted to plug a gaping hole – the friends or family of Chinese citizens who lived abroad that it could not control. The Chinese government's first state-run cyberattacks coincided, in July 1999, with an attempt to silence Falun Gong practitioners and other Chinese living overseas.

The first known Chinese state-run cyberattacks against the West targeted networks in four countries – two in the US, two in Canada, one in the UK, and one in Australia. All of the targets were websites that explained what Falun Gong is and how it began to be persecuted in China. According to a January 2002 RAND Corporation report, the attacks took place within a close time frame that aligned with the persecution of the group in China and several of the cyberattacks were traced to networks under the Chinese MSS.

112

As the government continued using cyberattacks to try to quell the free flow of information abroad, it recognized that the new tool could have other applications. Security researchers began seeing cyberattacks originating from China that served multiple uses. They were used to spy on dissidents, and the same methods were used to steal from Western companies and gain intelligence from foreign governments. Google revealed, in 2010, that China was targeting its networks, but documents later leaked by WikiLeaks revealed that the attacks were part of a larger campaign that had been occurring since 2002. The Chinese regime was also targeting government networks of the US and its allies, as well as networks belonging to the Tibetan Dalai Lama and e-mail accounts of Chinese artist Ai Weiwei. An attack from 2006 to 2007 breached computers of two US congressmen and stole documents about dissidents critical of the Chinese regime.

Mastering the Game

With US intelligence agencies focused on terrorism in the first decade of the twenty-first century, Chinese spies and their hackers were not a primary focus. Chinese hackers launched successful attacks in Taiwan and, in 2005, were able to carry out the Titan Rain cyberattacks that targeted everything from military contractors to the Pentagon and the US National Aeronautics and Space Administration (NASA). In 2007, *Chinese hackers were able to carry out the Byzantine Hades cyberattacks with little more than a peep of condemnation from US officials. The attacks, which were traced to the Chinese military, ended up getting broad media attention years later, in part because part of the theft of designs of the F-35 fighter jet (which enabled China to produce its own stealth fighter, the Chengdu J-20).*[11]

During the Obama administration, the US devoted more resources to the problem and began to respond more robustly. In 2014, the US Justice Department indicted five Chinese military hackers from Unit 61398 for their alleged role in economic theft, but Chinese cyberespionage has grown to become a goliath. *The whole system runs through a corrupt nexus among government officials, military officers, business executives, and academics throughout China. It makes money back by developing products based on the stolen information.*

The system even extends to 'transfer centers' that process stolen information and transforms them into usable designs.

Many of the Chinese products based on stolen American research and development are resold back in the US at a fraction of the price of the original American product. Chinese law states that any company greater than 50 people in size must have a government liaison assigned to it, blurring the lines separating government from private industries, military from government, and the private sector from the military. The systems in place to accommodate economic theft take place across all three of these sectors.

During the Cold War, if a Soviet spy had stolen designs for a US spy camera, for example, the designs would have been transferred to a research facility where Soviet engineers would have attempted to directly reproduce the technology. China's approach was different, given its acknowledgement about its technological gap with other countries at the time. While the Soviets would start their counterfeit process from the top, the Chinese started theirs from the bottom.

If a Chinese spy were to get her hands on the same hypothetical spy camera, she would similarly transfer it to a research facility but, rather than try to duplicate the camera, the researchers would find earlier generations of the technology and build those first. They would send spies to gather publicly available information for the earliest models of the targeted technology, buy the next generations in stores, and send students to study and work abroad in the targeted industry. The process would give them a foundation of knowledge and, when they were ready to reverse engineer the modern generation of the gadget, they could easily see which parts had been upgraded and which changes had been made from the technology's previous generations. The Chinese approach was significantly faster and more cost effective than the Soviet approach.

Unbridled Access to Technology

The Chinese government's current system for processing and reverse engineering stolen designs has grown significantly larger than it was during the Cold War and has developed from a strictly military operation into a system permeating the entire Chinese government. *It is an elaborate, comprehensive system for identifying foreign technologies, acquiring them by every means imaginable, and converting them into weapons and competitive goods.* The departments in charge of reverse engineering are officially called China's National Technology Transfer Centers (or National Demonstration Organizations) and became established by policy in 2007. Among their names are the State Administration of Foreign Experts Affairs (under the State Council), the Science and Technology Office (under the Overseas Chinese Affairs Office), and the National Technology Transfer Center (under the East China University of Science and Technology).

These organizations do not attempt to hide their purpose; their charters explicitly name 'domestic and foreign technology' as targets for 'commercialization'. The transfer centers play several roles, which include processing stolen technology, developing cooperative research projects between Chinese and foreign scientists, and running programs designed to 'encourage' Chinese nationals who have studied abroad to become part of the organizations. *China's meteoric economic rise can, in part, be attributed to this system of minimal investment in basic science through a technology transfer apparatus that worked to suck in foreign proprietary achievements while most of the countries which they were stealing from had no idea what they were doing.*

China could not have experienced the dramatic economic transformation it has experienced in the twenty-first century, nor have sustained its progress, without inexpensive and unrestricted access to other countries' technology. A 2010 report from the US Defense Threat Reduction Agency noted that modernization in the Chinese military depends heavily on investments in China's science and technology infrastructure, reforms of its defense industry, and procurement of advanced weapons from abroad. It added that the Chinese regime's theft of technology is unique in that, under the system, autonomy is given to research institutes, corporations, and other entities to devise collection schemes according to their needs.

State Theft as a Business

The PLA is required to cover a portion of its own costs. Its decades-long focus on building external sources of cash has made its military leaders some of the most powerful people in China. With only 70% of its operating expenses covered by the state budget, the PLA must make up the difference and generate supplemental funds for its modernization. Just as is the case regarding the nexus between government and private business, the lines between the military and the state and the military and the private sector are thin. *The PLA maintains thousands of front companies in the US, whose sole reason for existing is to steal and exploit US technology.* According to the US Defense Threat Reduction Agency, the Chinese regime operates more than 3,200 military front companies in the US dedicated to theft.

Project 863 (also called the 863 Program) was started by former CCP leader Deng Xiaoping in 1986. According to a report from the US Office of the National Counterintelligence Executive, it provides funding and guidance for efforts to clandestinely acquire US technology and sensitive economic information. Project 863 originally targeted seven industries: biotechnology, space, IT, automation, laser technology, new materials, and energy. It was updated to include telecommunications and marine technology.

The Chinese government also runs the Torch Program to build high-tech commercial industries, the 973 Program for research, the 211 program for 'reforming' universities, and countless programs designed to attract Western-trained scholars back to China. Each of these programs relies on foreign collaboration and technologies to cover key gaps, encouraging Western-trained experts to help China's technological development by returning to China or 'serving in place' by providing needed information gained while working for their Western employers. Project 863 maintains a library of tens of millions of open source articles in scores of databases that contain more than four terabytes of information gleaned from American, Japanese, Russian, and British publications, military reports, and standard specifications.

One of the most powerful organizations behind economic theft is the 61 Research Institute, under the Third Department of the GSD. The man in charge of it, Major General Wang Jianxin, has some powerful connections at the most senior level of the Chinese government. The names of many known military hacker units in China begin with the number '61', and there are at least 11 units under the GSD's Third Department with that designation, including Unit 61398, under which five military hackers who were indicted by the DOJ in 2014 operated.[12]

Attacks Against Japan

Since 2013, China is believed to have targeted Japan in a large-scale hacking operation similar to campaigns against the US. Among the hundreds of victims targeted were the Japanese pension system and government organizations, as well as companies in the research, manufacturing, and finance arenas. Dubbed 'Blue Termite', the CCP was thought to be responsible, based on similarities to its attacks against the US. The Japanese pension service was consistent with previous targets of CCP hackers – while their primary target used to be intellectual property and data used for monetary gain, their preferred target shifted to personal information useful for spies.

Modeled after its domestic spy program (the 'Social Credit System'), which rates Chinese citizens based on perceived good or bad behavior and then rewards of punishes them based on access to goods and services within China, the CCP was believed to be creating a database on US citizens. The attacks on Japan suggested that the CCP was expanding its database to include Japanese citizens. The hackers gathered geopolitically and technologically significant information on Japan during the attack. The hackers targeted Japanese industries in construction, robotics, manufacturing, communication, media, information services, satellites, electricity, and energy.

The methodology used corresponded with changes made in Chinese state-run cyberattacks at the time. The hackers were using spear phishing attacks (by infecting e-mails tailored for each victim) to gain access to computers in targeted networks. A few days prior to the start of the attack, a group of hacker activists leaked information on an Italian company which provides hacking services for governments. The leak included was a zero-day vulnerability – a type of cyberattack that cannot be stopped since it has not yet been identified by security companies – that the group had used in its own attacks. This attack involved infecting websites frequented by the intended victims (known as a 'watering hole attack') and included code to filter out unwanted targets.

Shortly after the zero-day vulnerability used was revealed, CCP hackers obtained it and began using it in their attacks. The malware they used was a specific remote access trojan (RAT), which gave them full control over the computers, previously used by the Chinese group in other targeted attacks against governments. The hackers behind the Blue Termite attack then installed a RAT on the computers of their victims, which allowed them to monitor all activity on the computers and control the computers at will. Many of the documents and tools used by the hackers were written in Chinese. The hackers used a graphical user interface for their command and control server and had technical documents related to the malware used in the attacks – both of which were in Chinese.[13]

Containment?

Numerous Chinese-attributed attacks have occurred in the US – ranging from the OPM breach in 2014 (which succeeded in gaining the personal and government-oriented information of every US government employee at the time and their relatives), to the Anthem breach (in which an estimated 80 million medical records were stolen, to the Equifax breach (which targeted 145 million working age adults), to the Marriott breach (which provided access to the travel habits (and in some cases, passport information) of tens of millions of Americans). This has given the Chinese government the most sensitive information of individuals at every level of US society. *The Chinese government now has the ability to build a profile on specific individuals based on a range of information it has obtained through hacking.*

According to the NSA, nearly 700 Chinese cyberattacks designed to steal corporate or military secrets in the US had already occurred between 2009 and 2014.[14] As an example of this, in 2011, the US Chamber of Commerce was attacked through a newly installed Internet-enabled thermostat in Washington, DC. The installation created a back door to its corporate network. Chamber officials discovered that the thermostat had been secretly communicating with an Internet address in China. The hackers made a mistake when instructing a Chamber printer used by executives and, instead of sending themselves documents, the printer ended up spontaneously printing pages with Chinese characters –

another indication of the origin of the hacking. They were ultimately successful in obtaining highly sensitive information related to financial and budgetary matters, as well as to trade policy issues in Asia.[15] The scope and scale of Chinese hacking in the US is mammoth.

When, in 2015, the US signed a cyber agreement with China, it sent a list of Chinese hackers identified as having stolen commercial secrets from US businesses to President Xi, requesting their arrests. Chinese authorities made some arrests but, *by passing evidence against Chinese hackers to Chinese authorities, the US unintentionally helped the Chinese government close gaps in its system of economic theft.* The Chinese authorities presumably took this information as a road map for how US investigators detect attacks and used the information to adjust their methods and make cyberattacks progressively more difficult to identify.

The agreement stated that neither country would "conduct or knowingly support cyber-enabled theft of intellectual property, including trade secrets or other confidential business information, for commercial advantage."[16] The cyber agreement also established a system for high-level dialogue between the US and the CCP, which, on the US side, included the Secretary of the Department of Homeland Security and the attorney general. However, *it only prohibited "cyber-enabled theft of intellectual property," which did nothing to address intellectual theft through other means, rendering it relatively toothless. And it failed to forbid economic theft more generally – only one method of economic theft – while leaving unmentioned that the CCP itself is behind so many of the attacks against the US.*[17]

Acknowledging America's own capabilities in this arena, President Obama said at the time that, "although the Chinese and Russians are close, we are the best at this, and if we wanted to go on the offense, a lot of countries would have some significant problems, but we don't want to see the Internet weaponized in that way. We are preparing a number of measures that will indicate to the Chinese that this is not just a matter of us being mildly upset, but is something that will put significant strains on our bilateral relations if not resolved. We are prepared to take countervailing actions in order to get their attention, but my hope is that something can get resolved short of that."[18] It was a little late for that by 2015.

Buyer Beware

In terms of government actions, it is also worth pointing out that, in 2016, the Chinese government passed new laws enforcing its national security abroad by including Chinese law in the terms of service (ToS) of Chinese name brand products. For example, *by purchasing a Xiaomi smartphone, the buyers agree to assume full legal liability not to engage in activities China has banned. The terms ban purchasers from opposing the principles of the Constitution of the People's Republic of China, from leaking state secrets, or subverting the government. Some of the terms of the agreements have actually been there for several years but broadened in scope in 2016.*

By being a citizen of Tibet, Taiwan, or Hong Kong, a purchaser is technically violating Xiaomi's user agreement, which forbids undermining national unity. An author writing about Tibetan Buddhism may violate its rules on "cults". The agreement also forbids "spreading rumors"[19] by discussing news. And by using Xiaomi's products, buyers give Xiaomi the right to access their accounts. Other Chinese tech firms, such as Huawei, Foream, Condenatcenter, Adbox, and Decathlon, have similar user agreements. Under Decathlon's agreement, users are not allowed to do anything that could damage the reputation of government organizations.

In 2015, German writer Christoph Rehage uploaded a YouTube video that referred to Mao Zedong as "China's Hitler".[20] A Communist Youth League website then called for him to be punished for violating Chinese law, even though he lives in Hamburg. It argued that Rehage, who speaks Chinese, made the video to circulate in China, which the League said undermined the sovereignty of its Internet. In 2015, the National People's Congress Standing Committee passed the National Security Law, which emphasized that "China must defend its national security interests everywhere" and would "affect almost every domain of public life in China."[21] The law's mandate covers politics, the military, finance, religion, cyberspace, ideology, and religion.

The Counterterrorism Law was also passed in 2015, which requires foreign tech firms to cooperate with Chinese investigations and its brand of 'counterterrorism', the definition of which includes "any thought, speech, or activity that, by means of violence, sabotage, or threat, aims to generate social panic, influence national policymaking, create ethnic hatred, subvert state power, or split the state". Any company that wants to do business in China must uphold these rules.[22] This raises the larger issue of ToS agreements, how few consumers actually read them, how few thereby necessarily legally abide by them, and whether governments are willing and able under international law to pursue those who do not (wittingly or unwittingly).

The Chinese government will completely block access to much of the Internet inside the country as part of its effort to suppress dissent and maintain the CCP's control on power. In 2017, the government ordered China's three telecommunications companies – China Mobile, China Telecom, and China Unicom (all state-owned) – to block access to Virtual Private Networks (VPNs) by 2018. Millions of Chinese citizens have for years circumvented China's censorship system, known as the Great Firewall, by using a VPN, which allows unfettered access to any website. Beijing's directive follows a year-long effort to promote its version of 'Internet sovereignty'.[23] In doing so, the Chinese government is doubling down on its effort to maintain control of the Internet within its borders, while also endeavoring to increase the amount of control it has over the Internet outside of its borders.

Based on China's approach to cyber and military strategy, it seems unlikely that trade, diplomacy, and common interests between the US and China will necessarily avert a real conflict. Part of the reason is China's Assassin's Mace program, which, as previously noted, is designed to fight a technologically superior adversary. The program includes cyberwarfare, space warfare, and other systems that could disable the fighting ability of the US military. Many experts refer to the Chinese breach of the US OPM as America's 'Cyber Pearl Harbor', but the breach is nothing compared to what a real military cyberattack would look like. Such an attack would very quickly move a war beyond borders and into the homelands of rival nations in ways never seen before.[24]

In 2015, China published its first official military guidelines under Xi Jinping, officially shifting its focus toward "winning informationized local wars." Under the new strategy, the space and cyber domains are thought of as the "commanding heights of strategic competition."[25] IT will play a larger role in all aspects of military operations for all elements of the PLA's combat-related activities. The new guidelines focus on the central objective of 'winning' informationized local wars, indicating that high technology will become the basic form of warfare in the twenty-first century.[26] In some ways, it already has.

The Chinese economy has become so reliant on the theft of intellectual property to power its growth that it cannot simply switch it off, even if it wanted to. It is simply too ingrained in the practice of Chinese government and business. Another contributing factor to the problem is that, despite all the noise around Chinese economic theft, *there is an air of quiet tolerance among Western businesses – a kind of blind acquiescence and grudging acceptance that it is the price that must be paid in order to do business with the most populous country and second largest economy in the world.* Compounding this, of course, is that *neither the US nor any other country has a meaningful strategy or policy framework for addressing Chinese cyberattacks because, based on the current state of affairs, the attacks are simply too numerous and ubiquitous.*

As an example of some of the challenges US and other businesses face when operating in China, the US firm American Superconductor had its software stolen there, prompting the company to fire 600 of its nearly 900 employees there and costing the company more than a billion dollars. Sinovel, the company partly owned by the Chinese government that allegedly stole it, now exports wind turbines that run on American Superconductor's technology. The Chinese were even able to sell one of the turbines to the state of Massachusetts, which paid for it with federal stimulus funds. The case is a clear example of what a cyber agreement with China needs but lacks – sanctions that actually discourage *theft.*

When American Superconductor began doing business with China, the company made sure its data systems were locked tight. It used strong encryption and had a solid system for cybersecurity. When, in 2011, it tested its software on Sinovel's turbines, although the system had been programmed to shut down after the test, the blades kept spinning because its Chinese corporate partner had successfully broken

American Superconductor's encryption. It turned out that the breach took place through one of its employees – an Austrian named Dejan Karabasevic would later spend a year in jail for his crime. The Chinese offered him women, an apartment, and money. All it took for the company to lose its key product to China was for Karabasevic to say 'yes'.

The CCP has reduced its cyberattacks against the US since the agreement was signed, although many of its hacker units remain active. In 2016, cybersecurity company FireEye reported that, since mid-2014, it had seen a notable decline in China-based groups' overall intrusion activity against entities in the US and 25 other countries. The CCP's revised program on state-sponsored cyberattacks has two points of focus: to expand the reach of Chinese factories and to steal intellectual property from competitors directly.

It builds on existing programs for economic theft the CCP already had in place, which run parallel to its cybertheft operations. All of these programs leverage foreign collaboration and technologies to cover key gaps and use methods that include encouraging skilled experts to return to China or to have them serve in place, providing information gained from Western employers. This is being combined with selectively pushing foreign companies out of China if their own domestic products are at a level where they can compete with each other in global markets. The companies they allow to remain in China are those they can still learn from.[27]

President Obama signed an executive order giving him the ability to sanction companies that commit economic theft and the threat of sanctions was believed to be one of the incentives used to arrive at the cyber agreement with China, but *sanctions were not mentioned directly in the agreement. In essence, the cyber agreement gave China a platform for dialogue with the US on the subject while continuing to pretend it is not part of the problem nor having it pay a price for cybertheft.*

The problem of economic theft seems complicated on the surface but, when you boil it down, it is really simple: *governments will use any means they have to steal intellectual property and grab market share. To address the problem, every nation needs to broaden its view of economic theft beyond cybersecurity, implement laws with enforcement and sanctions teeth, and be willing to hold other nations accountable for their actions.* [28] Clearly, that is easier said than done.

May I Please Give You My Encryption Keys?

The CCP's National Security Law from 2015 addresses nearly every facet of Chinese society. Part of it is aimed at foreign companies and proclaims that all information systems in China must be secure and controllable.[29] Under it, *every company operating in China is required to give Chinese authorities their source code, encryption keys, and back door access to their computer networks in China.* In other words, businesses must now simply hand Chinese agents the lifeblood of their companies and products, while also giving the CCP a free pass to spy on their networks.

The Chinese government has arranged that, in order to do business in China, the information that Chinese agents once had to steal through cyberattacks is now automatically provided for the 'privilege' of doing business there. Incredibly, even the largest, best known, and most influential foreign companies that operate in China are doing just that.

IBM became the first major US tech company to agree to the new rules. At one of IBM's Chinese facilities, agents with the Chinese Ministry of Industry and IT were invited into a secure room where IBM allowed them to look at some of their source code. It was not clear which IBM products they opened up for review nor how long the Chinese agents were allowed to review it. While the agents were not allowed to take the code out of the room, it is unclear what, if any, security precautions were taken by IBM to ensure the agents were not recording the process with hidden cameras.

IBM began delivering its technical knowledge to Chinese companies that had clearly stated their objective of replacing IBM's markets in China. The company passed information about how to build its high-end servers and the software that runs the servers to Beijing-based Teamsun, which proudly declared its strategy to 'absorb and then innovate', enabling it to eliminate the capability gap between Chinese and American companies and create products that could replace those sold by companies in the US.[30]

That was not the first time IBM had done something similar. In 2014, IBM sold its x86 server division to Chinese computer company Lenovo. The $2.1 billion sale included the x86 BladeCenter HT servers used in some critical US Navy systems, including its Aegis Combat System, which controlled the Navy's ballistic missile and air defense systems. When a business with products used in critical government and military networks reveals its code to another government, it becomes a national security issue.

The US Navy was subsequently forced to identify and purchase new servers, concerned that Chinese government agents could remotely access the systems by compromising routine maintenance. A vulnerability on Lenovo computers was subsequently discovered, which took advantage of the Lenovo System Update, leaving the door open for hackers. The servers were used by Navy assets, including its guided missile cruiser and destroyer fleets, and ballistic missile and anti-air defenses.[31]

In 2015, Hewlett-Packard (HP) sold more than half of its networking and server operations to China, whose restrictions on foreign technology vendors pushed its banks, military, and major companies to stop buying foreign technology. HP gave up control of its then $4.5 billion business to remain in the Chinese market, selling 51% of its networking and server operations in the country to an arm of Beijing's Tsinghua University.[32] Presumably, the reason HP was being allowed to remain was because the Chinese government had not yet acquired what it perceived to be all of HP's intellectual and material capital. Once that has been accomplished, HP will presumably be asked or told to leave, either directly or via passage of a new law, for which it will be found to be non-compliant.

China's first Cybersecurity Law, enacted in 2017, increases costs for multinationals while leaving them vulnerable to industrial espionage and ultimately giving some Chinese companies an unfair advantage. Aspects of the measure have been widely welcomed as a milestone in much needed data privacy, but it could also have the effect of helping Beijing steal trade secrets or intellectual property from foreign companies. The law is both extremely vague and exceptionally wide in scope, potentially putting companies at risk of regulatory enforcement that is not related to cybersecurity.

The law is part of a drive by Beijing to shield Chinese data from the eyes of foreign governments. Under it, companies must introduce data protection measures – a novelty for many Chinese businesses – and data relating to the country's citizens or national security must be held on *Chinese* servers. Companies must submit to a review by regulators before transferring large amounts of personal data abroad.

'Critical' companies – whose designation encompasses sensitive entities such as power companies or banks, but also any company holding data that, if breached, could "harm people's livelihoods" – must store all data collected in China within the country. These companies, and any services bought by them, must go through a "national security review" to ensure they and their data systems are "secure and controllable". A supplementary law on encryption allows the government to demand 'decryption support' in the interests of national security, meaning the government can force companies to decode encrypted data.

Among its key provisions are:

• Government departments and companies gathering private information must protect digital data (for example, through encryption);

• Collecting "citizens' personal information" without permission is a criminal offense.

• All companies must undertake a security assessment before moving data out of China if it contains the personal information of more than half a million users or data is "likely to affect national security or social public interests";

• "Critical infrastructure" companies must store "personal information and other important data" collected in China inside the country; and

• "Important network products and services" must undergo a "national security review" before being sold in China.

The measure allows Beijing to request computer program source code (usually known only by the software developer) and national security reviews may also permit

China to delve even further into companies' intellectual property. On this basis, fast-food delivery companies could be considered critical infrastructure, Shanghai regulators ruled during a pilot run for the law, because they hold information about millions of users. Multinational corporations will be hardest hit, as the data localization measures prevent them from pooling client data in cloud storage databases across the world, creating data fragmentation and adding significantly to data storage costs.[33]

China's Alternative Glimpse into the Future

As a contrast to Europe's General Data Protection Regulation, which seeks to protect individual rights and reign in the actions of large corporates, China's Cybersecurity Law gives an alternative vision about how nations may choose to apply the law toward cyberspace in the future. The law requires network operators to cooperate with Chinese crime or security investigators and allow full access to data and unspecified 'technical support' to the authorities upon request.

The law also imposes mandatory testing and certification of computer equipment for critical sector network operators. These tests and certifications require network operators to formulate internal security management systems and implement network security protections, adopt measures to prevent viruses or unspecified forms of cyberattacks, monitor and record the safety of a network, and undertake data classification, back-ups of important data, and encryption.

On one hand, these security measures form part of what might otherwise be considered best practice recommendations for firms that gather and store important company and client data. On the other hand, the law requires network operators in critical sectors to store within China all data that is gathered or produced by the network operator in the country. It includes a ban on the export of any economic, technological, or scientific data that could pose a threat to national security or the public interest (with a broad interpretation of what that might be).

International law firms have warned that companies could be asked to provide source code, encryption, or other crucial information for review by the government, increasing the risk of this information being lost, passed on to local competitors, or kept and used by the government itself. Article

9 of the Law states that "network operators must obey social norms and commercial ethics, be honest and credible, perform obligations to protect network security, accept supervision from the government and public, and bear social responsibility."[34]

The vagueness of this provision, as well as undefined concepts of national security and public interest contained within the law, increases the government's grounds to make wide assertions about the need for investigation, and reduces a foreign company's ability to contest a government demand for data access. Spot checks can be initiated at the request of the government or a trade association, meaning domestic competitors can request spot checks on foreign firms.

To comply with the data localization requirements, foreign firms will have to either invest in new data servers in China – which would be subject to government spot checks – or incur new costs to hire a local server provider (such as Huawei, Tencent, or Alibaba, which have spent billions of dollars in recent years establishing domestic data centers). The substantial investment by these Chinese technology firms is one of the reasons critics of the new law believe it is partly designed to bolster the domestic Chinese data management and telecommunications industry against global competitors. An alternative explanation is that the requirement is a legal move by Beijing to bring data under Chinese jurisdiction to make it easier to prosecute entities seen as violating China's Internet laws.[35]

Prior to implementation of the law, a foreign firm would monitor its energy turbines in China from its headquarters, using its real-time global data to optimize operations, and a provider of global online education would send data on Chinese users overseas to allow them to access its courses abroad. Now such firms must reconfigure their IT systems to keep such data inside China. Critics worry that the new law could be a Trojan horse designed to promote China's aggressive policy of indigenous innovation. As previously noted, doing so prompted Microsoft to enter into a local joint venture and reveal its source code to officials in order to sell a local version of its Windows operating system. Other foreign technology firms worry that they will be forced to divulge intellectual property to government inspectors, with no knowledge of or control over what may happen to the data once it is released.[36]

In 2017, Apple announced it was setting up its first data center in Guizhou, China (in partnership with Guizhou-Cloud Big Data Industry Co. Ltd.) in order to comply with the new Cybersecurity Law. Apple put a public relations face on the move, stating that it would allow the company to improve the speed and reliability of its products and services, while also complying with China's new regulations, which require cloud services be operated by Chinese companies. Apple was the first foreign firm to announce amendments to its data storage for China following the implementation of the new law. It insisted that no 'back doors' would be created into any of its systems.[37] That month, Apple also silently removed VPN apps from its app store in China, which had given Chinese citizens the ability to access the unfiltered Internet.

While at first glance the law appears to give the Chinese government and Chinese companies a built-in advantage – given that interest in investing in China is strong and is likely to remain so well into the future because of the size of the domestic marketplace – China's companies and its consumers may lose out in the end. While many of the companies that operate in China will accede to 'moving legal goal posts' by implementing the Cybersecurity Law and enforcing increasingly burdensome regulatory requirements, some foreign firms will no doubt be pushed to the brink, decide they have had enough, and leave the country. If that occurs, it will hurt Chinese consumers by creating a less vibrant and less competitive marketplace.

China's Cybersecurity Law is masquerading as an attempt to enhance cybersecurity but it is so much more. *The danger is that other countries may adopt a similar approach, in a brazen attempt to gain commercial advantage for indigenous firms, while clearly crossing a legal and regulatory boundary that far surpasses what is required to be considered consistent with best practices.* That has already occurred in countries across the world where China has shared its surveillance methodology, especially in Africa.

So, there are two sides of the cybersecurity legal pendulum – the Chinese version and the EU version. Given the evolutionary state of the cyber landscape, the reactive nature of the legal regime, and that best practices constitute a moving target, *it is anyone's guess in which direction the cyber legal sphere will move in the longer term. The Chinese model may well prevail, and the majority of companies may eventually succumb to the new normal.*

Digital Social Control

All signs are that China has begun the most ambitious experiment in digital social control in the world. The CCP appears to be on its way to creating its own futuristic dystopia – what it calls a 'social-credit system' (as noted earlier) – which aims to rate and manage the social and political behavior of its citizens. It is not yet clear how extensive the system will be, whether it will even work, nor if it can withstand the criticism it will inevitably receive when it becomes fully operational, but an outline is complete and some of the building blocks are in place.

A pilot scheme in Suining county (in Jiangsu province, north of Shanghai) gives clues about what such a system might mean in practice. In 2010, the local government began awarding people points for good behavior (such as winning a national honor of some kind) and deducted points for everything from minor traffic offenses to illegally petitioning authorities for assistance. Those who scored highest were eligible for rewards such as fast-track promotion at work or being able to jump the queue for public housing. Amid a public backlash, the project turned out to be a failure.

Despite that, the CCP and government seemed undaunted, issuing plans for a nationwide social credit system, with about 30 local governments collecting data that would support it, as of 2016. The plan appears hugely ambitious, aiming to explicitly influence the behavior of the whole of Chinese society. The project is a response to one of the Party's biggest problems: the collapse of confidence in public institutions and the need to keep track of the changing views and interests of China's population (without letting them vote, of course).

Almost every Chinese citizen has a *hukou* (household registration) document that determines where he or she can get public services. Wholesale surveillance (increasingly digital) is a central pillar of CCP rule. A system of block-by-block surveillance called 'grid management' is being set up in several parts of the country. Newer forms of monitoring involve the ubiquitous use of closed-circuit television (CCTV) cameras

(China has overtaken the US as the country with the largest number of CCTV devices).

As Internet use has grown, so have China's comprehensive controls in cyberspace – from the Great Firewall (the system that blocks access to tens of thousands of websites) to the Golden Shield (an extensive online surveillance system) and the Great Cannon (a tool to attack hostile websites). The scale of the data collection effort suggests that the long-term aim is to keep track of the transactions made, websites visited, and messages sent by all of China's 700 million Internet users. Given that the NSA can already collect 42 billion Internet records per month and 5 billion mobile phone location records each day, China's data collection ambitions should not prove too challenging.

To undertake such surveillance work, the government must match the owners of devices with the digital footprints they leave behind, so laws passed in 2012 and 2016 require Internet firms to retain their customers' names and other personal information (it is unclear how censors plan to tackle VPNs). The list at the heart of the social credit system is called the 'judgment defaulter's list', composed of those who have defied a court order. People on the list can be prevented from buying tickets to travel; selling, buying, or building a house; enrolling their children in elite fee-paying schools; joining or being promoted in the Party and army; or from receiving honors and titles. If the defaulter is a company, it may not issue shares or bonds, accept foreign investment, or work on government projects.

By 2016, defaulters had already been stopped from buying airline tickets about 5 million times. Other types of 'untrustworthy behavior' meriting attention include conduct that seriously undermines normal social order, such as cyberspace transmissions and endangering national defense interests. Such broad categories imply that the system could be used to punish dissent, expressions of opinion, and perceived threats to security. Regulations on video games say that individuals or firms that violate the rules could be blacklisted and inscribed in the social credit database. The social credit project could well become a 360-degree digital surveillance panopticon.

Although Western governments, companies, data-brokers, and marketing companies all hold vast quantities of personal information without causing serious harm to civil liberties, China treats personal information differently. In conventional democracies, laws limit what companies may do with it and the extent to which governments can get their hands on it. China's National Security Law and Cybersecurity Law give the government unrestricted access to almost all personal data. Civil liberty advocates who might protest are increasingly thrown in jail, and companies that hold data (such as Alibaba, Baidu, and Tencent) routinely obey government demands to access data.

While big data systems in democracies are not designed for social control, China's is, and since its leaders consider the interest of the CCP and society to be one in the same, instruments of social control can be used for political purposes. In 2016, the Party asked China Electronics Technology Group (one of the country's largest defense contractors) to develop software to predict terrorist risks on the basis of people's job records, financial background, consumption habits, hobbies, and data collected from surveillance cameras. Sifting through data ostensibly to seek terrorists can easily morph into hunting down dissidents. Western intelligence agencies have tried to use data mining schemes to identify individual terrorists but have generally failed because of an excess of false positives.

Can such a vast social credit system actually work? The Chinese face two big technical hurdles: the quality of the data and the sensitivity of the instruments to analyze it. Big data projects everywhere – such as the attempt by Britain's National Health Service to create a nationwide medical database – have stumbled over the issue of how to prevent incorrect information from contaminating the system. Problems associated with the processing and interpreting of bad data would be even more onerous in a country of 1.4 billion people. Analyzing all that data would no doubt be an issue, and such a repository of data would also provide incentives for cybercriminals to steal or alter information.

Acknowledging such challenges, the Chinese government has allowed an unusual amount of discussion about them in state-run media. A 2016 high-level 'social credit summit' in Shanghai talked about how scores can be checked and mistakes rectified. Much about the social credit system remains unclear. The government has apparently not yet determined whether it wants to use the system primarily to crack down on crooks or greatly enhance its surveillance state, but the government has already created the capacity for a *1984*-esque national system of social control.

Many of the elements are already in place: the databases, digital surveillance, system of reward and punishment, and the 'state knows what is best for you' paternalism. All that remains is for the government to join the pieces together. When that is done, China will have the world's first digital totalitarian state.[38]

The Outer Space Weapons Race

The Chinese government's cyber ambitions stretch around the world and even into outer space. Satellites will play a crucial role in any satellite-enabled country's ability to mount a robust offense or defense in the wars of the future, so satellite-enabled countries are naturally making their opponents' satellites a primary target. For that reason, the entire network of US military and intelligence satellites is in the process of being controlled through a single command center, jointly operated by the US Department of Defense (DoD) and the broader intelligence community. The new center will help defend these satellites from attack by ensuring that all US military and intelligence satellites are visible and controllable. If an adversary tries to deny the USG access to its satellites, the government wants to be able to respond in an integrated and coordinated manner.

Space and cyberspace were named as the primary focus for fighting future wars by the Chinese PLA in its guiding military strategy announced in 2016. China's real goal is apparently to gain control of the Earth–Moon system, a concept that has also been around since the Cold War between the US and Soviet Union. While the US decided in the 1960s and 1970s that long-term survival on the Moon was technologically impossible, the Chinese have committed themselves to that goal, which makes its 2019 landing of a spacecraft on the dark side of the moon seem less like a benign bit of space exploration and more like a deliberate enhancement of its potential military capabilities in outer space. To be clear, *Beijing's ambitions for space missions are not just about science; China is developing assets for its space programs that will enable it to militarily control parts of space.*

China sees space warfare as its best chance to directly compete with the US militarily, since it has nowhere near the assets and firepower capability that the US military has. Rather than trying to match the US Navy and Air Force, China believes it could gain an advantage through production of specialized missiles, spacecraft, and platforms to send to the moon. *Many Chinese military analysts see space warfare as inevitable, and argue that since it will become the center of gravity in future wars it must be seized and controlled so as to achieve space supremacy.*

As part of a push to develop weapons meant to cripple the core strengths of the US military, in 2007, China destroyed one of its own weather satellites using a SC-19 anti-satellite (ASAT) missile. In 2013, the country claimed it had launched a 'sounding' (research) rocket, but it was later revealed to have been China's Dong Ning-2 ASAT missile, and in 2014, Beijing did the same, portraying it at the time as an 'anti-intercept test'. *China's subsequent ASAT tests have used targets at lower altitudes. The US is particularly vulnerable to such weapons because of its reliance on systems that use low-earth orbit, which is a primary reason why NASA is forbidden from cooperating with China in space. China is developing a larger missile defense system that some analysts expect to be deployed by the early 2020s.*[39]

Chinese scientists have also achieved success in their development of a high-power microwave (HPM) weapon, a form of directed energy weapon that combines 'soft kill' (electronic countermeasures that alter the electromagnetic, acoustic or other signature of a target, thereby changing the tracking and sensing behavior of an incoming threat) and 'hard kill' (measures that physically counterattack an incoming threat, thereby altering or destroying its payload in such a way that the intended effect on the target is severely impeded[40]) capabilities through the disruption or even destruction of enemy electronics systems. HPM is a type of weapon that possesses unique advantages in speed, range, accuracy, flexibility, and reusability. The PLA's future HPM weapons could have multiple defensive and offensive functions that would enhance its combat capabilities. HPM systems are able to destroy electronic equipment, and in an age when most combat systems rely on electronics, such weapons could change the way wars are fought.

The PLA's breakthrough in HPM weapons reflects a track record of consistent progress over the course of decades. Until the past several years, the decades-long research on HPM weapons had, apparently, reached a dead end, until the US Air Force Research Laboratory successfully developed its Counter-electronics High-Powered Microwave Advanced Missile Project, which could target an enemy's electronics from an aircraft or missile. While the full extent of current US program is, of course, classified, the PLA's reported advance in the development of HPM weapons appears to indicate that Chinese capabilities have the potential to keep pace with those of the US in disruptive military and space technology.

The eventual fielding of the PLA's HPM weapons will serve as a critical force multiplier for its war-fighting capabilities. In the near term, deployment of this weapon could be as a ship-borne anti-missile system (or a way to reinforce China's air defense systems). Such a weapon system has the potential to undermine the efficacy of even the most advanced US missiles, such as the Long-Range Anti-Ship Missile under development. Used on its own, and especially if it were used in conjunction with Chinese ASAT weapons (or incorporated with missiles to overcome enemy air defenses), HPM weapons can likely degrade and/or damage the electronics of an incoming missile by interfering with data links, GPS receivers, and other guidance mechanisms.[41]

This shift toward the areas of cyberwarfare, electronic warfare, and space warfare using autonomous weapons was formally introduced through the Chinese military's Strategic Support Force (SSF) branch in 2015. The SSF brings the military's new weapons under one roof and demonstrates a bold move toward the weaponization of outer space and broad information capabilities. During the Cold War, the US, UK, and Soviet Union signed the Outer Space Treaty (in 1967), which was either ratified by or acceded to by 105 countries (including China). It set in place laws regarding the use of outer space and banned any nation from stationing nuclear warheads, chemical, or biological weapons in space. However, *the Treaty does not prohibit the placement of conventional weapons in orbit, so such weapons as kinetic bombardment (i.e. attacking Earth with a projectile) are not strictly prohibited.*[42]

In addition to HPW, China's military is developing powerful lasers and electromagnetic railguns for use in a future war involving space-based attacks on satellites. Laser attack systems have significant advantages over more conventional weapons – including those with fast response speed, robust counter-interference performance and high target destruction rates – especially for space-based ASAT systems. An ASAT attack in space would employ ground-based radar to identify a target satellite, a special camera to provide precision targeting, and a deployable membrane telescope that would focus the laser beam on the target satellite. Chinese researchers have proposed building a 5-ton chemical laser that will be stationed in low-earth orbit as a combat platform capable of destroying satellites in orbit. Given the amount of funding devoted to that objective by the Chinese military, the satellite-killing laser could be deployed as soon as *2023*.

Beijing clearly wants the world to believe that it can rapidly militarize space. Developing dedicated space combat systems is in line with China's long-term goal of achieving global strategic ascendency. China's space program is dual-use, supporting both civilian and military needs. For example, China's Shenzhou and Tiangong manned spacecraft were used to perform military missions; its coming space station and plans for a future base on the moon also will have military applications. The combat space station could attack key US satellites, preventing the US from communicating with its military forces and interfering with its ability to conduct surveillance, blinding the US military in the event of war.

In 2015, the PLA published the book *Light War*, which assigned a central role to fighting future wars using lasers. The book argues that *future warfare will be dominated by combining big data analytics using cyber warriors armed with AI, robot lasers, and directed energy weapons*. The Chinese effort could neutralize decades of investment by the US in its own directed-energy weapons, which are also expected to be deployed in the early 2020s (high-powered compact laser guns are slated for deployment in the 2030s). China's disclosures about the coming 'weaponization of space' should greatly concern US and allied defense planners. *The US really has no choice but to change its long-held policy of not deploying arms in space.*[43] The Trump administration did just that in 2018.

Russia appears to be making a similar move with the creation, in 2015, of a new branch of the Russian armed forces – the Aerospace Forces – which brought its air force and Aerospace Defense Forces under a unified command. The focus of the Russian joint command center is somewhat different from the US, however. In addition to space forces, it will also oversee the Russian air force and its anti-missile defenses so as to defend Russian airspace from airborne and space-borne attacks. The Russian government said at the time that a key reason for proceeding with the Aerospace Forces was that Russia, the US, and China were all working on ASAT weaponry that could bring war into space, prompting the imperative of new defensive strategies.[44]

Quantum Entanglement, Anyone?

To control this bold new world of space warfare, the Chinese government seeks to build an entirely new kind of Internet that is completely secure and impervious to hackers. In 2017, Chinese scientists set a new distance record for beaming a pair of entangled particles – photons of light that behave like twins and experience the exact same things simultaneously, even though they are separated by great distances. The principle is called quantum entanglement, which is one of the subatomic world's strangest phenomena.

China smashed quantum entanglement's previous distance record. In a groundbreaking experiment, a laser on a satellite orbiting 480 kilometers above the earth produced entangled photons that were transmitted to two different ground-based stations 1,200 kilometers apart, without breaking the link between the photons. That distance was 10 times greater than the previous record for entanglement and was the first time that entangled photons had been generated in space.[45]

By launching a group of quantum-enabled satellites, China hopes to create a super-secure network that uses an encryption technique based on the principles of a field known as quantum communication. While traditional forms of encryption rely on mathematical functions that are very difficult to be reversed, scientists have demonstrated a far better way to transmit secret data, by demonstrating encryption techniques that rely on the law of physics rather than mathematical complexity (called quantum key distribution). Without getting too technical, for the process to work, laser beams send 'quantum information' held in a 'quantum system' to receivers, which work together to find a protocol to secure the communication.

In a 2016 experiment, a 600-kilogram Chinese satellite was launched and a crystal at the center of the spacecraft produced pairs of entangled photons which were used like a laser beam imbued with information. Once in orbit, the satellite sent its partners entangled photons to bases on the ground in Beijing and Vienna (Austria being a partner in the launch) to create a secret key used to access the information carried in the transmission. *The reason it cannot be hacked is because the information carried in the quantum state of a particle cannot be measured or cloned without destroying the information itself.* While, as of 2016, it could be proven that quantum encryption works in a city-sized radius (or at most between two nearby cities), China believes the atmosphere in space will allow the photons to travel further without disruption because in space there is nothing to attenuate light.

Quantum technology is a major focus of China's five-year economic development plan. While other space agencies have been experimenting with similar technology, none has seen the level of financial support being provided by Beijing. Although China has not disclosed how much money it has spent on quantum research, its funding for basic research, which includes quantum physics, was US $101 billion in 2015; by contrast, in 2005, it spent less than US $2 billion on quantum research. Scientists in the US, Canada, Europe, and Japan are also rushing to exploit the power of particle physics to create truly clandestine communication, but China's launch puts them far ahead of their global counterparts.[46]

As evidence that the Chinese government is peering far into the future, it plans to create an entire system of quantum-enabled, satellite-based communication that relies on entanglement. Beijing is already well on its way to creating a new form of neocolonialism – cyber neocolonialism – which relies of its Information Industrial Complex to project its cyber power on to the world, and beyond.

7 The Race for AI Supremacy

In some countries, the pursuit of supremacy in the Artificial Intelligence (AI) arena would be a simple, straight forward process – the government, and large national companies would compete on the global chessboard playing more or less by the same set of rules as everyone else to become more economically or militarily competitive. But that is not how China plays the game. China does not merely aspire to be a leader in AI to become more economically and militarily competitive – it seeks to do so as part of a well-defined and executed plan to acquire what it needs from other countries in order to make up for any competitive deficiencies it may have so as to protect China, project its businesses, and prolong the power of the CCP. China's acquisition of AI technology from other countries fits neatly into that framework. There is no way to sugar coat this: *China's path toward AI supremacy is an extension of its well-crafted strategy to use unrestricted warfare and state theft to achieve its objectives.*

Harnessing the Power of Big Data

Given the size of China's population, it has an inherent advantage in harnessing the power of data into AI applications. Every time someone enters a search query into Baidu (China's Google), pays a restaurant bill with a WeChat wallet, shops on Taobao (China's Amazon), or catches a ride with Didi (China's Uber), that data can be fed back into algorithms, not only to improve their accuracy but, of course, to keep tabs on where Chinese citizens go and what they do. A similar phenomenon is occurring in the US and many other countries around the world, but China now has in excess of 750 million people online, and more than 95% of them access the Internet using mobile devices. In 2016, Chinese mobile payment transactions totaled $5.5 trillion – about *50 times* more than in the US.

China's State Council issued an ambitious policy blueprint in 2017 calling for the nation to become the world's primary AI innovation center by 2030, by which time, it believed, China's AI industry could be worth about *$150 billion*. China has been investing tens of billions of dollars in all aspects of information technology, from quantum computing to chip design, and Chinese government and industry have launched multiple simultaneous initiatives in an effort to commence its drive to achieve AI supremacy. By contrast, according to In-Q-Tel, a US not-for-profit venture capital firm run by the US Central Intelligence Agency, the US government's total spending on unclassified AI programs in 2016 was about *$1.2 billion*.

Facial recognition is the rage in China and is now used routinely for shopping and to gain access to some public services. In 2018, Alibaba led a $600 million investment in SenseTime, a Chinese firm that develops technology for tracking individuals, working with 40 local governments in China. It was estimated at the time that the company was the world's most valuable AI company, worth approximately $4.5 billion.

Throughout China, customers can authorize digital payment in some fast food restaurants via facial scan. Baidu's facial recognition systems confirm passenger identity at some airport security gates. Recent advances in AI have made it possible to identify individuals in video – a far more complex task than in photographs. The government has deployed facial recognition technology in Xinjiang, a Muslim-majority region in western China where tensions between ethnic groups erupted in riots in 2009. Facial recognition checkpoints operate throughout Xinjiang, from gas stations to shopping centers to mosque entrances. Even toilet paper in public restrooms is now being dispensed (in limited amounts, of course) after a facial scan.[1]

In its quest to achieve AI supremacy, the government is proceeding full throttle. As of 2016, Chinese researchers published more Deep Learning (DL)–related papers in journals around the world than researchers from any other country. China plans to expand the number of universities offering dedicated AI and Machine Learning (ML) departments.

Chinese industry continues to bet heavily on AI. In 2017, Alibaba announced plans to invest $15 billion in research over 3 years to build 7 labs in 4 countries that will focus on quantum computing and AI. That same year, China's Ministry of Science and Technology (MST) issued a 3-year plan to guide AI development, naming several large companies as 'national champions' in key fields; for example, Baidu, in autonomous driving, and Tencent, in computer vision for medical diagnosis.[2] *China intends to be, and will indeed become, the world leader in AI and ML in the next decade.*

Digital Leninism

China's transition to a 'great power' in AI has raised a host of fundamental issues the country's leadership must address, from the transformation of labor markets and diminishing human control over critical decision-making processes to the increasing influence of those who develop and deploy AI and potential changes in the power structure in a country where the CCP reigns supreme. Of course, any country with such ambitions would need to address a similar set of issues but, where China is concerned, *the potential of AI to dramatically transform Chinese society is a tiger being unleashed that the CCP may come to regret, for it has the potential to upend the command and control structure the Party has worked so hard to put in place since the 1940s.*

At the turn of the century, the Internet revolution posed a threat to authoritarian rulers, which they methodically turned to their own advantage by creating a surveillance state on steroids. The current big data revolution has been warmly embraced by the CCP as an opportunity, rather than a threat, and the country's leaders are reconfiguring many aspects of Chinese society to align with AI. In this reconfigured system, central co-ordination and control (fondly referred to as 'top-level design' by Xi Jinping) are intended to become an asset that propels technological innovation and enhances economic performance, while maintaining political stability.

The prospect of reaching a goal that has historically eluded Communist rulers – the perfection of centralized control – propels the CCP's intense and long-term commitment to digitization. All of China's major development strategies now rely on big data-driven solutions. 'Healthy China 2030' seeks to expand online health services that can generate diagnoses and treatment advice with the help of big data. Local governments are investing heavily in the provision of public services by way of IT applications. China's Social Credit System, announced in 2014, judges individuals' trustworthiness and aims to nudge citizens (and companies) into rule-abiding behavior by evaluating data ranging from payment morale and compliance with traffic rules to environmental regulations and opinions voiced in online chat rooms. *Algorithms – rather than laws, policemen, or judges – will assume regulatory and enforcement powers in China's future.*

China's leaders have more flexibility to experiment with the technologies of the future than elected leaders in the West, and they are doing so with vigor. *China's top-down authoritarian approach to governing meshes well with a compliant, bottom-up enthusiasm for new technologies in Chinese society.* From facial recognition to compulsory sharing of consumer data, China has become a laboratory for everything from mobile payment systems to online surveillance. *It is not incentivized to share new technology with the rest of the world because it seeks technological supremacy, which is one way of compensating for its lack of military supremacy vis-à-vis the US and West.* This applies in particular to AI and cyber-oriented technology and capabilities.

China's future success as a digital superpower is, of course, not guaranteed. The success of 'smart' economic and social planning will ultimately depend on the quality, integration, and processing of the data that feed it, but also on the government's responsiveness and agility that is essential to make use of feedback from data analysis. President Xi has advanced his 'digital Leninism' further than most had thought possible within a short time. Other authoritarian regimes around the world are watching the CCP's approach closely. If China manages to harness big data technologies to build a top-down yet responsive system of governance that turns out to be politically effective, economically productive, and socially stable, it has the potential to become a global model[3] that could further threaten democratic systems of government.

China's 2030 Vision

China's leadership sees technological innovation generally, and AI in particular, as a core element of its international competitiveness. Beijing has embarked on an agenda of 'intelligentization' to take advantage of the transformative potential of AI throughout its society, economy, government, and military. As noted above, the Chinese government has not exactly been shy about declaring its intention to be the world's leading AI power by 2030. In 2017, it issued a bold AI plan[4] to proceed toward that objective in characteristic 5-year increments, which can be summarized as follows:

- By 2020, China will be on par with other advanced nations in the pursuit of AI supremacy. AI will become a focal point of economic growth, will improve Chinese citizens' livelihoods, and China will have made significant progress in developing a new generation of AI theories and technologies.

- By 2025, China will have achieved major breakthroughs in basic theories for AI and will become the primary driving force for China's ongoing economic transformation. A new generation of AI will be widely used in intelligent manufacturing, medicine, agriculture, defense, and other fields. By then, China will have established laws, regulations, and ethical norms governing the use of AI.

- By 2030, China's AI theories, technologies, and applications will lead the world and provide an important foundation for becoming a leading power in AI innovation.[5]

Despite the country's noteworthy rise in AI, the plan candidly acknowledges that, as of 2017, China had not produced major original results in AI and had lagged well behind leading AI nations in critical components such as high-performance chips for ML. At that time, there had not been systematic high-level design for research and development, and Chinese research institutions and enterprises had yet to establish AI influence internationally.

The plan called for the leveraging of global innovation resources while acquiring what it needed to become competitive via overseas mergers and acquisitions, equity investments, the deployment of venture capital, and the establishment of research and development centers abroad. As a result, China will likely become less dependent upon foreign innovation resources as its becomes more capable in the space. Chinese investments in Silicon Valley AI start-ups prompted a debate in the US about whether to broaden the remit of the CFIUS in order to expand reviews of Chinese high-tech investments, particularly in AI (discussed in more detail below).

The plan calls for progress in new 'AI 2.0' technologies, including big data intelligence, cross-media intelligence, swarm intelligence, hybrid-augmented intelligence (human-machine symbiosis or brain-computer collaboration), and autonomous intelligent systems. China appears to be particularly focused on approaches that could enable paradigmatic changes in AI, such as high-level Machine Learning (ML) (self-adaptive or autonomous learning), brain-inspired AI, and quantum-accelerated ML. As the government enhances national competitiveness, of course, it also plans to bolster its capacity to ensure state security and national defense, in accordance with the CCP's imperatives. *The country's AI will therefore have a range of applications intended to maintain public security, social stability, and national defense.*[6]

While the plan formalizes and points to a national-level focus on AI, local governments and companies were, as noted above, already engaging in subnational planning on AI before the plan was announced. Additionally, crucial elements of the AI plan are rooted in previously adopted science and technology plans. So, while the central government plays an important guiding role in the plan's execution, bureaucratic agencies, private companies, academic labs, and subnational governments are all pursuing their own interests and staking their own claims to China's AI platform.

Although the rest of the world might be inclined to believe that ethics and safety considerations will be largely absent from Beijing's planning efforts, substantive discussions about AI safety and ethics are emerging in China. In fact, a wide range of Chinese AI researchers are participating in the Global Initiative for Ethical Considerations in AI. That said, it seems clear that China will not want to be part of any global arrangement which restricts its freedom of movement in the AI sphere. While there is no consensus about the endpoints of AI development in China – which will remain a work in progress for some time to come – it appears equally clear that the State Council's AI plan is not intended to be the totality of China's AI strategy.

The 2020 benchmark for the core AI industry's gross output (RMB150 billion or approximately US $24 billion) represents a tenfold increase from 2017. Four factors are driving the overall development of China's AI: hardware (in the form of chips designed for training and to execute algorithms); data as an input for AI algorithms, research and algorithm development; and the commercial AI ecosystem. There are important similarities and differences between China's current approach to AI development and its past efforts to guide scientific and technological innovation in other areas. These include a strong degree of state support and intervention, transfer of both technology and talent, and investment in long-term, society-level measures. However, the plan differs from previous approaches because of AI's 'omni-use' potential – the breadth of actors involved is much wider than for other technologies. As a result, international private tech giants and vigorous start-ups are leading players in driving innovation.

The Chinese government has adopted a 'catch-up' approach to obtain the hardware necessary to train and execute AI algorithms. It has supported national corporate 'champions' by providing substantial funding, encouraging domestic companies to acquire chip technology through overseas transactions, and making long-term bets on supercomputing facilities. Access to large quantities of data is an obviously important driver for AI systems. While China's data protectionism favors Chinese AI companies (which access domestic data), it simultaneously inhibits the cross-border pooling of data. This may prove to be an important impediment as China's AI industry matures.

The AI plan outlines a two-pronged 'gathering' and 'training' approach, wherein national and local-level talent programs accumulate AI researchers to work in China, while the country's tech giants set up their own overseas AI institutes to recruit foreign talent. The government has begun to take a more active role in funding AI ventures, helping promote the fourth driver of AI development, the commercial AI ecosystem. By disbursing funds through Government Guidance Funds established by local governments and state-owned enterprises, the government has already invested more than US $1 billion in domestic start-ups, with much of the investment directed toward AI. The government is also exploring ways to exert more influence over large technology companies, including through the establishment of party committees and 'special management shares'.[7]

A Multiplicity of Purposes and Applications

With such a diverse platform having been established to ramp up China's AI ambitions, AI serves a multiplicity of purposes for the Chinese government. *While helping to make China more competitive commercially and militarily, AI is also a vehicle through which the government can be perceived to provide better governance for the Chinese people, using AI to drive smart cities, manufacturing, government, and forming the infrastructure for a smart society.*

Consistent with the government's lofty aspirations, AI applications in agriculture, transportation, social security, pension management, public security, and a host of other government functions will enable the government to provide a range of new benefits to its people. Should the application of AI tools throughout Chinese society become as successful as the government envisions, *it could create a comprehensive new power source within the CCP's architecture, further deepening and strengthening the Party's power.* Doing so could also enhance the influence the technology industry within Chinese society and politics,[8] not unlike what is already the case in the US and other advanced nations.

The truth is, *China is particularly well placed to achieve its stated objectives and assume the global lead in AI. It has capital, people, and computing power in abundance.* In addition, China has two other resources that make China a promised land for AI. China already has approximately 40% of the world's trained AI scientists and most large universities have launched AI programs, meaning that number can only increase.

Then there is the data component: China's enormous population generates more data than any other nation, given its 750+ million daily Internet users. Almost all of them go online from smartphones, which generate far more valuable data than desktop computers, primarily because they contain sensors and are mobile. In its big coastal cities, cash has all but disappeared for small purchases: the Chinese make purchases with their devices using services such as Alipay and WeChat Pay.

Moreover, *unlike in the West, where citizens are preoccupied with civil liberty protections, the Chinese are not necessarily concerned about privacy, which makes openly collecting data easier.* The country's popular bike-sharing services not only provide cheap transport but what is known as a 'data play' – when riders hire a bicycle, some firms keep track of renters' movements using a GPS device attached to the bike. This would likely be frowned upon in the West (even though, although most people do not think about it, nearly everyone riding a shared bike carries a smart phone that is broadcasting their location to their apps and service providers), but the average Chinese person may either care a great deal about location (or other forms of privacy) or could not really care less.

Young Chinese are particularly enthusiastic about their AI-powered services, while being relaxed about who uses their data. Xiaoice, a chatbot operated by Microsoft, has more than 100 million Chinese users. Most talk to the bot frequently about the problems they may have had during a given day. Each time they do so, the bot is learning from its interactions and becoming cleverer. Xiaoice no longer just provides encouragement and tells jokes – it has created the first collection of poems written with AI, which caused a heated debate in Chinese literary circles about whether there should be such a thing as artificial poetry.

While the country has more than 40 laws containing rules about the protection of personal data, they are rarely enforced. *Technology firms are working closely with government agencies to develop AI and ML, so it is unlikely that the government will burden AI firms with overly strict regulation.* Entrepreneurs are taking advantage of China's data strengths and lax regulatory environment. While many Chinese AI firms have only recently started up, a good number of them have progressed more rapidly than their Western counterparts. As a result, China already has a herd of AI unicorns (start-ups valued at more than US $1 billion). Baidu, Alibaba and Tencent, collectively referred to as BAT, are working on many of the same services as their smaller counterparts, including speech- and face-recognition, while also trying to become dominant in specific areas of AI, consistent with their comparative advantages.

Tencent is poised to develop a big presence in AI, given that it possesses more data than the other two. Its WeChat messenger service has almost 1 billion accounts and is the platform for thousands of services, from news to legal assistance to payments. It is also a world leader in games, with more than 100 million players for each of its most popular games. Alibaba is already a behemoth in e-commerce, investing billions of dollars to become number 1 in cloud computing. It already boasts traffic optimization software and AI-powered services to discover drugs and diagnose diseases from medical images.

However, Baidu's fate is mostly tied to AI in part because the technology may be its best opportunity to catch up with Alibaba and Tencent. It is putting most of its resources into autonomous driving, hoping to provide technology for fully autonomous vehicles by 2020. While its rivals – such as Waymo (Google's subsidiary) and Tesla – jealously guard their software and the data they collect, Baidu is sharing its data. The idea is to encourage carmakers that use Baidu's technology to do the same, creating an open platform for data from self-driving cars. That could shake up the autonomous vehicle marketplace globally.[9] Imagine that – a Chinese company leading the way in data transparency in one of AI's most significant sectors.

Don't Trust and Verify

The government began a nation-wide surveillance project, Skynet, in 2005. Today, as facial recognition has become omnipresent throughout the country, cameras track passengers at railway stations, identify homeless people on the streets, and monitor worshippers in state-approved churches. A 2017 documentary co-produced by the CCP claimed that the country had the largest network of CCTV cameras in the world (more than 200 million). That same year, some 55 cities became part of a plan called Xio Liange ('sharp eyes'), which entailed footage from surveillance cameras in public and private properties being centrally processed to monitor people and events. The intelligence collected from the video footage became part of what powers China's Social Credit System.

In 2017 alone, 530 patents related to video surveillance and surveillance cameras were published in China,[10] compared to just 96 in the US during the same period[11]. China has also seen a rise in facial recognition patents, with more than 900 patents published in 2017. Applicants included government-supported academic institutions, big tech companies, and start-ups whose clientele includes government agencies. As the government adds a layer of AI to its surveillance operations, start-ups have come to play an important role in providing the government with foundational technology.

Although facial recognition has been in use for some time in many railway stations for ID verification, AI-enabled smart glasses developed by a start-up are now being used to enable law enforcement authorities to identify criminals. Using Intel's Movidius Myriad vision processing chip, the technology matches faces with a database of known and wanted criminals stored on the device. By storing images on the device (as opposed to sending images to a central server on the cloud), it can function faster. One start-up led by the Chinese state government's venture capital fund had access to 1.3 billion face data records on Chinese citizens stored in the Ministry of Public Security's database.

As previously noted, China has a strong mobile payment market with WeChat (owned by Tencent) and Alipay (Alibaba's financial arm) having 1 billion and 500 million users, respectively. These payment giants have become digital ID repositories. At least three provinces in China are issuing electronic ID cards for their citizens using WeChat or Alipay's facial recognition technology. The mobile IDs can be used for authentication instead of carrying physical ID cards (mandatory for citizens at all times in China) for travel booking, name registration at Internet cafés, and for other security checks.

Alibaba and Tencent are also working with the government on smart city projects, offering their cloud processing and AI capabilities. The projects involve online and offline surveillance, in conjunction with smart city projects, to help monitor traffic, waste and water level management, and real-time monitoring of surveillance footage for crime prevention. Approximately 500 smart city projects were underway in China in 2017.[12]

AI with Chinese Characteristics

In some respects, the real race in AI between China and the US will be between the two countries' big cloud companies, which will compete to be the provider of choice for companies and cities that want to dive deeply into AI. China's tech giants are ready to compete with Google, Amazon, IBM, and Microsoft to serve up AI. While Alibaba's core business remains selling goods and providing a platform for business-to-business trade, it has spawned other lucrative operations, including a platform for logistics and shipments, an advertising network, and cloud computing and financial services. The company's ubiquitous mobile payments app, Alipay, is run by a sister company, Ant Financial, which also offers loans, insurance, and investing via a smartphone.

Alibaba announced in 2017 that it would spend $15 billion over the following three years on a research institute called the DAMO (Discovery, Adventure, Momentum, and Outlook) Academy, dedicated to exploring fundamental technologies. This is evidence, as if it were needed, that China long ago dispensed with a reputation for simply copying Western innovations. According to the Organization for Economic Cooperation and Development, research and development (R&D) spending in China grew tenfold between 2000 and 2016, rising to $412 billion.[13] The US still spends more ($464 billion in 2016), but its total has increased by only a third since 2000. Very soon, China will be the leader in that category, as well.

DAMO will effectively triple Alibaba's research budget, to more than $7 billion. This most likely means that Alibaba will overtake IBM, Facebook, and Ford, and will narrow the gap with the world's leaders – Alphabet and Amazon – which spent $16 billion and $14 billion on R&D in 2017, respectively. DAMO will include a portfolio of research groups working on fundamental and emerging technologies including blockchain, computer security, fintech, and quantum computing, with AI being the biggest focus with the greatest commercial potential.

Alibaba appears to be inspired by the way the DARPA funds different teams competing on the same project, and it is clearly learning from Alphabet and Amazon, as well. It has released a cloud ML platform, just as they have (the first from a Chinese company), which was launched in 2015 and has been upgraded significantly since then. The tools it offers are similar to those on Google Cloud and Amazon Web Services, including off-the-shelf solutions for such services as voice recognition and image classification. Developing these tools was a major technical undertaking for Alibaba and signals both how ambitious the company is to shape the future of AI and how big a role cloud computing will play.

Alibaba's cloud already supports several other companies' DL frameworks, including Google's TensorFlow and Amazon's MXNet. By supporting its competitors' frameworks, Alibaba gives developers a reason to use its platform instead, but Alibaba is creating its own Deep Learning framework. In 2017, the company released an AI program capable of reading a piece of text and answering simple questions about that text more accurately than anything ever built before. Alibaba has already used the program to improve its automated customer support on its online marketplace and it plans to deploy language understanding across all of its platforms and technologies.

Alibaba's AI researchers are working on other cutting-edge projects, such as generative adversarial networks, an ML approach developed by a Google researcher wherein two neural networks compete against one another, with one trying to generate data that seems as if it comes from a real data set, while the other tries to distinguish between real versus fake examples. Most Westerners may not realize it, but Alibaba is already exporting AI technology as the world's fifth-largest cloud computing provider (after Amazon, Google, IBM, and Microsoft). Alibaba is arguably already ahead of the competition in some areas. In 2017, it announced a collaboration with the Malaysian government to provide smart city services, including a video platform that can automatically detect accidents and help optimize traffic flow. Alibaba may have already done more to change the way business is done in China than any other organization.[14] It is ambitious on every front.

While the quantity of Chinese AI research has grown dramatically, researchers in the US remain responsible for a lot of the most fundamental groundbreaking work. *What Chinese researchers have been very good at doing is focusing on an idea and expanding on its different applications.* In fact, the Chinese have become prominent in adding value to existing research, with researchers in China wasting no time to produce papers on various applications, which can then be further developed.

Chinese researchers usually speak English, so they have the benefit of access to all the work disseminated in English. By contrast, the English-speaking AI research community is much less likely to have access to work within the Chinese AI community, and the velocity of work is much faster in China than in most of Silicon Valley[15] – among the many distinct advantages China possesses.

A Plethora of Concerns

Baidu's call for data transparency aside, there are a number of additional concerns about how China will manage its rise to be a great AI power. Among them is the potential that the benefits of Chinese technological breakthroughs will be muted by data protectionism. In 2017, a cyber security law came into force requiring foreign firms to store the data they collect on Chinese customers within the country's borders; foreigners cannot use Chinese data to offer services to third parties. If data cannot be pooled, the algorithms that run autonomous cars and other products may not be the most efficient. There is also, of course, the risk of reprisals from foreign firms on Chinese firms and citizens outside of China.

On the subject of ethics and safety, in the US the technology giants of Silicon Valley have pledged to work together to ensure that any AI tools they develop will be safe. All the leading AI researchers in the West are signatories to an open letter from 2015 calling for a ban on the creation of autonomous weapons. Equivalent Chinese discussions about the limits of ethical AI research are more opaque, however. Chinese AI companies have incentive to think about some of these issues, since rogue AI would be a problem for the planet wherever it may emerge. There is a self-interest case to be made for the formulation of global safety standards, but it is hard to imagine that Beijing will lead the charge on that.

China's AI plan is clearly about maximizing AI's value to the state. AI techniques are ideally suited to identifying patterns in the massive amounts of data that Chinese censors sift through on a daily basis in order to maintain the government's grip on its citizenry. It is easy to imagine how the same data may be used to enhance the government's plans to create the Social Credit system that scores individuals based on their behavior and its perceived desirability. Once perfected, such algorithms would likely be of interest to autocratic regimes around the world. China's tech firms are in no position to prevent the government from taking advantage of such tools.

While Baidu preaches data transparency in public, it has been appointed by the government to lead a national laboratory for DL. That ought to cause a severe case of cognitive dissonance to AI ethicists in China and beyond. Western firms and governments are no angels in the areas of data collection and espionage, but at least they are engaged in an open debate about the ethical implications of AI, and intelligence agencies in many other countries are constrained by democratic institutions.[16] Neither is true of China.

When, in 2014, the US Air Force wanted help making military robots more perceptive, it awarded Boston-based AI start-up Neurala the contract, but when Neurala needed money to finance the project, it got no help from the American military. The company ended up turning to China's Haiyin Capital,[17] backed by state-run Everbright Group, for an undisclosed sum to support the Air Force contract. Everbright was initially owned by China's State Administration for Foreign Exchange[18], the wholly government-owned entity that manages the country's foreign exchange reserves. In 2008, it was sold to the China Investment Corporation,[19] the country's wholly government-owned sovereign wealth fund. So, *the Chinese government ended up partially funding the US Air Force's contract to make military robots more perceptive*.

In fact, Chinese firms have routinely become investors in American start-ups, particularly those working on cutting-edge technologies with potential military applications. These are companies that make rocket engines for spacecraft, sensors for autonomous navy ships, and printers that make flexible screens that can be used in fighter-plane cockpits. Many of the Chinese firms are owned by state-owned companies or have direct connections to Chinese leaders. According to the DoD, Beijing actively encourages Chinese companies with close government ties to invest in American start-ups specializing in critical technologies such as AI and robots to advance China's military capacity, as well as its economy.

US government controls intended to protect potentially critical technologies against countries like China have fallen short. It took a while, but such transactions eventually started ringing alarm bells in Washington. US lawmakers raised broad questions about the nature of China's economic relationship with the US well before the Trump administration started applying tariffs on Chinese products, in an effort to reduce the inherent inequity in bilateral trade between the two nations.

Neither the high-tech start-ups nor their Chinese investors had been formally accused of malfeasance, and some experts admit that much of the activity could indeed be perfectly innocent. Chinese businesses have money and are, after all, looking for returns, but the fund flows fit China's pattern of using state-guided investment to support its industrial policy, enhance its technology holdings, and acquire military-related technology. Yet, some start-ups—especially those making hardware rather than revenue producing mobile apps—have said that Chinese money has at times been the only available funding. If one is inclined to give them the benefit of the doubt, some Chinese investors appear to have a bigger appetite for risk and a willingness to get things done quickly, which is exactly what most start-ups need.

Although Neurala apparently made efforts to ensure that Haiyin Capital had no access to its source code or other important technological information, Haiyin's participation raised enough concern inside the Pentagon that some in the DoD argued that the US government should steer clear of the contract that it awarded to the company. To address concerns that it was not tapping a sufficient amount of innovation from start-ups, in 2015 the Pentagon set up Defense Innovation Unit Experimental, to enable investments into promising new companies. That same year, Haiyin Capital also invested in XCOR Aerospace, a US commercial space-travel company that makes spacecraft and engines and has worked with NASA. Haiyin Capital's founder later admitted that part of his firm's goal is to build Chinese industrial capabilities, noting the difficulty with which Chinese firms are able to obtain space technology from abroad because of American export controls.[20]

The Race for Faster Neural Network Processors

Part of China's race with the US for AI supremacy is in 5G wireless technology and includes Beijing's drive to achieve mass-production of neural network processors by 2020, with the intention of applying the chips to improve manufacturing, while putting into hyperdrive its move into smart cities. America's NVIDIA is the leader in neural processor chips, which are used by the world's largest tech companies to power everything from AI data centers to semi-autonomous cars. The company estimates that its total AI-related revenue will reach nearly $40 billion by 2025. China has taken notice of NVIDIA's AI chip dominance and has specifically named the company as one that it would like its domestic companies to challenge. China's MST wants a chip that delivers performance and energy efficiency 20 times better than that of NVIDIA's M40 chip, branded as an 'accelerator' for neural networks. Although it was first produced in 2015, the M40 is still used in a plethora of AI projects.

Chinese officials and tech companies each have good reason to target NVIDIA, which has provided chips for robots, drones, and autonomous vehicles, and has partnered with such auto makers as Toyota and Volvo. In response, in 2017, an investment fund owned by China's State Development and Investment Corporation led a $100 million funding round in Cambricon, a Beijing AI chip start-up. Cambricon subsequently announced the creation of two server chips that could substitute for NVIDIA chips in some AI projects, while Huawei began collaborating with Cambricon to produce AI chips for phones and other devices. Plenty of other Chinese companies are jumping into the fray, with Horizon Robotics having raised $100 million and Deephi raising $40 million in 2017.

Although it wants to rely far less on foreign chip makers for commercial and military applications, China has struggled for years to make its chip industry more competitive. The US and other governments closely scrutinize proposed acquisitions of domestic semiconductor technology by Chinese companies. The US government has canceled multiple proposed purchases of US chip makers on national security grounds.[21] The concern is that cutting-edge technologies developed in the US could be used by China to bolster its military capabilities and gain a competitive advantage in strategic industries. The USG is strengthening the CFIUS, the inter-agency committee that reviews foreign acquisitions of US companies on national security grounds.

An unpublished 2017 Pentagon report warned that China was skirting US oversight and gaining access to sensitive technology through transactions that did not trigger CFIUS review, including joint ventures, minority ownership stakes, and early-stage investments in start-ups. The Trump administration recognizes that the CFIUS is outdated and inadequate for the new landscape the US faces with China and other countries. AI and similar technologies are so new that existing regulatory mechanisms related to export control and national security have not found a way to account for them. Legislation proposing revision of CFIUS guidelines would require the Committee to heighten scrutiny of buyers from nations identified as potential threats to national security. The legislation would provide a mechanism for the Pentagon to lead that ID effort, with input from the US technology sector, and the Commerce and Energy Departments.

As the legislation was making its way through Congress in 2018, a contentious issue was a provision that would give the CFIUS increased jurisdiction over a wide variety of transactions between US companies with 'critical' technology (innovations that will sustain a US competitive edge in the future) and any foreign company. US technology company lobbyists tried to water down provisions that the industry deemed to be too restrictive on non-sensitive transactions, such as computer hardware sales and software licensing. Other industry lobbyists were concerned that stronger US regulations may not succeed in halting technology transfer and could trigger retaliation by China in the process.[22] The truth is that, in the absence of a lobbying effort by US technology firms, the CFIUS would have swiftly passed in Congress in 2018, lending credence to the argument that the Chinese have a distinct advantage when it comes to passing legislation and getting things done. They do not engage in a long drawn out debate about it – they just do it.

In 2018, President Trump signed into law the Foreign Investment Risk Review Modernization Act (FIRRMA), which establishes more vigilant reviews of foreign investments into American companies on national security grounds. Now that start-ups and minority investors are specifically included in the vetting process, countries such as China will no longer be given a free pass to slip under the radar undetected when making investments into sensitive areas of industry. According to the US Defense Innovation Unit Experimental, in 2015 alone, Chinese investors invested between $3 and $4 billion in early-stage venture transactions. Between 2015 and 2017, the Unit estimated that China contributed 13% of its total investment funds into US-backed companies, ranking second only to Europe as the largest foreign source of capital for start-ups.

Part of the reason this becomes so important is that China's sovereign, provincial, and local governments, along with state-owned enterprises, firms, and individual investors often form their own funds and pool their capital into each other's investment vehicles. Some have also adopted Western-sounding names, making it even more difficult to distinguish between Chinese and non-Chinese sources of investment. The US government believes that, in many cases, Chinese investments into US start-ups are not simply innocent investors seeking high returns on their capital but, increasingly, seeking information and insight into the inner workings of these start-ups.

Some analysts also believe that investing in start-ups may help prevent the ideas and technology they represent from becoming part of the US military. The DoD does not use technologies supplied by early stage companies with foreign investors, for fear that they could either share or steal information or clandestinely offer a back door into sensitive government computer systems. The implementation of FIRRMA will give the CFIUS enhanced discretion to review a host of new types of cross-border transactions in sensitive sectors and/or businesses. However, to fall within the purview of FIRRMA, investment must either include seats on a board of directors or access to sensitive material. And, just what constitutes 'critical technology' will remain somewhat ambiguous. Some Chinese and other foreign investment that should fall within the purview of FIRRMA will remain outside its scope.[23]

There is certainly an argument to be made that *the US and other countries should focus at least as much on accelerating their own AI development as on restricting access to it*. Much of the work that is done on AI, ML, and DL takes place out in the open and is highly transparent. Companies such as Google and Facebook not only publish numerous papers detailing their latest ideas, but also the open source software and hardware that they use to do so. *America's best hope of staying ahead in AI is to keep alive the type of vibrant, open R&D culture that has made Silicon Valley the global hub for the blossoming of ideas and investment in the field.*[24] That may prove increasingly difficult with the tightening of protective legislation, in combination with a more competitive and combative tone having been set by Washington toward Beijing specifically, with respect to trade, and more generally.

Warp Speed

While the Obama administration sought to *increase* support for AI R&D in its final years and planned a range of initiatives to embrace AI in the future, in its first year in office, the Trump administration proposed *cutting* AI research to a variety of institutions supporting it. Funding for AI research at the National Science Foundation was cut by 10%, to a mere $175 million. By contrast, and at the same time, China was spending enormous sums on technology. In 2014, the Chinese government created a 1 trillion renminbi (US $150 billion) investment fund to turn the Chinese semiconductor industry into a global powerhouse. That was just an initial foray into the space.

While the US civilian sector races ahead of the US government in money spent and innovation achieved, and the government remains indecisive about how best to embrace the private sector to achieve AI supremacy, China has not been shy about pursuing AI in a manner deliberately designed to fuse together the most AI-capable aspects of its civilian and military sectors in AI. Beijing is proceeding full steam ahead, having created a Military-Civilian Fusion lab at its equivalent of America's MIT (Tsinghua University), to provide a formal platform for dual-use AI. In 2017, China also established its first national DL laboratory, through Baidu, in partnership with three universities. Baidu has enthusiastically embraced AI technology, in essence reinventing itself around AI. As of 2017, the company had a 1,300-person strong AI team working on a range of cutting-edge initiatives.

While the USG slowly ramps things up in the AI space, China's government is proceeding at warp speed, rapidly making up for any lag it has with Western firms and governments. *It would not be surprising if it took the lead well before 2030.* Chinese companies believe that, by rotating Chinese staff to Silicon Valley and American staff to Chinese campuses, they can accelerate the timeline for reaching parity with the US. For the time being, however, the size and experience of China's AI workforce is a fraction of that of the US. *Half of the top 10 employers of AI talent in China are US firms – including IBM, Intel, and Microsoft – who are integral to the development of China's human capital in AI.*

Governments around the world are beginning to grapple with the potential implications of AI on a range of societal sectors. As was the case under the Obama administration in the US, the Chinese plan also calls for government action to mitigate the economic pain and social instability of worker displacement. Given China's government-led transition of hundreds of millions of laborers from the agriculture to manufacturing sectors, it clearly has meaningful experience in this area, but its AI-related efforts have only just begun.

Unfortunately, under the Trump administration, the US is no longer attempting to plan for these challenges. The White House Office of Science and Technology Policy, which was instrumental in leading AI policy work during the Obama administration, has been depleted of 70% of its staff in Trump's first year in office, depriving the administration of critical expertise and insights on AI, while China is using the Obama playbook to plan its own AI revolution.[25]

China's Game Plan

China lags behind the US and the UK in terms of fundamental research capability, which is a big reason why there is a shortage of talent. Despite its recent push to devote serious resources toward achieving AI supremacy, fewer than 30 university research labs in China are focused on AI, and they are unable to develop enough talent to meet the recruiting needs of China's AI industry. Chinese AI scientists have also disproportionately specialized in areas such as computer vision and voice recognition, creating gaps in some other areas. Beijing knows that, in order to turn the tide, one of the things it must do is increase the number of universities focused on AI, in order to produce more graduates prepared to contribute to the nation's AI effort.[26]

Another area where China has fallen behind, as previously noted, is its dependence on foreign suppliers for microchips. For some types of high-value semiconductors, China has had to rely on imports for virtually all of its needs. To address this, as previously noted, the Chinese government implemented its Made in China 2025 policy, an initiative to comprehensively upgrade Chinese industry and become the global leader in manufacturing, while at the same time achieving self-sufficiency and reducing reliance on other countries. The policy outlines a wide-ranging strategy for harnessing and promoting the acquisition of foreign technology through outbound investment, including the use of industrial funds, state-owned capital dividends, and other channels to support the creation of advantageous manufacturing capacity to implement overseas investment acquisitions[27] and counteract China's comparative manufacturing disadvantages.

That said, many countries have become concerned that Made in China 2025 is not simply an effort by a country that lags behind to become more competitive. Governments around the world are increasingly concerned that such investments by Beijing, inside and outside of China, are not simply a product of market forces but are guided by the CCP (rather than the private sector), particularly where high-tech is concerned. Circumstantial evidence confirms this suspicion. For example, Chinese investment in the US and elsewhere has skyrocketed since 2015. *Between 1990 and 2015, Chinese investment in the US totaled $64 billion. In 2016 alone, Chinese investment in the US totaled $45 billion – triple the amount in 2015 – with another $21 billion awaiting either regulatory of financing approval.*[28]

Such investments reveal a broader coordinated strategy by Beijing – to appear to have transparent and straightforward ambitions, and be playing by the rules, when not necessarily doing so. For example, Fujian Grand Chips is an ostensibly 'private' Chinese company that attempted to acquire German machine maker Aixtron in 2016. Shortly before it attempted the public takeover, another Fujian-based company – San'an Optoelectronics – unexpectedly canceled a critical order from Aixtron on dubious grounds, sending its stock tumbling and presenting Fujian Grand Chips with an opportunity to purchase Aixtron for substantially less.

It turned out that both Fujian Grand Chip and San'an Optoelectronics shared a common investor: a national semiconductor fund controlled by Beijing. Aixtron makes which produce crystalline layers based on gallium nitride that are used as semiconductors in weapons systems. The acquisition was stopped by the US and German governments at the last hour but is illustrative of how Beijing can drive Chinese foreign direct investment in a highly coordinated manner. As the stakes associated with acquiring cutting edge AI technology become higher, such concerns can only become even more sensitive with time.[29]

Algorithmic Governance

Beijing is producing software to predict instability before it arises, based on the volumes of data mined from Chinese citizens about their friends, families, jobs, and habits. Taking a page from the film Minority Report, such predictive policing is used to deploy law enforcement or military units to places where crime (or anti-government political protests) is *likely* to occur. Predictive policing was actually first created and used in 1994 by the New York City Police Department, which embraced a pioneering and deeply controversial effort to pre-deploy police units to places where crime was expected to occur on the basis of crime statistics. It was highly controversial and ultimately deemed to be unconstitutional because minority youth in the wrong place at the wrong time were frequently targeted and harassed by the police. It did, however, reduce crime by 37% in 3 years.

China is putting predictive policing on steroids by rolling it out on a national level to create a unified information environment whose applications go well beyond simply sending police to a specific street corner. The government's control over the Internet places it in a unique position to extend the reach of surveillance and data collection deeply into the lives of citizens. Since Chinese authorities face far fewer privacy limits on the type of information they are allowed to gather on citizens, they can deploy police forces much more precisely. They might, for example, decide to target an individual who received and deposited a large payment in his or her bank account, or who reads pro-democracy news sites, or who is displaying a change in purchasing habits – labeling them as a 'potential' threat to peace, stability, or the state.

Following the Arab Awakening in 2011, the Chinese government substantially increased spending on internal security, compelling 650 cities to improve their ability to monitor public spaces via surveillance cameras and other technologies. Collecting massive amounts of data inevitably leads to the question of how to analyze it at scale.

The Chinese government does not seek to keep its ongoing efforts to create a hyper-surveillance state hidden. On the contrary, it regularly updates (and sometimes overstates) its capabilities in an effort to maintain a sense of fear, uncertainty, and control over the Chinese people. It is based on the well-established notion that only strong authority can bring order to a potentially turbulent country.

Since President Xi assumed power in 2012, he has launched a significant upgrade of the Chinese surveillance state. China has become the world's largest market for security and surveillance technology, with analysts estimating that the country will have nearly 400 million cameras installed by 2020.[30] Chinese buyers will purchase more than three-quarters of all servers designed to scan video footage for faces, and China's police will spend another $30 billion in the coming years on snooping-oriented hardware and software.

Government-sponsored contracts are promoting research and development into technologies that track faces, clothing, and even a person's gait. As the country spends heavily on surveillance, a new generation of start-ups has risen to meet the demand. Chinese companies are developing globally competitive applications in image and voice recognition. Start-up Yitu took first place in a 2017 contest to develop facial recognition algorithms held by the US government's Office of the Director of National Intelligence. The halls of Yitu's offices are filled with cameras searching for faces and tracking employees' paths from their desks to break rooms to exits.

China's public security market was valued at more than $80 billion in 2017 but will be worth considerably more as the country continues to build its impressive surveillance capabilities. China's national database of individuals it has flagged for surveillance includes up to 30 million people, which is too many people for today's facial recognition technology to parse. But when citizens do not know if they are being monitored, the uncertainty it creates tends to make them more generally obedient.[31] Those who are not can be quickly discerned from among the majority who are.

China has become a world leader in the use of AI and ML for national security and is leading the way in predictive policing research. It is developing systems to more easily recognize faces by compressing a Deep Neural Network to a smaller size, to enable cameras to recognize faces without calling up a distant database, and to use the datasets of thousands of disruptive occurrences to predict how and when others may occur. Beijing has the resources, will, data and inclination to turn predictive policing into something incredibly powerful.[32] No doubt this will prove to be another area of intense interest among governments from round the world.

Battlefield Singularity

As AI and robotics become more pervasive in warfare, some in the PLA anticipate battlefield 'singularity' – when human cognition may no longer be able to keep pace with the decision speeds and tempo of combat in an AI-driven battlefield. That could result in humans shifting command and supervisory roles to machines. Limitations in the capabilities of current military AI systems preclude higher degrees of autonomy and automation for the time being, but there are, even now, missions and contexts in which they are either desirable or imperative – such as for air or missile defense operations. PLA planners have already highlighted the importance of human-machine collaboration, manned-unmanned teaming, and human-machine hybrid intelligence.

While the future trajectory of China-US strategic competition in AI remains uncertain, it is clear that the PLA has emerged as a true peer competitor to the US military in the AI sphere. As the PLA attempts to overtake (rather than simply catch up with or match) the US, *China's implementation of military-civil AI fusion could ultimately provide the PLA with a structural advantage by being able to rapidly adapt and integrate the latest advances in AI weaponry*. Accordingly, US competitive strategy and defense innovation initiatives should focus on a more nuanced understanding of the PLA's strategic thinking about, and development of, military applications of AI. The US (and other militaries) should also further explore the risks and advantages of developing 'counter-AI' capabilities.[33] This is something that is likely to receive greater attention in the future.

In 2018, the PLA's Navy (PLAN) declared (presumably for propaganda or other purposes) that it was developing a nuclear submarine with AI-augmented brainpower, designed to give Beijing a comparative advantage in battle. The project involved updating the computer systems on nuclear submarines with an AI decision-support system that can think for itself, reducing commanding officers' workloads. The plan was for AI to take on 'thinking' functions on nuclear subs, which could include, at a basic level, interpreting and responding to signals picked up by sonar, through the use of convolutional neural networks. The application of ML to acoustic signal processing has, at a basic level, been an active area of research in China for a number of years.

The PLAN is also pursuing the development and deployment of unmanned underwater vehicles (UUVs) such as Sea Wing, a new generation of underwater glider using hybrid propulsion technology to support submarines engaged in military missions. In the future, the PLAN could seek to use such UUVs, in conjunction with submarines, in an attempt to advance its anti-submarine warfare capabilities and shift the undersea balance. As the deep sea battlespace becomes even more complex and contested, the use of AI to support commanders for acoustic signal processing, underwater target recognition, and even more direct decision support, seems plausible.

It is too soon to say whether putting 'superintelligence' on nuclear submarines could ultimately unleash killer AI with nukes, but such a question must be asked and addressed. When (not if) such technology is fully developed, would there ever be a situation in which any country may consider ceding such decision-making authority to a machine? As any military seeks to use AI to enhance its response and fighting capabilities, there is always a risk that it may rely too heavily upon, or overestimate the superiority of, machine intelligence over the judgment of humans.

Past experience (such as with the Patriot missile system) has demonstrated that such complex systems can end up creating greater challenges for their operators, requiring nuanced understanding of their advantages and limitations through specialized training. In addition, the dynamic of 'automation bias' can result in compromised decision-making when humans rely too heavily on automated systems, at the expense of their own judgment.

The use of AI on the battlefields of the future will necessarily create new and unexpected operational risks, which may include potential malfunctions, adversarial interference, or unexpected emergent behaviors. AI remains brittle and vulnerable to manipulation. As the world's major militaries start to rely more upon AI systems, the development of 'counter-AI' capabilities to disrupt them will take on new importance.

While the PLA's pursuit of decision support systems is not new, possessing the capabilities to develop command decision-making capabilities that are made intelligent via AI may serve to fast forward the progress already made in developing cutting edge AI technologies. Beyond submarines, the PLAN also appears to be working on the development of systems to augment command decision-making and, at the tactical level, for the pilots of fighter jets. Having the capability to leverage AI-enabled support to command decision-making could become critical to achieving decision superiority and dominance[34] in the longer term, on land, in the sea, and in the air.

Conclusion

Many in the West may find China's way of doing business distasteful, but there is more than one way to achieve AI supremacy and, like it or not, China is well on its way to getting there. There are, after all, no universally-accepted set of rules dictating how to do so. Similarly, those outside of China may detest the institutionalized state theft of intelligence, data, and industry secrets, but what is worse – to be stolen from or to give a thief the easy ability to steal? The Chinese government and Chinese companies undoubtedly see the world in these terms and would retort, if you do not want your secrets stolen, then do not allow me to steal them, for I will take what you cannot protect. If that is what they think, then they have a point.

It will do the West no good to simply complain about how China gets to the AI finish line. Perhaps it should play the game in a similar fashion. Maybe it already does and we are unaware of it. Regardless, the stakes are rather high and, in the end, it will not matter so much *how* a country achieves AI supremacy, but *that* it does so. *China deserves credit for recognizing early on the importance AI fluency implies for national competitiveness in the coming decades. The West should either find a way to maintain its lead or get out of the way, because nothing will stop Beijing in its quest to achieve AI supremacy.*

8 A World with Chinese Characteristics

In December 2018, the Communist Party marked the 40th anniversary of the 'reform and opening up' policies that have transformed China from a primarily rural and agricultural country into the global manufacturing powerhouse that it is today. Rather than marking the beginning of a period of enhanced reform, the anniversary served to emphasize just what a tight grip on power the CCP continues to hold over the Chinese people, and how President Xi is tightening his, and the Party's grip, rather than loosening it. The pro-democracy movement of 1989 was the closest the Party ever came to political liberalization following Mao's death, and the crackdown that ensued at the time was the furthest it has gone toward overt repression and control since then. President Xi has more than succeeded in concentrating power in his hands, having established himself as ruler for life by abolishing the presidential term limit, and is in the process of replacing selective repression with something more ominous.

The Party has always been vigilant about crushing potential threats but, with some exceptions, it has generally hesitated to interfere too deeply into its citizens' personal lives, giving them enough freedom to ensure the maintenance of economic growth. But that is in the process of changing, with the Social Credit System, enhanced oversight by the government of state-owned companies, and the establishment of censorship 'minders' in many of China's private companies.

While China is certainly not alone in managing the nexus between authoritarian rule and a free market economy, it has done so for longer, at greater scale, and with more convincing results than any other country.

Prosperity has created an enormous and growing middle class, and along with it, rising expectations in China. Today, the Chinese people want more than mere economic growth; they want cleaner air, safer food and medicine, better health care and schools, greater equality, and a visible, effective fight against corruption. While President Xi and the CCP understand this, and are making efforts to deliver on all fronts, much of the effort either appears to be half-hearted, too little too late, or likely to be ineffective because they waited so long to tackle some of these issues earnestly or are battling a rising tide. Chinese youth, and the country's middle class, understand the difference between fact and fiction. Put another way, many of them have no particular reason to be compliant toward the CCP, and they know the difference between words and deeds.

As Chinese economic growth continues to slow down – with 2018 having marked the slowest official growth rate since 1990 – public confidence is being shaken. President Xi himself has acknowledged that the Party must adapt, having declared that the nation is entering a new era requiring new methods. But he also appears to believe that China has become so successful that the Party can afford to return to a more conventional authoritarian posture,[1] and that the successful execution of China Vision requires that repression replace a modicum of individual freedoms. The CCP long ago made a tacit agreement with the Chinese people: in exchange for their loyalty to the Party, it will deliver reliable economic growth, and they will live a better life than their parents did. That has generally worked well as a quid pro quo until recently. The question is, will it continue to work in the coming decade and beyond?

The CCP and its leaders have been adept at shaping a politicized nationalism that reinforces the primacy of the party and defends the authoritarian model as the best bulwark against theoretical societal chaos. Yet, *Chinese nationalism binds its citizens with the state, not with each other. Since communist ideology long ago lost its appeal to the public, President Xi is drawing on Chinese tradition to reinforce the idea that the country needs a strong leader to prevent chaos and guard against foreign threats outsiders.[2] But a growing percentage of the Chinese people do not see much in the way of a foreign threat, leaving President Xi's and the CCP's drumbeat ringing increasingly hollow.*

Is the Foreign Threat Real or Imagined?

To the extent that a threat against the Chinese state is real, it largely emanates from within China itself rather than from foreign powers. The freedom movements in Xinjiang and in Tibet are the result of Beijing seeking to impose its will on these neighboring regions, not the other way around. Had Beijing not sought to do so, these freedom movements would undoubtedly not have materialized or maintained their appeal among the local populace. *So the CCP has created its own bogeyman, which happens to mesh nicely with its own narrative about threats to the state. The same is true with respect to opposition to the CCP. To use George W. Bush's phrase, "either you're with us or you're with the terrorists."[3] From the CCP's perspective, the 'terrorists' may be any Chinese person who opposes the Party or seeks to prevent it from exercising its will upon the Chinese people.* Since approximately 90 million Chinese (roughly 6% of China's population) are CCP members, from the CCP's perspective, the 'terrorists' in this case could actually be considered the 94% of the Chinese people who are not CCP members, whose loyalty to the Party may be questionable, or who may actually oppose the CCP.

Beijing and Washington's relationship has, since the post War era began, largely been one of mutual convenience and comparative advantage; both have seized the opportunity to embrace one another whenever possible while pursing areas of singular and joint interest. Even as the trade war between the two nations raged on in 2018 and 2019, there was never any real likelihood that their disagreements would turn into a full-fledged and permanent trade war, much less a military conflict. The stakes were simply too high, and both sides knew it.

Having ceded control of the South China Sea to Beijing with little more than a public objection, the most obvious recent source of prior military conflict between them has faded away. Beijing and Washington reached a stalemate over Taiwan long ago. America and China have, in reality, agreed to become permanent sparring partners, but even that turned out to be for their mutual benefit, since it allowed both Presidents Xi and Trump to stir up nationalist sentiment and wave their respective flags at home.

With regard to Russia, *Beijing and Moscow have been transactional and situational allies for decades*. Their shared border has meant that they are unlikely to ever engage in formal military conflict, and their respective spheres of influence have implied that they tacitly acknowledge where each other's backyard is, and that, to the extent that they overlap in Central Asia, there are plenty of spoils for both sides to derive without stepping on the other's toes. During and following the Cold War, things never got too hot nor too cold for either side to become unduly concerned. There is little reason to believe that that reality would change in the future. Again, there is simply too much at stake.

So, if neither Washington nor Moscow are the source of a genuine foreign threat to China, is there one? The short answer is, no. Certainly, no Asian country represents any kind of significant threat to Beijing. Quite the contrary – *most of China's Asian neighbors either fear Beijing or seek its partnership*. And no such threat exists from any African, European, Latin American, or Middle Eastern country. President Xi and the CCP can rest easy, because they know that *there is no real foreign threat to China – they merely want the Chinese people to believe that there is*.

And yet, any major military power, such as China, is likely to be the object of attack in some fashion abroad, particularly when it takes actions beyond its own borders, as Beijing has increasingly done. As Beijing has become more engaged around the world – economically and militarily – it has certainly opened itself up to such attack. A good recent example of this was the suicide bomber who targeted the Chinese consulate in Karachi, in 2018. The Baluch Liberation Army claimed responsibility for the attack, stating that China was exploiting the region's natural resources and threatening Pakistan's sovereignty with its many infrastructure projects in the China Pakistan Economic Corridor.[4] As the BRI continues to significantly impact countries around the world, Beijing should expect more such attacks – one of the prices of establishing its new Silk Road – but likely more of a threat to Chinese interests outside of China than inside it.

China's European Port Buying Spree

One of the primary objectives of the BRI, of course, is to help transform China from a continental power to a maritime power. Much of Beijing's investment activities around the world are consistent with that objective. India has already made its concerns about Beijing's investment in Indian Ocean ports and the resulting 'string of pearls' clear to the international community. But Beijing's investment activities in ports have stretched well beyond that.

It is estimated that the Chinese state has at least a 10% equity stake in ports throughout Europe (including in Belgium, France, Greece, Italy, the Netherlands, and Spain), and a growing investment portfolio of at least 40 ports in Africa, the Americas, Central and Eastern Europe, the Middle East, South and Southeast Asia, Australia, and the Pacific. Beijing's sometimes stealth approach to investing has resulted in its 35% stake in the Euromax terminal at Rotterdam, a 20% stake in the Port of Antwerp (Europe's two busiest ports), and 100% ownership of Zeebrugge in Belgium.

Chinese interest in global ports is consistent with Beijing's desire to tilt the global economic playing field in its favor while helping to ensure that commercial processes and standards preferred by China start to become normalized. Another purpose of the BRI is to bind consumer markets to Chinese exporters through the Initiative's physical, financial, and digital networks, which all lead back to China.

In nominal terms, the EU is the largest economy in the world, constituting about 22% of global GDP. Europe will remain the most important destination for finished goods throughout the BRI for the foreseeable future. The Made in China 2025 policy cannot succeed without bringing Europe into the Chinese economic orbit through the BRI.

While Beijing has ensured that it extracts its pound of flesh from Europe in return for essentially making the EU the centerpiece of the BRI, it is worth adding, in fairness, that a number of European ports have benefitted directly from the Chinese investment. For example, when China's COSCO Shipping Corporation took over the Greek container and passenger port of Piraeus in 2008, fewer than 900,000 containers passed through its facilities; by 2016, it reached 3.7 million containers, and Piraeus rose in container port rankings from 93rd in 2010 to 44th in 2015 to 38th in 2017. Chinese-invested ports will eventually be connected to the *maritime* Silk Road accompanying the BRI and become part of a network of freight lines belonging to the Eurasian economic corridor. This will link European economies with the entire BRI economic ecosystem, from China through to the Mediterranean.

Those entities that are familiar with how Beijing does business will know that China Vision is certainly at play with respect to Chinese infrastructure investment. According to the CSIS Reconnecting Asia database[5], *89% of contractors participating in strictly Chinese-funded BRI-related projects are Chinese companies, with only 7.6% being local companies and 3.4% being foreign companies.* By contrast, of the BRI projects funded by MDBs, just 29% of contractors were Chinese, 41% were local firms, and 30% were non-Chinese foreign firms.

There is also growing discomfort on the part of non-Chinese entities with the close funding arrangements between Chinese firms and government-controlled financial organizations. This stands at odds with the EU's liberal notion of political economy, which depends on there being significant distance between the political and strategic objectives of the government, versus the objectives of commercial enterprises.

China's official *Blue Book of Non-Traditional Security*, produced annually by state-sanctioned academics and researchers, stated in 2015 that *two of the purposes of the BRI are to mitigate American-led geopolitical machinations and ideas, and to promote a new international order that enhances China's national power and soft power.* Investment in ports and other assets are therefore considered in the context of 'strategic support states', achieved through regional cooperation and the provision of economic goods as China expands westward. One of the principles of cultivating a strategic support state is to ensure that China has the ability and resources to guide the actions of the country so that they fit Beijing's strategic needs.[6]

Beijing is gradually asserting de facto control and dominance over European ports just as it did with the islands of the South China Sea but, in this case, Beijing is using a divide-and-conquer strategy to prevent the EU from taking a common stance against Beijing by offering substantial amounts of funding and investments to countries throughout the region. While Beijing's actions in the South China Sea were judged to be illegal by The Hague, its actions in Europe are legal and, as noted, create some economic benefits, even though the biggest net beneficiary will, of course, ultimately be China.

European nations should remember that President Xi's goal of making China a moderately prosperous society by 2021 (when the country celebrates the 100th anniversary of the formation of the CCP), and to become a fully developed, rich and powerful nation[7] by 2049 (when China celebrates its 100th anniversary as the People's Republic of China) require that Europe play along. As noted, the BRI cannot be completed without the active participation of Europe, so European leaders may want to consider taking a page out of President Trump's playbook and find a way to establish a more equal footing with Beijing. They, too, will have a stake in the success of the BRI. Cross-border investment is *supposed* to be a two-way street.

The EU should consider putting pressure on countries such as Greece and Hungary to agree to a common set of guidelines with respect to screening how Chinese investments are made and how Chinese-owned assets are run and operated. The sale or lease of any asset-but especially strategically important assets-should follow a set of guidelines adhered to by all EU states. Foreign entities should abide by the same set of rules. More broadly, all EU member states should take collective responsibility for protecting European interests, the adherence to international law, and the preservation of a regional and economic system which does not prioritize a China-centric view of the world while ensuring that special advantages are baked in for China.

There are also stakes, as usual, for the US. Chinese port operators will undoubtedly be passing sometimes sensitive information about the movement of American naval vessels to Beijing. Gaining access to such information may even be an unspoken part of the reason Beijing has taken such an interest in European ports. Such information could include important details about the combat readiness of ships, the type of munitions they store, the logistics networks used by these vessels, and even highly sensitive details about the tactics used for naval patrols. The US Navy regularly makes calls to such ports as Piraeus in Greece, Zeebrugge in Belgium, and Valencia in Spain, which are all majority-owned by COSCO.[8] Should it desire to keep such information from the Chinese, the American navy may need to modify which ports its chooses to visit in around the world in the future.

As an example of how Beijing is seeking to expand its port-related infrastructure elsewhere in the world, Hanjin Heavy Industries and Construction Philippines had been operating an industrial shipyard in Subic Bay-site of the former Spanish and US naval bases-for years, but the company, a shipbuilding unit of the South Korean Hanjin Heavy Industries and Construction company, declared bankruptcy in 2019 after defaulting on loans of more than $400 million from Philippine banks, in addition to $900 million of outstanding loans from South Korean banks. Believed to be one of the largest corporate defaults in Philippine history, Hajin Philippines asked the Philippine government to help identify investors to assume ownership of the shipyard operations. Two Chinese firms quickly expressed interest in purchasing Hanjin Philippines, raising concern in Manila about the Chinese government extending its reach into ports around the world to the Philippines. While at the time of the bankruptcy there were calls in the Philippine government for the state to assume control of the company so as to prevent Chinese companies from stepping in, the government did not have the funds to do so. Corporate entities in other countries were interested in assuming control of the shipyard, but the outcome of the bankruptcy remains unclear.[9]

Global Shipping with Chinese Characteristics

It will come as a surprise to no one that Beijing was making a play on global ports before the BRI came into existence. In 2013, a Chinese company teamed up with Nicaraguan President Daniel Ortega to revive an old idea – create an alternative to the Panama Canal that would traverse through Nicaragua. As soon as the Nicaraguan legislature approved construction of a trans-oceanic canal through the country, a draft agreement was signed between a Hong Kong registered company and the government. The government and the project's developers saw the project as economically transformational for Nicaragua, the region, and global consumers, who in theory stood to benefit from reduced shipping costs.

They apparently did not consider the fact that the proposed 155-mile-long waterway would be three times longer than the Panama Canal, would cost an incredible $40 billion to construct, and would take an estimated 11 years to build, at the same time that the Panama Canal had finished doubling its own capacity to accommodate larger ships and heavier traffic. The developers believed that, in the decades to come, shippers would mostly prefer to transport their cargo on super-sized ships and that, despite doubling its capacity, the appeal of the Panama Canal would eventually wane. While true that, at the time, some supertankers and military vessels were already too large to pass through even the expanded Panama Canal, the number of such vessels would surely not be sufficient to justify such capital expenditure, and it would undoubtedly take decades of heavy use of such a canal to ever recoup the original investment.[10]

The very idea that a Chinese investor would ignore all this and commit funding to pursue such a pie-in-the-sky project is illustrative of the lengths some Chinese entities are willing to go in order to grab a piece of global commerce, even if it makes little sense. While many Chinese investors may be generally characterized as savvy and sophisticated, not every Chinese megaproject passes the smell test, as we have seen in many of the examples noted earlier. That this particular investor also chose to hold its nose and partner with Daniel Ortega is equally troublesome, but it should be well understood by now that *neither common sense nor moral considerations necessarily enter into the equation where China is concerned.*

Will China's Approach for Foreign Direct Investment Change?

So, just how is China's approach to foreign investment likely to evolve over time? Will it become even further entrenched, incorporating China Vision into the process, or will it become more normalized and consistent with global best practices? As it continues to rise as a great power, China is likely to gravitate toward best practices, but not necessarily in those parts of the world where there is the least amount of governance and regulatory oversight. *In the poorest of the poor countries, Beijing's inclination will probably be to carry on doing what it has been doing there.* Despite the fact that more pushback to the BRI should be expected, many of the host governments will continue to welcome Chinese funding and other resources in the longer term, particularly given the absence of a plethora of choices in some cases.

Although China's growth model is shifting away from natural resource-intensive investment towards more reliance on domestic consumption, its reliance on raw materials to power its economy may decline, but its domestic demand will not exactly disappear. The flip side is that many private Chinese firms are investing abroad in a wide range of sectors and countries, many of which, particularly in the developed world, will require that Chinese investors adhere to the same set of investment criteria and jump through the same regulatory hurdles as investors from anywhere else in the world. And the investment requirements of any project that involves an MDB are the same for any participatory country, which requires that Chinese firms have the same ability to pivot, depending on the investment destination and range of partnerships, as any other firms.

If there is to be a substantive change in how Chinese firms invest abroad, it may originate with Chinese SOEs. As unlikely as such a proposition may appear at first glance, as the Chinese government continues to refine how it manages SOEs and how it allows them to operate, it may require that, in order to continue to receive governmental support in the future, these firms should become better aligned with international best practices. It will be easier for China to maintain a healthy growth rate if SOEs are better to able to operate more efficiently and become more competitive internationally.

It would be nice to believe that Beijing will eventually decide to just throw out its China Vision-driven playbook, but this is as unrealistic as it is wishful thinking. China Vision, and the frame of reference that comes with it, were derived from China's history and experience. Common sense, or a desire to think like much of the rest of the world thinks about such issues as cross-border investment, are simply not in Beijing's lexicon. Rather, there is every reason to believe that Beijing will continue to act as it has since President Xi came to power and for as long as he remains in power, which could be for a very long time.

Expanding Influence

Beijing is expanding its soft power influence in a range of ways, none more important than its growing influence in the Western press. As part of Beijing's attempt to exert influence in foreign affairs, its state-run media companies are expanding their integration with Western news outlets. The CCP has rapidly expanded its efforts to influence discussion about China beyond its borders to attempt to suppress criticism of the Chinese government and mold international media to refer to China in a positive light. In 2018, Xinhua, China's largest state-run news agency, announced that it was expanding cooperation with the US news service The Associated Press (AP), declaring that the two news agencies had established broad cooperation in such areas as new media, economic information, and the application of AI.

At the time, the US-China Economic and Security Review Commission warned that Xinhua was rapidly expanding globally in an effort to discredit Western media outlets. The AP maintained, in response to a Congressional inquiry on the scope of the agreement between AP and Xinhua, that Xinhua would not influence its reporting or have access to sensitive information in AP's possession. In the wake of Russia's interference in the 2016 US presidential election, no US media outlet would subsequently agree to partner up with RT or Sputnik. Some US members of Congress were of the view that Beijing's influence operations inside the US represented a similar threat.[11]

Like other powerful countries (including, first and foremost, of course, the US), China utilizes aid, cultural programming, and the media to boost its global image. But for Beijing, the current influence offensive, is on a much greater scale. Beijing can more easily shape global narratives through state media that reaches hundreds of millions of people around the world. It is pouring money into such outlets as the China Global Television Network, turning them into major global media players, as Russia did with RT and Sputnik. Chinese social media and messaging platforms have also spread globally, making it easier for Beijing to push Xinhua and other state-run platforms on to more social media users outside China.

Beijing is also seeking to shape media coverage of China by using state-owned media to train foreign journalists, especially from developing countries, inviting reporters from Southeast Asia to Latin America to visit China to participate in workshops and courses that offer an officially sanctioned view of Chinese foreign and economic policies. Recent purchases of local media outlets in South Africa, for example, by pro-

China business tycoons are providing Beijing with direct access to target markets.

Pro-China business owners are also donating funds to influence research institutes, universities, and think tanks abroad. China's Confucius Institute project, run by the Ministry of Education, helps set up Chinese language and culture studies programs at universities around the world, including many in the US. It appears to have been successful not only in promoting language and cultural studies but also in creating a climate of self-censorship at many universities around issues deemed sensitive to Beijing. A 2017 report[12] concluded that the arrival of more than 100 Confucius Institutes in the US had led schools to self-censor programming about Taiwan, Tibet, and the 1989 Tiananmen crackdown.

More pro-Beijing think tanks are also being created all over the world, some directly funded by the government and others endowed by pro-Beijing businesses. Nowhere has China been more successful in swaying research institutions and business organizations than in Southeast Asia. In Thailand, for example, the Chinese Embassy has established close links to several prominent business and cultural organizations that, over the past decade, have become regular mouthpieces for Beijing's policy objectives in the kingdom and around the region. The German government levied that charge against China in 2017, claiming that Beijing had used LinkedIn and other social media to target more than 10,000 of its citizens, including lawmakers and other government employees, posing as leaders of think tanks and headhunters, and offering all-expenses-paid trips to China and meetings with influential clients.

Many countries spend money projecting soft power in a similar manner. The challenge is to differentiate between benign types of cultural and political promotion versus more direct and potentially meddlesome influence-peddling and interference. While many Western intelligence agencies are focused on Russia's information warfare, comparatively few of them are presumably devoting a similar scale of resources to understand China's influence operations and how the country is projecting its soft power abroad.[13] One could easily argue that Beijing's influence operations are far more important, given that this is China's century.

In addition to punching above its weight in influence peddling, Beijing is also punching above its weight in science. Success in modern science requires institutions of higher education, capable researchers, and a lot of money. Since China has all the necessary ingredients, it is rapidly climbing the rankings of scientific achievement. Apart from its achievement on the dark side of the moon, Beijing has spent many billions of dollars to detect dark matter, make great advances in quantum communications, and become a leader in renewable energy and advanced materials. *In 2018, Nikkei and Elsevier found that more scientific papers originated from China than from any other country in 23 of the 30 most active fields of study.* While the quality of American research has been consistently higher, China is nipping at its heels.

The looming prospect of a dominant China in science alarms Western governments not only because of the new weaponry Beijing is in the process of developing, but because of the implications for how else it may be used-whether for repression at home, AI development, or purposes of spying. Science may end up changing China, and the world, in ways no one is anticipating,[14] but for China to be all it can be in the scientific realm implies granting its scientists an unprecedented degree of freedom to be all that they can be. That implies that President Xi and the CCP will need to ease up on the reins of the scientific community in China. Are they capable of doing that?[15] It remains to be seen, but President Xi has already proven himself to be masterful at adapting when needed to accommodate new realities and keep China Vision on course.

Why China Defies the Pundits

Depending on which pundit you may have listened to most recently, China is either about to conquer the world or fall flat on its face. Some analysts maintain that China has found its footing and is running circles around the US on the global stage. Others believe that The World According to Xi is riddled with inherent contradictions and is finally being seen for what it really is – a house of cards waiting for the right set of circumstances to come tumbling down. The truth appears to be somewhere in the middle, for Beijing and President Xi must maneuver around numerous bumps along the road to China Vision nirvana while reveling in the knowledge that China is well on its way to run circles around the US and the rest of the world in the political, economic, and technology arenas. *As has increasingly become the case when reporting the news, more and more geopolitical and economic analysts are succumbing to using a sledge hammer and taking one extreme side of an issue or the other. Doing so in the case of China often completely misses the point, however, for pontificating about China does not lend itself to extremism, but rather, nuance.*

What we are witnessing in the slugfest between China and the US is neither the imminent demise of the US-led postwar global order nor the swift imposition of a new order based on China's unique view of the world. The postwar order was not created and did not come to define the global legal, regulatory, trade, and investment regime of the past 70 years in one fell swoop. It was the result of decades of carefully crafted multilateral diplomacy that will not simply be unraveled by a single Chinese or American president. *If it is truly to be redefined, that, too, will take decades, and implies the ongoing complicity of scores of countries.*

On the assumption the China Vision reigns supreme, that does not imply that the US simply withers away and dies, or that the postwar order it was so instrumental in creating becomes suddenly irrelevant. Quite the contrary – it will either be modified or enhanced, but not replaced on a wholesale basis. Let us also not forget that *the existing order has been absolutely critical to China's rise. It would not be in China's interest to see it entirely replaced*, nor would it be for almost any other nation.

Despite China's dramatic and undeniable economic rise – which, it is worth adding, has for at least the past 20 years been catalogued based on some dubious economic statistics published by the Chinese government – its GDP in 2017 was still roughly two thirds that of the US (approximately $13 trillion versus $19 trillion). In 2016 and 2017, China's official growth rate (as declared by the government) was 6.7 and 6.8%, respectively. Yet, the World Bank published a report in 2017 stating that China's actual annual GDP growth rate in 2016 was just 1.1%. So, just when will China become the world's largest economy, and based on whose statistics will that title be formally awarded?

Many countries are adept at manipulating statistics, and China is certainly not alone in that department, but, Beijing has been crafting an alternate statistical universe for a long time.

Despite this, analysts of many persuasions have unquestionably used China's official statistics to craft their analyses, either willfully ignorant of the view of multilateral institutions or having chosen to ignore them. The more non-Chinese analysts jump on the Chinese government's statistical bandwagon, the more they perpetuate China Vision, helping make it a self-fulfilling prophecy.

In recent years, some in the Western press have highlighted the many challenges the Chinese economy faces as President Xi pivots from Deng's reformist agenda to one more akin to Mao's Stalinist model. China does indeed face some severe economic and political headwinds, some of which are entirely of its own making, with massive debt accumulation, the real estate bubble, and the ongoing challenge of reigning in state-owned enterprises being prominent among them. But, in fairness, these are not new issues, and, every time economists have predicted a hard or soft landing, it has usually resulted in no landing at all – the result of the Chinese government's ability to drink its own Kool Aid and craft its own reality. *President Xi's challenge is to continue to keep all the plates spinning while the Chinese economy marches on, as it has done for decades, in spite of the ongoing headwinds.* Chances are better than not that he will be successful in doing that.

At the same time, the US is rapidly hurtling further into the arena of the unknown, but it is taking much of the world with it. If it, or the global bodies it helped create, were no longer relevant, the world would not care quite so much about what happens in Washington. While plenty of countries around the world are embracing Beijing and the BRI, many are doing so with a wary eye, at the same time wondering what will happen next in America. Should its political fortunes change in 2020, some of these countries will be glad they held their options open. On the other hand, the very idea that America would so deliberately throw itself into an abyss of its own making is deeply and perhaps permanently unsettling to much of the rest of the world.

Some of the pundits that so many of us rely upon to interpret what is happening in the world at times cast it in black and white terms, forgetting that there is, or ever was, a middle ground. Many of them are going the way of much of the global media, taking one side or another, whether for ratings, for applause, or to adhere to their own political persuasion. They are not doing anyone, much less themselves, a favor. Let us hope that, going forward, nuance will be reintroduced into political and economic punditry – not just vis-à-vis China, but more generally. If the pundits cannot seem to get it right, and if news consumers cannot tell the difference, perhaps the Chinese model of state-run media will in the end prevail. After all, what many countries – certainly the US – have now is little more than pre-fabricated partisan news creation, drip fed to individuals who do not appear to care at all about whether the news is truly fair or balanced (or know the difference), on either side of the political spectrum.

An Evolving World Order

As of 2019, the BRI was one mammoth construction project, China and the US were engaged in the most serious trade dispute the world has seen in generations, English remained the world's predominant language, the US was the world's largest economy, the dollar remained its reserve currency, Google was the world's primary search engine, and Facebook was its largest social media platform. Fast forward 30 years and things could look very different. Once the BRI is completed, China's ability to project its soft and hard power will be greatly enhanced. Since China will have, decades previously, become the world's largest economy, and parents around the world will ensure that their children speak Mandarin (many already do).

Once the Chinese government makes the yuan fully convertible, it could well become the world's reserve currency. And given the growth in Chinese speakers, it could be Baidu that becomes the world's predominant search engine and Weibo that supplants Facebook. The growth in the Chinese middle class, already larger than the US and EU population *combined* by some estimates (which is the reason you will *already* find Chinese tourists in literally any travel destination you will ever visit), will help ensure that China weens itself of overdependence on exports to sustain growth and becomes increasingly self-reliant for economic growth.

If President Xi and the CCP have their way, and China Vision results in the kind of changes in the global order they would like to see, there will be no distinct center of gravity. More likely, China, India, the EU, and the US will be competing for supremacy, but, much as is the case in the race for AI supremacy, there will be no single victor, and any country that may hold the top spot in politics, economics, technology, or as a military power will not stay there for long. *As the US continues on its downward trajectory and China continues it inexorable rise, the world order will continue to be multipolar.*

The coming Chinese world order is likely to be devoid of the kinds of checks and balances the world has come to take for granted in the postwar world order. Rather, it is more likely to be akin to a transaction-driven landscape where the strongest party rules and the weak are considered collateral damage. The Chinese order will likely see a break with the Western model by moving decisively away from the Enlightenment ideal of transparency in exchange for the opacity of power.[16] This transformation has already begun, and as it is occurring, the US, and many other countries, are essentially asleep at the wheel. As domestic crisis upon crisis piles up, the world's leading Western economies continue to turn their attention inward, preoccupied with political and economic crises at home and functioning with unipolar blinders on. Many of the world's leaders fail to see all that President Xi and the CCP are doing, and fail to appreciate its implications for the future.

Not since the modern liberal order was born in the 1940s has the world had to grapple with the possibility of its demise, at the hand of a rising China. Just at a time when the world is in need of the stability and governance it has had the luxury of relying upon for decades, it must contemplate transitioning to a world order not of the West's choosing. Clearly, the era of US hegemony is coming to an end. Will the global institutions it was so instrumental in creating become less relevant and forceful with time? Will Beijing be successful in crafting new institutions derived from a Chinese footprint. If so, will good governance and rule of law be consistent with such organizations? Only time will tell, of course.

What is certain is that Beijing's realization of the Chinese century is sure to be infused with precepts and applications that are uniquely Chinese. The world has yet to fully contemplate all that this portends, but President Xi and the CCP want to ensure that China Vision achieves, at a minimum, the perpetuation of the CCP, its continued domination over the Chinese people, and a pathway that guarantees the supremacy of China throughout this century and beyond.

If the Chinese government is to be encouraged to modify the manner in which it engages with the rest of the world, it is up to the world's nations to enhance the manner in which they challenge Beijing, for the CCP is unlikely to become incentivized to do so without some externally-derived inspiration. The USG has taken an important first step by not only strenuously objecting to Beijing's incessant theft of intellectual property on an institutionalized basis, and being willing to endure some pain on a sustained basis in order to focus minds in Beijing. But any leveling of the playing field will have only limited appeal, impact a small percentage of the world's countries, or be likely to endure for a limited period of time before Beijing finds other ways to create yet another uneven playing field somewhere in the global economic system.

It is also not only America's battle to fight, though there are plenty of other nations around the world who are perhaps only too happy for Washington to lead the charge and endure much of the pain of seeking change in how the Chinese government interacts with the rest of the world, without themselves either joining the battle or enduring the pain. This book should be a clarion call for all nations-rich, poor, developed, developing, and middle income alike-to join hands to take collective action to help ensure that Beijing adheres to the letter and spirit of international and domestic law in the future.

Countries (and companies) should strenuously object each and every time Beijing acts in an illegal or outrageous manner. In the absence of such sustained and collective action, Beijing will continue to implement China Vision in any manner, and using any tactic it can get away with. This is China's century, but that does not mean it should be able to thwart the law, create its own set of rules, or avoid sanction when it acts in a manner contrary to established norms. If the world is successful in inspiring Beijing to change its ways, China Vision *could* become a force for good and generally mutual benefit. If not, it will continue to be a means of expanding Chinese influence in every corner of the world primarily for Chinese benefit, with potentially negative consequences for much of its population.

Notes

Prologue

[1] Leslie Hook and Lucy Hornby, "China Emerges as Powerbroker in Global Climate Talks, *Financial Times,* Nov. 16, 2018, https://www.ft.com/content/7c1f16f8-e7ec-11e8-8a85-04b8afea6ea3.

1 China and the World

[1] Elena Holodny, "The Rise, Fall, and Comeback of the Chinese Economy over the Past 800 years," *Business Insider,* Jan. 8, 2017, https://www.businessinsider.com/history-of-chinese-economy-1200-2017-2017-1?r=UK&IR=T.

[2] The Globalist, "12 Facts on China's Economic History," The Globalist Research Center, Nov. 10, 2014, https://www.theglobalist.com/12-facts-on-chinas-economic-history/.

[3] The World Bank, *The World Bank – Data – China*, World Bank Group, last updated 2019, https://data.worldbank.org/country/china.

[4] Corporate Secretariat, "IBRD Country Voting Table," *Siteresources.worldbank.org,* Sept. 30, 2018. http://siteresources.worldbank.org/BODINT/Resources/27802 7-1215524804501/IBRDCountryVotingTable.pdf.

[5] David Dollar, "China as a Global Investor," *Asia Working Group Paper 4,* May 2016, pp. 4, 16, https://www.brookings.edu/wp-

content/uploads/2016/07/China-as-a-Global-Investor_Asia-Working-Paper-4-2.pdf.

[6] Paul Midler, *What's Wrong with China* (Wiley, 2018), pp. 6-7.

[7] Ibid., p.7.

[8] Ibid., p. 9.

[9] Ibid., pp. 64-66.

[10] Ibid. p. 51.

[11] Ibid. p. 21.

[12] Ibid. p. 23.

[13] Ibid., p. 25.

[14] Edward R. Slack, *Opium, State, and Society: China's Narco-Economy and the Guomintang, 1924-1937* (University of Hawaii Press, 2000).

[15] Midler, pp. 184-185.

[16] Madison Freeman, "How Russia, China Use Nuclear Reactors To Win Global Influence," *Defence One*, July 13, 2018, https://www.defenseone.com/ideas/2018/07/china-and-russia-look-dominate-global-nuclear-power/149642/.

[17] Daniel Wagner, "China's Zero-Sum View of the World," *Huffington Post*, September 6, 2016, https://www.huffingtonpost.com/daniel-wagner/chinas-zero-sum-vision-of_b_11879206.html.

[18] A. Maddison, *Chinese Economic Performance in the Long-Run,* Second Edition (OECD Development Centre, Paris, 2007), http://piketty.pse.ens.fr/files/Maddison07.pdf.

[19] Lecture of Professor Andrew R. Wilson, US Naval War College, delivered at the Stamford World Affairs Council, December 12, 2018.

[20] Ben Lowsen, "Is China Inflicting a 'Century of Humiliation' on the World?," *The Diplomat,* February 4. 2018, https://thediplomat.com/2018/02/is-china-inflicting-a-century-of-humiliation-on-the-world/.

[21] Doug Tsuruoka, "Where the Chinese Live in Africa," *Asia Times,* Jan. 19, 2017, http://www.atimes.com/article/chinese-live-africa/.

[22] Mariama Sow, "Figures of the Week: Chinese Investment in Africa," *Brookings*, The Brookings Institution, Sept. 6, 2018, https://www.brookings.edu/blog/africa-in-focus/2018/09/06/figures-of-the-week-chinese-investment-in-africa/.

[23] Kai Schultz, "Sri Lanka, Struggling With Debt, Hands a Major Port to China," *The New York Times,* Dec. 12, 2017, https://www.nytimes.com/2017/12/12/world/asia/sri-lanka-china-port.html.

[24] The Economist, "Latin Lessons," *The Economist,* November 3, 2018, p. 46

[25] "Asian Development Bank and the People's Republic of China: Fact Sheet," Asian Development Bank, April 2018, https://www.adb.org/publications/peoples-republic-china-fact-sheet.

[26] The World Bank, *Where We Work – China -Projects and Programs,* World Bank Group, last updated 2019, http://www.worldbank.org/en/country/china/projects.

[27] Tyler Cowan, "Is the World Bank Lending Too Much to China?," *Marginal Revolution,* October 15, 2017, http://marginalrevolution.com/marginalrevolution/2017/10/world-bank-lending-much-china.html.

[28] The World Bank, *Annual Report 2017 – World Bank Lending (Fiscal 2017),* http://pubdocs.worldbank.org/en/982201506096253267/AR17-World-Bank-Lending.pdf.

[29] "Poverty in China," *Wikipedia,* last updated Feb. 2, 2019, https://en.wikipedia.org/wiki/Poverty_in_China.

[30] Pan Che and Wang Liwei, "China Still Needs Loans from World Bank, Expert Says," *Caixan*, Caixan Global Limited, Oct. 20, 2017, https://www.caixinglobal.com/2017-10-20/101159140.html.

[31] Ibid.

[32] Daniel Wagner, "China Cannot Have It Both Ways," *Lobelog*, February 5, 2018, https://lobelog.com/china-cannot-have-it-both-ways/.

2 Economic Considerations

[1] "Historical GDP of China," *Wikipedia,* last updated Feb. 3, 2019,

[2] Daniel Wagner and Dee Woo, "The Demise of the Beijing Consensus," *Huffington Post*, January 10, 2012, https://www.huffingtonpost.com/daniel-wagner/post_2819_b_1197508.html.

[3] "China Cement Production," *Trading Economics,* 2019, https://tradingeconomics.com/ china/cement-production.

[4] Ana Swanson, "How China Used More Cement in 3 Years than the U.S. Did in the Entire 20th Century," *The Washington Post,* March 24, 2015, https://www.washingtonpost.com/news/wonk/wp/2015/03/24/how-china-used-more-cement-in-3-years-than-the-u-s-did-in-the-entire-20th-century/?noredirect=on&utm_term=.eff32b23e37f.

[5] Martin Wolf, "The Future Might Not Belong to China," *Financial Times*, January 2, 2019, https://www.ft.com/content/ae94de0e-0c1a-11e9-a3aa-118c761d2745.

[6] Evelyn Cheng, "China's Overseas Investment Drops in 2017 For the First Time on Record," *CNBC,* Sept. 28, 2018, https://www.cnbc.com/2018/09/28/chinas-overseas-investment-drops-for-the-first-time-on-record.html.

[7] Stephen Goldsmith and Daniel Wagner, "FDI with Chinese Characteristics," *Huffington Post,* last updated May 25, 2011, https://www.huffingtonpost.com/stephen/fdi-with-chinese-characte_b_759903.html.

[8] Stephen Goldsmith and Daniel Wagner, "Think Tank: The Rise of China as an Outward Investor," *FDI Intelligence*, Dec. 10, 2010, https://www.fdiintelligence.com/Locations/Asia-Pacific/China/Think-Tank-The-rise-of-China-as-an-outward-investor.

[9] James Kynge, Michael Peel, and Ben Bland, "China's Railways Diplomacy Hits the Buffers," *Financial Times,* July 17, 2017, https://www.ft.com/content/9a4aab54-624d-11e7-8814-0ac7eb84e5f1.

[10] Nicolas Casey and Clifford Krauss, "It Doesn't Matter if Ecuador Can Afford This Dam. China Still Gets Paid," *The New York Times*, Dec. 24, 2018, https://www.nytimes.com/2018/12/24/world/americas/ecuador-china-dam.html?rref=collection%2Fspotlightcollection%2Fchina-reach.

[11] Daniel Wagner, "Don't blame China for the Carnage in Global Stock Markets," *South China Morning Post*, August 25, 2015, https://www.scmp.com/comment/insight-

opinion/article/1852371/dont-blame-china-carnage-global-stock-markets.

[12] Robert Muggah and Yves Tiberghien, "The Future Global Order Will Be Managed by China and the US - Get Used To It," *World Economic Forum,* Feb. 12, 2018, https://www.weforum.org/agenda/2018/02/the-future-global-order-will-be-managed-by-china-and-the-us-get-used-to-it/, accessed November 12, 2018.

3 Asia and the South China Sea

[1] Daniel Wagner and Edsel Tupaz, "China's Pre-Imperial Overstretch," *Huffington Post*, June 15, 2011, https://www.huffingtonpost.com/daniel-wagner/chinas-preimperial-overst_1_b_877720.html.

[2] The Economist, "Full Steam," *The Economist,* August 20, 2016, https://www.economist.com/asia/2016/08/20/full-steam.

[3] Bill Hayton, *The South China Sea: The Struggle for Power in Asia* (Yale University Press, 2014).

[4] The Economist, "Full Steam."

[5] Republic of the Philippines, *Position Paper of the Government of the People's Republic of China on the Matter of Jurisdiction in the South China Sea Arbitration Initiated by the Republic of the Philippines*, Dec. 7, 2014, http://www.fmprc.gov.cn/mfa_eng/zxxx_662805/t1217147.shtml.

[6] Daniel Wagner, "China's Nine-Dash Line and its Misplaced National Pride," *Huffington Post*, September 22, 2016, https://www.huffingtonpost.com/daniel-wagner/chinas-nine-dash-line-and_b_12136780.html.

[7] Daniel Wagner and Edsel Tupaz, "China's Territorial Claim at Risk in the South China Sea," *Huffington Post,* May 27, 2015, https://www.huffingtonpost.com/edsel-tupaz/chinas-territorial-claim-_b_7441514.html.

[8] Ibid.

[9] Daniel Wagner, Edsel Tupaz, Ira Paulo Pozon, China, the Philippines, and the Scarborough Shoal, Huffington Post, May 20, 2012, https://www.huffingtonpost.com/daniel-

wagner/china-the-philippines-and_b_1531623.html, accessed December 3, 2018.

[10] Daniel Wagner and Edsel Tupaz, "China and The Philippines' Dual South China Sea Challenge," last updated July 17, 2013,
https://www.huffingtonpost.com/daniel-wagner/china-and-the-philippines_b_10939574.html.

[11] "6,000 Meters Under Water: Beijing Plans AI-driven Deep-sea Base in Disputed South China Sea," *RT*, RT.com, Nov. 29, 2018,
https://www.rt.com/news/445088-china-ai-sea-base/.

[12] Daniel Wagner, "China Gets a Lesson in Realpolitik," *Huffington Post*, October 2, 2011,
https://www.huffingtonpost.com/daniel-wagner/china-gets-a-lesson-in-re_b_993363.html.

[13] Nan Lwin, "Chinese Company Lobbies Locals on Reboot of Suspended Myitsone Dam Project," *The Irrawaddy,*
https://www.irrawaddy.com/news/burma/chinese-company-lobbies-locals-reboot-suspended-myitsone-dam-project.html. accessed November 12, 2018.

[14] Daniel Wagner, "Energizing China-Myanmar Relations," *The Diplomatist*, March 2015,
http://www.diplomatist.com/dipo201503/article013.html.

[15] Hannah Beech, "'We Cannot Afford This': Malaysia Pushes Back Against China's Vision," *New York Times,* Aug. 20, 2018,
https://www.nytimes.com/2018/08/20/world/asia/china-malaysia.html?rref=collection%2Fspotlightcollection%2Fchina-reach.

[16] Nathan Vanderklippe, "A More Confident China Threatens to Use Military Force in Taiwan, Holds up Hong Kong as a Model," *The Globe and Mail*, Jan. 2, 2019,
https://www.theglobeandmail.com/world/article-a-more-confident-china-threatens-military-force-in-taiwan-holds-up/?cmpid=rss.

[17] James Griffiths, "Xi Jinping Warns Taiwan Independence is 'A Dead End,'" *CNN,* Jan. 2, 2019,
https://edition.cnn.com/2019/01/02/asia/Xi-jinping-taiwan-tsai-intl/index.html?no-st=1546530699.

[18] G. V. C. Naidu, "Looking East: India and Southeast Asia," *Asia Pacific Forum,* April 2005, available from

https://www.rchss.sinica.edu.tw/capas/publication/newsletter/
N27/2704_02.pdf.

[19] Daniel Jackman and Daniel Wagner, "China and India's Battle for Influence in Asia," *Huffington Post*, March 9, 2011, https://www.huffingtonpost.com/daniel-wagner/china-and-indias-battle-f_b_833371.htm.

[20] Ibid.

[21] Maria Abi-Habib, "China's 'Belt and Road' Plan in Pakistan Takes a Military Turn," *The New York Times,* Dec. 19, 2018, https://www.nytimes.com/2018/12/19/world/asia/pakistan-china-belt-road-military.html?rref=collection%2Fspotlightcollection%2Fchina-reach.

[22] "How Good is the Indian Navy in Comparison to the Chinese Navy?," *Quora*, Aug. 5, 2017, https://www.quora.com/How-good-is-the-Indian-Navy-in-comparison-to-the-Chinese-Navy.

[23] Daniel Jackman and Daniel Wagner, "China and India's Battle for Influence in Asia."

[24] Teddy Ng and Liu Zeng, "China and Philippines Sign Oil and Gas Exploration Deal as Xi Jinping Meets Rodrigo Duterte," *South China Morning Post,* Nov. 21, 2018, https://www.scmp.com/news/china/diplomacy/article/2174213/china-philippines-sign-oil-and-gas-exploration-deal-Xi-jinping.

4 The United States

[1] Sun Xi, "US-China trade war: toward the Thucydides Trap?," *Asia Times*, July 30, 2018, http://www.atimes.com/us-china-trade-war-toward-the-thucydides-trap/.

[2] Daniel Wagner and Sun Xi, "Realistic expectations must guide China-US relations," *South China Morning Post,* Aug. 7, 2016, https://www.scmp.com/comment/insight-opinion/article/1999600/realistic-expectations-must-guide-china-us-relations.

[3] Steven Lee Myers, "With Ships and Missiles, China is Ready to Challenge the US Navy in the Pacific," New York Times, August 29, 2018,

https://www.nytimes.com/2018/08/29/world/asia/china-navy-aircraft-carrier-pacific.html.

[4] The Economist, "America's New Attitude Towards China is Changing the Countries' Relationship," *The Economist,* Oct. 18, 2018, https://www.economist.com/briefing/2018/10/18/americas-new-attitude-towards-china-is-changing-the-countries-relationship.

[5] Office of the United States Trade Representative, *Update Concerning China's Acts, Policies and Practices Related to Technology Transfer, Intellectual Property, and Innovation,* Nov. 20, 2018, p. 49, https://ustr.gov/sites/default/files/enforcement/301Investigatio ns/301%20Report%20Update.pdf.

[6] Alan Wong and Alan Rappeport, "In a Race for Global Power, the US and China Push Nations to Pick a Side," *New York Times*, November 21, 2018, https://www.nytimes.com/2018/11/21/us/politics/usa-china-trade-war.html?action=click&module=News&pgtype=Homepage,

[7] Ellen Nakashima and David J. Lynch, "U.S. charges Chinese hackers in alleged theft of vast trove of confidential data in 12 countries," *The Washington Post,* Dec. 21, 2018, https://www.washingtonpost.com/world/national-security/us-and-more-than-a-dozen-allies-to-condemn-china-for-economic-espionage/2018/12/20/cdfd0338-0455-11e9-b5df-5d3874f1ac36_story.html?utm_term=.3d0608a43beb.

[8] White House Office of Trade and Manufacturing Policy, *How China's Economic Aggression Threatens the Technologies and Intellectual Property of the United States and the World*, June 2018, https://www.whitehouse.gov/wp-content/uploads/2018/06/FINAL-China-Technology-Report-6.18.18-PDF.pdf.

[9] Ibid., p. 2.

[10] Ibid., p. 6.

[11] Ibid., p. 12.

[12] Del Quentin Wilbur, "China 'Has Taken the Gloves Off' In Its Thefts of U.S. Technology Secrets," *LA Times*, Nov. 16, 2018, https://www.latimes.com/politics/la-na-pol-china-economic-espionage-20181116-story.html.

193

[13] Office of the United States Trade Representative, *Findings of the Investigation Into China's Acts, Policies, and Practices Related to Technology Transfer, Intellectual Property, and Innovation Under Section 301 of the Trade Act of 1974,* March 22, 2018, https://ustr.gov/sites/default/files/Section%20301%20FINAL.PDF.

[14] Adam Segal, Samantha Hoffman, Fergus Hanson, and Tom Uren, "Hacking for Ca$h," *Australian Strategic Policy Institute,* Sept. 25, 2018, https://www.aspi.org.au/report/hacking-cash.

[15] Eli Lake, "China Is Now the Greatest Threat to Americans' Privacy," *Bloomberg,* Dec. 13, 2018, https://www.bloomberg.com/opinion/articles/2018-12-13/marriott-hack-china-is-greatest-threat-to-americans-privacy.

[16] David E. Sanger, Julian E. Barnes, Raymond Zhong, and Marc Santora, "In 5G Race With China, U.S. Pushes Allies to Fight Huawei," *New York Times,* January 26, 2019, https://www.nytimes.com/2019/01/26/us/politics/huawei-china-us-5g-technology.html?action=click&module=Top%20Stories&pgtype=Homepage.

[17] Julia Horowitz, "US Unveils Its Criminal Case Against Huawei, Alleging China Giant Stole Trade Secrets and Violated Iran Sanctions," *CNN Business*, CNN, Jan. 29, 2019, https://www.cnn.com/2019/01/28/business/huawei-charges/index.html.

[18] Julia Horowitz, "Huawei CFO Meng Wanzhou Arrested in Canada, Faces Extradition to United States," *CNN Business,* CNN, Dec. 6, 2018, https://edition.cnn.com/2018/12/05/tech/huawei-cfo-arrested-canada/index.html.

[19] Aaron Mehta, "How the US and China Collaborated to get Nuclear Material out of Nigeria – and Away from Terrorist Groups," *Defense News*, defensenews.com, Jan. 14, 2019, https://www.defensenews.com/news/pentagon-congress/2019/01/14/how-the-us-and-china-collaborated-to-get-nuclear-material-out-of-nigeria-and-away-from-terrorist-groups/.

[20] BBC Monitoring, "His own words: The 14 principles of 'Xi Jinping Thought'," *BBC Monitoring,* Oct. 18, 2017, https://monitoring.bbc.co.uk/product/c1dmwn4r.

[21] Mehta.

[22] Daniel Wagner and Sun Xi, "Will China, US fall into Thucydides Trap?," *The Sunday Guardian Live,* July 28, 2018, https://www.sundayguardianlive.com/opinion/will-china-us-fall-thucydides-trap.

[23] The Economist, "China V America: The End of the Engagement," *The Economist, Oct. 18, 2018,* https://www.economist.com/leaders/2018/10/18/the-end-of-engagement.

[24] Henry Kissinger, *On China* (Penguin, 2012), pp. 539-542.

[25] Ibid, pp. 546-547.

5 Africa and the Middle East

[1] Abdi Latif Dahir, "China Now Owns More than 70% of Kenya's Bilateral Debt," *Quartz Africa,* July 10, 2018, https://qz.com/africa/1324618/china-is-kenyas-largest-creditor-with-72-of-total-bilateral-debt/.

[2] Duncan DeAeth, "China's African Debt-trap: Beijing Prepares to Seize Kenya's Port of Mombasa," *Taiwan News,* Dec. 27, 2018, https://www.taiwannews.com.tw/en/news/3605624.

[3] BBC World Service, "The Inquiry: Is the China-Africa Love Affair Over?," *BBC,* last updated November 1, 2018, https://www.bbc.co.uk/programmes/w3cswqv4.

[4] Feyi Fawehinmi, "The Unseen Hand of China in Africa's Largest Economy," *Quartz Africa,* June 20, 2018, https://qz.com/africa/1310072/china-in-nigerias-economy-from-huawei-to-small-businesses/.

[5] Kartik Jayaram, Omid Kassiri, and Irene Yuan Sun, "The Closest Look Yet at Chinese Economic Engagement in Africa," *McKinsey&Company*, June 2018, https://www.mckinsey.com/featured-insights/middle-east-and-africa/the-closest-look-yet-at-chinese-economic-engagement-in-africa.

[6] Carlos Martinez, "Is China the New Imperialist Force in Africa?," *Invent the Future*, Oct. 8, 2018, https://www.invent-

the-future.org/2018/10/is-china-the-new-imperialist-force-in-africa/#fn:43..

[7] Ibid.

[8] Mogopodi Lekorwe, Anyway Chingwete, Mina Okuru, and Romaric Samson, "China's Growing Presence in Africa Wins Largely Positive Popular Reviews," *Afrobarometer,* Dispatch No. 122, October 24, 2016, http://afrobarometer.org/sites/default/files/publications/Dispatches/ab_r6_dispatchno122_perceptions_of_china_in_africa1.pdf.

[9] Lu Hui, "Spotlight: Why China and Africa are Destined for a Shared Future," *Xinua*, XinuaNet, Sept. 4, 2019, http://www.Xinhuanet.com/english/2018-09/04/c_137444088.htm.

[10] Ibid.

[11] Ibid.

[12] Ibid.

[13] Ibid.

[14] Ibid.

[15] Trading Economics, "Nigeria Imports by Country," *Trading Economics,* 2019, https://tradingeconomics.com/nigeria/imports-by-country.

[16] Yomi Kazeem, "Nigeria has taken its first steps in adopting China's yuan as a reserve currency," *Quartz Africa,* Aug. 2, 2018, https://qz.com/africa/1346766/chinas-yuan-trades-in-nigeria-africa-top-economy/.

[17] "List of Countries by Oil Exports," *Wikipedia,* last updated Jan. 11, 2019, https://en.wikipedia.org/wiki/List_of_countries_by_oil_exports.

[18] Daniel Wagner and Giorgio Cafiero, "China and Nigeria: Neo-Colonialism, South-South Solidarity, or Both?," *Huffington Post*, July 19, 2013, https://www.huffingtonpost.com/daniel-wagner/china-and-nigeria-neocolo_b_3624204.html.

[19] Noah Smith, "The Future Is in Africa, and China Knows It," *Bloomberg Opinion*, Sept. 20, 2018, https://www.bloomberg.com/opinion/articles/2018-09-21/africa-economy-west-should-try-to-match-chinese-investment.

[20] Abdi Latif Dahir, "China is expanding its military footprint in Africa," *Quartz Africa,* June 5, 2018, https://qz.com/africa/1297093/china-will-host-the-china-africa-defense-forum/.

[21] Daniel Wagner, "China's Bold Moves on the Middle Eastern Chess Board," *International Policy Digest,* January 27, 2016, https://intpolicydigest.org/2016/01/27/china-s-bold-moves-on-the-middle-eastern-chess-board/.

[22] Daniel Wagner, "China Rewrites the Rules on How to Rise in Influence in the Middle East," *South China Morning Post,* January 31, 2018, https://www.scmp.com/comment/insight-opinion/article/2131328/china-rewrites-rules-how-rise-influence-middle-east.

[23] Reuters, "China Oil Demand Helps Saudi Arabia Challenge Russia's Export Crown," *Arab News,* Nov. 30, 2018, http://www.arabnews.com/node/1413301/business-economy.

[24] Trading Economics, "Saudi Arabia Imports by Country," *Trading Economics,* 2019, https://tradingeconomics.com/saudi-arabia/imports-by-country.

[25] Daniel Wagner and Ted Karasik, "The Maturing Saudi-China Alliance," *Real Clear World*, April 7, 2010, https://www.realclearworld.com/articles/2010/04/07/the_maturing_saudi-china_alliance_98904.html.

[26] Trading Economics, "Egypt Imports by Country," *Trading Economics,* 2019, https://tradingeconomics.com/egypt/imports-by-country.

[27] Daniel Wagner and Giorgio Cafiero, "Is the US Losing Egypt to China?," *Huffington Post*, November 28, 2012, https://www.huffingtonpost.com/daniel-wagner/losing-egypt-to-china_b_2202438.html.

6 Cyber Warfare

[1] Adam Segal, "When China Rules the Web," *Foreign Affairs,* September/October 2018, https://www.foreignaffairs.com/articles/china/2018-08-13/when-china-rules-web.

[2] "Silencing the Messenger: Communication Apps under Pressure," Freedom on the Net 2016, *Freedom House*, November 2016,

https:u//freedomhouse.org/sites/default/files/FOTN_2016_BO
OKLET_FINAL.pdf.
[3] Adam Segal, "Final Thoughts on China's World Internet
Conference," *Council on Foreign Relations*, Dec. 21, 2015,
http://blogs.cfr.org/cyber/2015/12/21/final-thoughts-on-chinas-
world-Internet-conference-2/.
[4] Emma Llansó, "Adoption of Traffic Sniffing Standard Fans
WCIT Flames," *CDT*, November 28, 2012,
https://cdt.org/blog/adoption-of-traffic-sniffing-standard-fans-
wcit-flames/.
[5] Philipp, "China Security: Under Veil of Cybersecurity, China
Looks to Govern Global Internet," *The Epoch Times*, last
updated April 4, 2016,
https://www.theepochtimes.com/china-security-under-veil-of-
cybersecurity-china-looks-to-govern-the-global-
internet_2006286.html?utm_expid=.5zxdwnfjSHaLe_IPrO6c5
w.0&utm_referrer=http%3A%2F%2Fwww.theepochtimes.com
%2Fn3%2Fauthor%2Fjoshua-philipp%2Fpage%2F5%2F.
[6] Richard A. Clarke and Robert K. Knake, *Cyber War: The Next
Threat to National Security and What to Do About it* (Harper
Collins, 2010), pp. 50-58.
[7] Ibid.
[8] Ibid.
[9] "Hybrid Warfare," *Wikipedia*, last updated Jan. 23, 2019,
https://en.wikipedia.org/wiki/Hybrid_warfare.
[10] Joshua Philipp, "Extensive Network of Secret Chinese
Military Units Attack US on Daily Basis," *The Epoch Times*,
November 21, 2014,
http://www.theepochtimes.com/n3/1094262-chinas-silent-war-
on-the-us/.
[11] Joshua Philipp, "How Silencing China's Dissidents Led to
Stealing the West's Secrets," *The Epoch Times*, January 30,
2015,
http://www.theepochtimes.com/n3/1230816-how-silencing-
chinas-dissidents-led-to-stealing-the-wests-secrets/.
[12] Joshua Philipp, "Exclusive: How Hacking and Espionage
Fuel China's Growth," *The Epoch Times*, September 10, 2015,
http://www.theepochtimes.com/n3/1737917-investigative-
report-china-theft-incorporated/.

[13] Joshua Philipp, "China's Fingerprints Are All Over Spy Operation Targeting Japan," *The Epoch Times*, August 24, 2015,
http://www.theepochtimes.com/n3/1734669-chinas-fingerprints-are-all-over-spy-operation-targeting-japan/.

[14] Robert Windrem, "Exclusive: Secret NSA Map Shows China Cyber Attacks on U.S. Targets," *NBC News*, July 30, 2015,
http://www.nbcnews.com/news/us-news/exclusive-secret-nsa-map-shows-chinacyberattacks-us-targets-n401211.

[15] Marc Goodman, *Future Crimes* (Anchor 2016) pp. 323-328.

[16] Joshua Philipp, "US-China Cyberpact: A Deal Built on Distrust," *The Epoch Times*, September 29, 2015,
http://www.theepochtimes.com/n3/1777875-a-deal-built-on-distrust/.

[17] Joshua Philipp, "China Security: Cyber Agreement Could Help China Perfect Cybertheft," *The Epoch Times*,
October 20, 2015,
http://www.theepochtimes.com/n3/1876649-china-security-cyber-agreement-could-help-china-perfect-cybertheft/.

[18] Joshua Philipp, "Obama Warns of Cyberwar During Comments on Chinese Hackers," *The Epoch Times*, September 16, 2015, accessed July 21, 2017,
http://www.theepochtimes.com/n3/1753476-obama-warns-of-cyberwar-during-comments-on-chinese-hackers/.

[19] Joshua Philipp, "China Security: Chinese Electronics Force You to Abide by Chinese Censorship," *Epoch Times,* December 18, 2018,
https://www.theepochtimes.com/china-security-chinese-electronics-force-you-to-abide-by-chinese-censorship_1939162.html.

[20] Didi Kirsten Tatlow, "A German's Video Likens Mao to Hiter," *New York Times*, September 1, 2016,
https://www.nytimes.com/2016/01/09/world/asia/china-mao-hitler.html.

[21] MMLC Group, "China's New National Security Law," *MMLC Group*, July 29, 2015, https://www.hg.org/legal-articles/china-s-new-national-security-law-36174.

[22] Joshua Philipp, "China Security: Chinese Electronics Force You to Abide by Chinese Censorship," *The Epoch Times*, Jan. 12, 2016, https://www.theepochtimes.com/china-security-

chinese-electronics-force-you-to-abide-by-chinese-censorship_1939162.html.

[23] Benjamin Haas, "China Moves to Block Internet VPNs from 2018," *The Guardian*, July 11, 2015, https://www.theguardian.com/world/2017/jul/11/china-moves-to-block-Internet-vpns-from-2018.

[24] Joshua Philipp, "Why a Novel on War with China has the Pentagon Talking," *The Epoch Times*, July 28, 2015, http://www.theepochtimes.com/n3/1648090-why-a-novel-on-war-with-china-has-the-pentagon-talking/.

[25] M. Taylor Fravel, "China's New Military Strategy: Winning Informationized Local Wars," *China Brief* (15:13) July 2, 2015, https://jamestown.org/program/chinas-new-military-strategy-winning-informationized-local-wars/.

[26] Joshua Philipp, "Chinese Military Officially Shifts Focus to Cyberwarfare and Space Warfare," *The Epoch Times*, June 26, 2015, http://www.theepochtimes.com/n3/1407686-chinese-military-officially-shifts-focus-to-cyberwarfare-and-space-warfare/?expvar=004&utm_expid=.5zxdwnfjSHaLe_IPrO6c5w.1&utm_referrer.

[27] Joshua Philipp, "China's New Industrial War," *The Epoch Times*, March 16, 2017, http://www.theepochtimes.com/n3/2232139-chinas-new-industrial-war-2/?utm_expid=.5zxdwnfjSHaLe_IPrO6c5w.0&utm_referrer=https percent3A percent2F percent2Foutlook.live.com percent2F.

[28] Joshua Philipp, "China Security: What Can Be Done to Stop Chinese Economic Theft?," *The Epoch Times*, last updated April 9, 2016, https://www.theepochtimes.com/china-security-what-can-be-done-to-stop-chinese-economic-theft_1944921.html.

[29] Samm Sacks and Manyi Kathy Li, How Chinese Cybersecurity Standards Impact Doing Business in China," *CSIS*, Aug. 2, 2018, https://www.csis.org/analysis/how-chinese-cybersecurity-standards-impact-doing-business-china.

[30] Joshua Philipp, "China Security: IBM Shows Chinese Agents Its Source Code," *The Epoch Times*, October 19, 2015,

http://www.theepochtimes.com/n3/1881004-china-security-ibm-shows-chinese-agents-its-source-code/.

[31] Joshua Philipp, "US Navy Cruisers and Destroyers Look to Ditch Lenovo Servers," *The Epoch Times*, May 7, 2015, http://www.theepochtimes.com/n3/1348839-us-navy-cruisers-and-destroyers-look-to-ditch-lenovo-servers/.

[32] "HP Partners with Tsinghua to Create a Chinese Technology Powerhouse," *HP*, May 21, 2015, http://www8.hp.com/us/en/hp-news/press-release.html?wireId=1950801#.WRxxM2jyvic.

[33] Yuan Yang, "China's Cyber Security Law Rattles Multinationals," *Financial Times*, May 30, 2017, https://www.ft.com/content/b302269c-44ff-11e7-8519-9f94ee97d996.

[34] Rogier Creemers, Paul Triolo, and Graham Webster, "Translation: Cybersecurity Law of the People's Republic of China," *New America Foundation*, June 29, 2018, http://www.newamerica.org/cybersecurity-initiative/digichina/blog/translation-cybersecurity-law-peoples-republic-china/.

[35] Jack Wagner, "China's Cybersecurity Law: What You Need to Know," *The Diplomat*, June 1, 2017, http://thediplomat.com/2017/06/chinas-cybersecurity-law-what-you-need-to-know/.

[36] "China's New Cyber-security Law is Worryingly Vague," *The Economist,* June 1, 2017, https://www.economist.com/news/business/21722873-its-rules-are-broad-ambiguous-and-bothersome-international-firms-chinas-new-cyber-security.

[37] Reuters, "Apple Sets Up China Data Center to Meet New Cyber-security Rules," *Reuters*, July 12, 2017, https://www.reuters.com/article/us-china-apple-idUSKBN19X0D6.

[38] The Economist, "China Invents the Digital Totalitarian State," *The Economist*, December 17, 2016, https://www.economist.com/news/briefing/21711902-worrying-implications-its-social-credit-project-china-invents-digital-totalitarian.

[39] Joshua Philipp, "China Covers Up Anti-Satellite Test, Again," *The Epoch Times*, August 3, 2014,

http://www.theepochtimes.com/n3/838700-china-covers-up-anti-satellite-test-again/.

[40] "Active protection system," *Wikipedia*, last updated November 13, 2018, https://en.wikipedia.org/wiki/Active_protection_system.

[41] Elsa B. Kania, "The PLA's Potential Breakthrough in High-Power Microwave Weapons," *The Diplomat*, March 11, 2017, http://thediplomat.com/2017/03/the-plas-potential-breakthrough-in-high-power-microwave-weapons/.

[42] Joshua Philipp, "China Makes Advances in Space Lasers, Microwave Weapons," *The Epoch Times*, March 22, 2017, http://www.theepochtimes.com/n3/2234510-china-advances-assassins-mace-warfare-program/.

[43] Bill Gertz, "How China's Mad Scientists Plan to Shock America's Military: Super Lasers, Railguns, and Microwave Weapons," *The National Interest*, March 10, 2017, http://nationalinterest.org/blog/the-buzz/how-chinas-mad-scientists-plan-shock-americas-military-super-19737.

[44] Joshua Philipp, "World Powers Are Preparing for Space Warfare," *The Epoch Times*, September 6, 2015, http://www.theepochtimes.com/n3/1741095-world-powers-are-preparing-for-space-warfare/.

[45] Nick Whigham, "China Sets New Record for Quantum Entanglement to Build New Communication Network," *News.com*, http://www.news.com.au/technology/science/space/china-sets-new-record-for-quantum-entanglement-en-route-to-build-new-communication-network/news-story/e528da0cf68b2e63bbe093cab49ec507.

[46] Nick Whigham, "China Takes Major Step in Creating a Global Network for Quantum Communication," *news.com.au,* Aug. 16, 2016, https://www.news.com.au/technology/science/space/china-takes-major-step-in-creating-a-global-network-for-quantum-communication/news-story/b7e5ec8cdd47b353bba8be886e7d1562.

7 The Race for AI Supremacy

[1] Margi Murphy, "Chinese Facial Recognition Company Becomes World's Most Valuable AI Start-Up," *The Telegraph,* April 9, 2018, https://www.telegraph.co.uk/technology/2018/04/09/chinese-facial-recognition-company-becomes-worlds-valuable-ai/.

[2] Christina Larson, "China's Massive Investment in Artificial Intelligence Has an Insidious Downside," *Science,* Sciencemag.org, February 8, 2018, http://www.sciencemag.org/news/2018/02/china-s-massive-investment-artificial-intelligence-has-insidious-downside.

[3] Sebastien Hielmann, "Big Data Reshapes China's Approach to Governance," *Financial Times*, Sept. 28, 2017, https://www.ft.com/content/43170fd2-a46d-11e7-b797-b61809486fe2.

[4] "China's New Generation of Artificial Intelligence Development Plan," *State Council Notice on the Issuance of the Next Generation Artificial Intelligence Development Plan,* (translated by New America Foundation), China's State Council, July 20, 2017, https://flia.org/notice-state-council-issuing-new-generation-artificial-intelligence-development-plan/.

[5] Ibid., pp. 4-5.

[6] Graham Webster, Rogier Creemers, Paul Triolo, and Elsa Kania, "China's Plan to 'Lead' in AI: Purpose, Prospects, and Problems," *New America*, Aug. 1, 2017, https://www.newamerica.org/cybersecurity-initiative/blog/chinas-plan-lead-ai-purpose-prospects-and-problems/.

[7] Jeffery Ding, *Deciphering China's AI Dream* (Future of Humanity Institute & University of Oxford, March 2018), https://www.fhi.ox.ac.uk/wp-content/uploads/Deciphering_Chinas_AI-Dream.pdf.

[8] Webster et al.

[9] The Economist, "Artificial Intelligence," *The Economist,* July 13, 2017, https://www.economist.com/topics/artificial-intelligence.

[10] Espacenet - Bibliographic Data, https://worldwide.espacenet.com/

[11] Based on keyword searches of title and abstract.

[12] "China's Surveillance State: AI Startups, Tech Giants Are At The Center Of The Government's Plans," *CB Insights,* March

27, 2018, https://www.cbinsights.com/research/china-surveillance-ai/.

[13] Organization of Economic Cooperation and Development, Gross Domestic Spending on R&D, *OECD*, 2018, https://data.oecd.org/rd/gross-domestic-spending-on-r-d.htm.

[14] Will Knight, "Inside the Chinese Lab That Plans to Rewire the World with AI," *MIT Technology Review,* March 10, 2018, https://www.technologyreview.com/s/610219/inside-the-chinese-lab-that-plans-to-rewire-the-world-with-ai/.

[15] Sarah Zhang, "China's Artificial-Intelligence Boom," *The Atlantic*, February 27, 2017, https://www.theatlantic.com/technology/archive/2017/02/china-artificial-intelligence/516615/.

[16] The Economist, "Why China's AI Push Is Worrying," *The Economist*, July 27, 2017, https://www.economist.com/news/leaders/21725561-state-controlled-corporations-are-developing-powerful-artificial-intelligence-why-chinas-ai-push.

[17] "Central Huijin Investment," *Wikipedia*, August 30, 2018, https://en.wikipedia.org/wiki/Central_Huijin_Investment.

[18] "State Administration of Foreign Exchange," *Wikipedia,* August 30, 2018, https://en.wikipedia.org/wiki/State_Administration_of_Foreign_Exchange.

[19] "China Investment Corporation," *Wikipedia*, August 26, 2018, https://en.wikipedia.org/wiki/China_Investment_Corporation.

[20] Paul Mozur and Jane Perlez, "China Bets on Sensitive U.S. Start-Ups, Worrying the Pentagon," *The New York Times*, March 22, 2017, https://www.nytimes.com/2017/03/22/technology/china-defense-start-ups.html.

[21] Tom Simonite, "China Targets Nvidia's Hold on Artificial Intelligence Chips," *Wired*, November 20, 2017, https://www.wired.com/story/china-challenges-nvidias-hold-on-artificial-intelligence-chips/.

[22] Phil Stewart, "U.S. Weighs Restricting Chinese Investment in Artificial Intelligence," *Reuters*, June 14, 2017, https://www.reuters.com/article/us-usa-china-artificialintelligence/u-s-weighs-restricting-chinese-investment-in-artificial-intelligence-idUSKBN1942OX.

[23] The Economist, "Silicon Valley Gets Queasy about Chinese Money," *The Economist*, August 09, 2018, https://www.economist.com/business/2018/08/09/silicon-valley-gets-queasy-about-chinese-money.

[24] Tom Simonite, "The Trump Administration Can't Stop China From Becoming an AI Superpower," *Wired,* June 30, 2017, https://www.wired.com/story/america-china-ai-ascension/.

[25] Gregory Allen and Elsa B. Kania, "China Is Using America's Own Plan to Dominate the Future of Artificial Intelligence," *Foreign Policy*, September 8, 2017, http://foreignpolicy.com/2017/09/08/china-is-using-americas-own-plan-to-dominate-the-future-of-artificial-intelligence/.

[26] *Artificial Intelligence: Implications for China*, McKinsey Global Institute, April 2017, https://www.mckinsey.com/~/media/McKinsey/Featured%20In sights/China/Artificial%20intelligence%20Implications%20for %20China/MGI-Artificial-intelligence-implications-for-China.ashx .

[27] Office of the United States Trade Representative, *Findings of the Investigation Into China's Acts, Policies, and Practices Related to Technology Transfer, Intellectual Property, and Innovation Under Section 301 of the Trade Act Of 1974*, Executive Office of the President of the United States, March 22, 2018, https://ustr.gov/sites/default/files/Section%20301%20FINAL.P DF, p. 67.

[28] Echo Huang, "Chinese Investment in the US Skyrocketed Last Year," *Quartz*, January 3, 2017, https://qz.com/876693/chinese-investment-in-the-us-skyrocketed-in-2016/.

[29] Lorand Laskai, "Why Does Everyone Hate Made in China 2025?," Council on Foreign Relations, March 28, 2018, https://www.cfr.org/blog/why-does-everyone-hate-made-china-2025.

[30] Jon Russell, China's CCTV Surveillance Network Took Just 7 Minutes to Capture BBC Reporter, *TechCrunch*, n.d., https://techcrunch.com/2017/12/13/china-cctv-bbc-reporter/.

[31] Paul Mozur, "Inside China's Dystopian Dreams: A.I., Shame and Lots of Cameras," *The New York Times*, July 8, 2018, https://www.nytimes.com/2018/07/08/business/china-surveillance-

technology.html?rref=collection/spotlightcollection/china-reach.

[32] Patrick Tucker, "Thanks, America! How China's Newest Software Could Predict, Track, and Crush Dissent," *Defense One*, March 7, 2016, http://www.defenseone.com/technology/2016/03/thanks-america-china-aims-tech-dissent/126491/.

[33] Elsa B. Kania, "China Is on a Whole-of-Nation Push for AI. The US Must Match It," *Defense One*, December 8, 2017, http://www.defenseone.com/ideas/2017/12/us-china-artificial-intelligence/144414/.

[34] Elsa B. Kania, "Chinese Sub Commanders May Get AI Help for Decision-Making," *Defense One*, February 12, 2018, http://www.defenseone.com/ideas/2018/02/chinese-sub-commanders-may-get-ai-help-decision-making/145906/.

8 A World with Chinese Characteristics

[1] Philip P. Pann, "The West Was Sure the Chinese Approach Would Not Work. It Just Had to Wait. It's Still Waiting." *Part 1: The Land that Failed to Fail. The New York Times*, Nov. 18, 2018, https://www.nytimes.com/interactive/2018/11/25/world/asia/china-rules.html.

[2] Amy Qin and Javier C. Hernández, As China Grew Richer, the West Assumed, Political Freedoms Would Follow. Now It Is an Economic Superpower – And the Opposite Has Happened," *Part II: How China's Rulers Control Society: Opportunity, Nationalism, Fear…,* Nov. 25, 2018, https://www.nytimes.com/interactive/2018/11/25/world/asia/china-freedoms-control.html.

[3] "Bush: 'You Are Either With Us, Or With the Terrorists' - 2001-09-21," *VOA*, Oct. 27, 2009, https://www.voanews.com/a/a-13-a-2001-09-21-14-bush-66411197/549664.html.

[4] "Pakistan Points to India After Attack On Chinese Consulate in Karachi," *South China Morning News,* Nov. 25, 2018, https://www.scmp.com/news/asia/south-asia/article/2174863/pakistan-points-india-after-attack-chinese-consulate-karachi.

[5] Jonathan E. Hillman, "The Belt and Road's Barriers to Participation," *Reconnecting Asia*, Centre for Strategic and International Studies, Feb. 7, 2018, https://reconnectingasia.csis.org/analysis/entries/belt-and-road-barriers-participation/.

[6] Evin Thorne and Ben Spevack, *Harbored Ambitions,* (CVADS 2017), https://daisukybiendong.files.wordpress.com/2018/04/devin-thorne-ben-spevack-2018-harbored-ambitions-how-chinas-port-investments-are-strategically-reshaping-the-indo-pacific.pdf.

[7] Paul Hodges, "President Xi Focuses on Pollution, Not Growth, as Key Party Congress Nears, *ICIS*, September 18, 2017, https://www.icis.com/chemicals-and-the-economy/2017/09/chinas-growth-slows-tackling-pollution-tops-xis-agenda/.

[8] John Lee, "China's Trojan Ports," *The American Interest,* 14:14 (Nov. 28, 2018), https://www.the-american-interest.com/2018/11/29/chinas-trojan-ports/.

[9] Nyshka Chandran, "A Bankruptcy in the Philippines Sparks Concerns of Chinese Firms Taking Over a Former US Naval Base," *CNBC*, Jan 25, 2019, https://www.cnbc.com/2019/01/25/philippines-sabic-bay-fears-chinese-may-take-over-old-us-naval-base.html

[10] Daniel Wagner, "China, Nicaragua, and the Canal: Global Shipping with Chinese Characteristics," *Huffington Post*, June 13, 2013, https://www.huffingtonpost.com/daniel-wagner/china-nicaragua-and-the-c_b_3436149.html.

[11] Josh Rogin, "Commentary: Congress Demands Answers on AP's Relationship with Chinese State Media," *The Bulletin,* Dec. 26, 2018, https://www.bendbulletin.com/opinion/6800778-151/commentary-congress-demands-answers-on-aps-relationship-with.

[12] Rachelle Peterson, *Outsourced to China*, (National Association of Scholars, April 2017), https://www.nas.org/images/documents/confucius_institutes/NAS_confuciusInstitutes.pdf

[13] Joshua Kurlantzick, "As China Extends Its Reach Abroad, When Does Influence Become Interference?," *World Politics Review,* Jan. 8, 2018,
https://www.worldpoliticsreview.com/articles/23935/as-china-extends-its-reach-abroad-when-does-influence-become-interference.

[14] The Economist, "How China Could Dominate Science," *The Economist,* Jan. 12, 2019,
https://www.economist.com/leaders/2019/01/12/how-china-could-dominate-science.

[15] The Economist, "Can China Become a Scientific Superpower?," *The Economist,* Jan. 12, 2019,
https://www.economist.com/science-and-technology/2019/01/12/can-china-become-a-scientific-superpower.

[16] Bruno Maçēas, "A Preview of Your Chinese Future," *Foreign Policy, Dec. 7, 2018,* https://foreignpolicy.com/2018/12/07/a-preview-of-your-chinese-future/.

Index

equipment: computer, 138; electronic, 145

era, postwar, 13, 95, 180

espionage: cyber-enabled, 82; industrial, 81, 136

ethical codes, 37

ethics, 19, 155, 163; commercial, 138

Europe, 18, 30, 38, 105, 110, 112, 116, 148, 167, 182–84

Everbright Group, 164

experts, 132, 164; nonproliferation, 89; skilled, 134

exports, 18, 28, 30, 40, 45, 100, 112, 115, 138, 193, 203

F

facial recognition, 151, 153, 159–60

facial recognition technology, 160, 173; deployed, 151

factories, 70, 87, 106

families, viii, 16, 123, 171

Fang Binxing, 118

FBI, 121

FDI (foreign direct investment), 12, 22, 24, 38, 103, 171, 186

fighter jets, 70, 175

financial support, 105, 148

financing, 35, 63, 68, 109

firms: foreign, viii, 138, 140, 163, 183; foreign tech, 131; giant, 39;

indigenous, 140; local, 183

FIRRMA (Foreign Investment Risk Review Modernization Act), 167–68

fiscal conservatism, 33

fiscal surpluses, 30

fiscal targets, 100

Five Eyes intelligence alliance, 79

Five-Year Plans, 38, 123

FOCAC (Forum on China-Africa Cooperation), 103

food, 103; safer, 179

force, ix, 17, 29, 37, 53, 62, 71, 82, 154, 163, 195; armed, 77, 79, 147; binding, 55; cheap labor, 115; deploy police, 172; important political, ix; mobilize, 118; modern fighting, 77; naval, 20, 77; positive, 50

foreign affairs, 187

foreign policy, 115; independent, 74; multi-tiered, 111

foreign powers, 20, 54, 107, 180

foreign technologies, 82, 125, 136, 170

foreign threat, real, 181

fossil fuels, 40

France, 57, 100, 182

freedom, 19, 47, 110, 155, 178–79, 190

hacking, 85, 129;
acceptable, 85;
unacceptable, 85
hacking services, 128
Hague, 52, 55, 57, 71, 183
Haiyin Capital, 165
Hambantota Development
Zone, 22
Hanjin Heavy Industries,
184
hardware, 120–21, 156,
165, 168
health care, 179
HEU (highly enriched
uranium), 89–90
high-speed railways, 42, 44
highways, 45, 70, 99;
major, 100
HIPCs (heavily indebted
poor countries), 38, 41,
50, 99
historical conflicts, vi
historical guilt, 17
historical ties, 56, 80
history: long, 61, 98;
maritime, 53; postwar,
93; recent, 32; recent
economic, 28; recent
regional, 74
Homeland Security, 130
Hong Kong, 20, 66, 131,
185
host, 24, 48, 61, 63, 70,
121, 152, 157, 168
housing, 34
HPM (high-power
microwave), 145
Hu Jintao (President), 112
Huangyan Island, 56

Huawei, 87–88, 131, 138,
166
humanitarian, 41
human rights violations,
alleged, 106
humiliation, 19–22;
national, 21, 53
Hungary, 184
Hussein, Gamal Abdel
Nasser (President), 114
hydropower projects, 22

I
IBM (International
Business Machines), 39,
135, 161–62, 169
ICJ (International Court of
Justice), 54
ideological interests, 80–81
ideology, 15, 41, 131;
communist, 179
image, 19, 50, 113, 173;
global, 188; positive,
109
imbalances, growing, 22
IMF (International
Monetary Fund), 28, 32,
100
importer, 30
imports, 30, 93, 100, 106,
115, 170
incentives, 34, 90, 134,
143, 163
income distribution, 36
incomes: national, 99;
rising, 35
India, vi, x, 13, 19, 22, 48,
53, 67–69, 71–72, 79–

intelligence, 79, 87, 122, 159, 176; cross-media, 155; human-machine hybrid, 174; hybrid-augmented, 155; machine, 175; swarm, 155

inter-agency committee, 166

interests: annum, 46; commercial, 84, 94; common, 132; foreign business, 80; national, 75, 94; national defense, 142; ownership, 42; social public, 137; strategic, 107, 109; vested, 34

interference: adversarial, 175; foreign, 20

international bodies, 50

International Court, 54

international law, 24, 52–53, 55–56, 60, 74–75, 122, 131, 184; established, 52

international order, 59

international structure, 19

Internet, 87, 108, 118–20, 123, 129–32, 141, 147, 151, 172, 204; unfiltered, 139

Internet networks, 82, 122

Internet users, 141; daily, 157

intervention, 156; foreign electoral, 122; human, 87; potential, 76

invasion, 67, 115

investment: asset, 30; early-stage, 166; equity, 154; fixed, 30, 34; high-tech, 155; inbound, 13; insured, 40; minimal, 126; natural resource, 40, 186; private sector, 80; spur, 39; state-guided, 165; state-sponsored, 84; ultra-high, 36

investment disputes, 101

investment diversification, 39

investment funds, total, 167

investors, 43–44, 48, 164, 167, 185–87; common, 171; forces, 92; global, 47; innocent, 168; minority, 167

IP. *See* intellectual property

Iran, 14, 19, 41, 43, 88, 110

Iraq, 110, 115

Iraqi government, 109

Iraq War, 16, 109

Irrawaddy River, 61

Islamabad, 69–70

islands, artificial, 63, 65

Israel, 113

Italy, 57, 182

ITU (International Telecommunications Union), 119

J

Jakarta, 44, 68

macroeconomic, 39; national, 172

liberalization, 17; political, 178

Libya, 22, 43

LinkedIn, 189

liquidity, 31, 35

livelihoods, 61, 154

loans, 18, 22, 25, 41, 43, 45–46, 50, 64, 98–101, 161, 185; concessional, 103; interest-free, 103; large, 100; market rate, 39; official, 98; soft, 40; sovereign, 25; total, 25; unpaid, 98

lobbyists, 47–48

location: geostrategic, 64; strategic, 65

luxury, 30, 194

M

machines, unrivaled, 121

Mahathir (Prime Minister). *See* bin Mohamad, Mahathir.

Malaspina, Alejandro, 56

Malaysia, 52, 57, 63–68, 71, 110

Malaysia Development Berhad, 64

Malaysian government, 63–64, 162

malware, 128–29

management: grid, 141; pension, 157; water level, 160

Manila, 52, 55, 57–58, 60, 71–72, 185

Manila Trench, 60

manufacturing, viii, 11, 29, 95, 102, 127–28, 157, 165, 170; domestic, 79; intelligent, 154; modern, 20

manufacturing capacity, 170

manufacturing facilities, 47

manufacturing powerhouse, global, 178

manufacturing powers, 101

Mao Zedong (Chairman), 74, 90, 105, 131

market countries, emerging, 40

market forces, 33, 171

marketplace, 39; autonomous vehicle, 159; competitive, 140; domestic, 139

markets, 15, 17, 34, 39, 47–48, 70, 120; consumer, 182; emerging, 39–41; global, 41, 68, 134; international, 17–18, 94; job, 33; open, 67; overseas, 30; public security, 173; sub-continental, 115; world's, 18

Marshall Plan, 43

Mauritania, 110

MDBs (multilateral development banks), 12, 18, 24–26, 50, 103, 183, 187

MSS (Ministry of State
Security), 85
MST (Ministry of Science
and Technology), 152
Mubarak, Hosni
(President). *See* El
Sayed Mubarak,
Muhammad Hosni
muscles, economic, 50
Muslims, 112
Muslim world, 70
Mutual Defense Treaty, 57
Myanmar, 19, 22, 43, 61–
63, 67–68, 71
Myitsone Dam, 61

N
Nairobi, 100
NASA (National
Aeronautics and Space
Administration), 124,
144, 165
Nasser (President). *See*
Hussein, Gamal Abdel
Nasser
National Security Law, 131
nations: advanced, 154,
157; poor, 24; powerful,
x, 95, 184; recipient, 38,
48, 60; rival, 132
natural resources, vii, 12,
21, 23, 55, 68, 70, 98,
101, 108–9, 120, 181
navy, 69–71, 77, 122, 135;
functional blue-water,
11
negotiations: bilateral, 92;
diplomatic, 75
neighbors, regional, 67

neocolonialism, 98, 102,
149
Nepal, vi, 19, 22, 68
net, freedom on the, 204
Netherlands, 182
networks, 78, 87–88, 123–
24, 134, 138, 143, 182;
advertising, 161;
cellphone, 87;
commercial, 85;
computer, 134;
corporate, 129;
cyberespionage, 120;
digital, 182;
distribution, 39; high-
speed, 43; logistics,
184; mobile, 88; neural,
162, 166, 174; railroad,
16; railway, 63; super-
secure, 148; targeted,
128
network security, 138
Neurala, 164–65
New Delhi, 19, 68, 71
New Development Bank,
12, 26, 50
New Zealand, 68, 79, 88
Nicaragua, 185
Nigeria, 22, 89, 105–7,
110, 203
Nigerian government, 105,
107
nine-dash line, 53–54, 57,
64, 199
non-compliance, 100
non-compliant, 136
non-interference, 19, 115
non-recognition, 58

quantum entanglement,
147

R

race, 89, 93, 95, 118, 150,
165, 193; new arms, 87
railway line, 65
railway stations, 159–60
RAT (remote access
trojan), 128
raw materials, critical, 82,
84
R&D, 161, 168
real estate, 34, 99, 102;
non-residential, 32
reforms, 30, 126
regime, 55; rules-based, 58
regulations, environmental,
153
regulatory enforcement,
inadequate, 47
relations: friendly, 61;
long-term strategic, 112;
multilateral, 109;
political, 13, 113;
public, 139
relationship: closer, 62;
cooperative, 75; deep
trade-based, 81;
historical, 110;
important strategic, 111;
long-term military, 70;
mixed postwar, 62;
political, 50, 110;
symbiotic, 16; working,
14
religion, 119, 131
reputation, 14, 131, 161

research: basic, 148;
decades-long, 145;
predictive policing, 173;
scientific, 60, 89
research collaborations, 50
research groups, 161
reserve currency, 31, 193
resource extraction, 100;
natural, 99
resources, vii, 18, 40, 58,
77, 101, 124, 157, 159,
170, 173, 183, 186, 189;
foreign innovation, 154;
global innovation, 154;
material, 122; strategic,
42
responsibilities, 64, 95;
claimed, 181; collective,
48, 184; increased
global, 16; social, 138
restrooms, public, 151
reunification, 66; forced,
66; peaceful, 66
rights: human, x, 13, 19,
108; invoking historical,
57; preferential trading,
vii; territorial, 71
riots, 151; pro-democracy,
62
risk, 14, 40, 45, 60, 80,
136, 138, 163, 165,
174–75, 199; financial,
45; managing, 48;
perceived political, 107;
potential national
security, 88;
reputational, 40, 61;
terrorist, 142;

services: active, 78; cloud, 139; financial, 161; messenger, 159; online health, 152; popular bike-sharing, 158; smart city, 162
service sectors, 29
SGR (Standard Gauge Railway), 100
Shanghai, 140, 143
ships, 69–70, 184–85; autonomous navy, 164; moving, 78; new, 77; super-sized, 186
shipyard, 185
short-circuit, systematic, 31
Shwe Gas Pipeline, 62
signals intelligence, 122
Silicon Valley, 155, 163, 168–69
Silk Road, new, 63, 181
Sinclair, Upton, 38
Singapore, 58, 61, 68, 110
Sinohydro, 45, 61
Sino-Indian relations, vi, 67
Sino-Pakistani cooperation, 69
Sino-Soviet disputes, 114
Sino-US relations, 75, 88
Sino-US relationship, 95
Sino-US trade war, 91
Sinovel, 133
skills, technical, 39
smartphones, 88, 157, 161; selling, 88
SMBs, 29
social control, 142–43

social credit system, 128, 141, 143, 163, 178
socialism, 17, 33, 90
social media users, 188
social security numbers, 86
society, 16, 104, 119, 142, 153, 196
SOEs (state-owned enterprises), 18, 29, 36, 39, 94, 98, 156, 167, 187, 192; large, 39; medium-sized, 39
software, 88, 133, 135, 159, 173; commercial, 82; open source, 168; traffic optimization, 159
source code, 83, 134–35, 138–39, 165
South Africa, 13, 21, 188
South China Morning Post, 199, 203
South China Sea, 41, 52–54, 56–58, 60, 63–64, 71, 74–78, 95, 180, 183, 199
Southeast Asia, 67, 182, 188–89, 200
South Korea, 57–58, 63, 68, 110
South Korean, 78, 185
South Sudan, 109
sovereignty, territorial, 57
Soviet Union, 78, 112, 144, 146
space, 127, 132, 143–44, 146–48, 155, 169; weaponization of, 146–47
space agencies, 148

superpower, 24, 74; digital, 153; global, 24–25; regional, 105

supertankers, 186

supply chains, global, 47, 84

suppression, 119

supremacy: digital, 118; economic, 18; technological, 153

surveillance, 141, 172–73; block-by-block, 141; digital, 143; offline, 160; pervasive, 123

systems: anti-missile, 145; automated, 175; centralized, 59; comprehensive, 125; cryptographic, 121; democratic, 153; developing, 173; financial, 35; global, vi, 84; international, 53; judicial, viii; missile, 71; moon, 144; national, 143; navigation, 69–70; political, 44, 67, 75; quantum, 148; radar, 70; railway, 15; social-credit, 140; transportation, 48; weapon, 145

T

tactics, 94, 120, 122, 184, 195

Taipei, 66

Taiping Rebellion, 20

Taiwan, 52, 66–67, 77, 91, 124, 131, 180, 189

tanks, 188–89

tax revenues, 16, 34, 102

technologies, 41–42, 82, 84, 119–20, 122, 125–27, 148, 150–51, 153–56, 159, 162, 166, 168–69, 171–73, 175; advanced military, 69; ballistic missile, 18; chip, 156; critical, 164, 167–68; cyber-oriented, 153; domestic semiconductor, 166; engineering, 42; foundational, 160; hybrid propulsion, 174; laser, 127; marine, 127; military-related, 165; new, 60, 153; nuclear, 19; railway, 42; sensitive, 166; wireless, 165

Tehran, 110–11

telecommunications, 23, 87–88, 127, 139

Tencent, 138, 142, 152, 158–60

territorial claims, 55, 58

terrorists, 89, 142, 180

Tesla, 159

Thailand, 57, 68, 189

theft, 82, 85, 124, 127, 133; cyber-enabled, 84; decades-long, 91; intellectual, 130; mandated, 123

About the Author

Daniel Wagner is the founder and CEO of Country Risk Solutions and has three decades of experience analyzing and managing cross-border risk in the private and public sectors.

He began his career at AIG in New York and subsequently spent five years as Guarantee Officer for the Asia Region at the World Bank Group's Multilateral Investment Guarantee Agency in Washington, DC. During that time, he was responsible for underwriting political risk insurance for projects in a dozen Asian countries. After serving as Regional Manager for Political Risks for Southeast Asia and Greater China for AIG in Singapore, Daniel moved to Manila, Philippines, where he served in a variety of capacities in the Asian Development Bank's Office of Co-financing Operations, including as Senior Guarantees and Syndications Specialist. He then became Senior Vice President of Country Risk at GE Energy Financial Services before founding CRS.

Daniel has published more than 600 articles on current affairs and risk management and is a regular contributor to the *South China Morning Post*, *Sunday Guardian*, and *The National Interest*, among many others. He is also the author or co-author of five previous books – *AI Supremacy*, *Virtual Terror*, *Global Risk Agility and Decision-Making*, *Managing Country Risk*, and *Political Risk Insurance Guide*.

He holds master's degrees in International Relations, from the University of Chicago, and in International Management, from the American Graduate School of International Management (Thunderbird), in Phoenix. Daniel received his bachelor's degree in Political Science from Richmond College in London.

daniel.wagner@countryrisksolutions.com.

linkedin.com/in/danielwagnercrs / twitter.com/countryriskmgmt

Made in the USA
San Bernardino, CA
16 July 2019